Practice on
Purpose

*Achieve the Financial Advice Practice
You Desire and Your Clients Deserve*

By Gary H. Schwartz, CLU®, ChFC®, CRPC®
*with Phillip C. Richards, CFP®, CLU®, RHU®
and Edward G. Deutschlander, CLU®, CLF®*

Cover and Interior Graphics Designer: Chialia Yang, CY Designs

© 2014 by North Star Resource Group

All rights reserved. Except as permitted under the US Copyright Act of 1976, no part of this publication may be reproduced, distributed, or transmitted in any form or by any means, or stored in a database or retrieval system, without the prior written permission of the authors.

Library Of Congress Control Number: 2014942207

ISBN: 978-0-692-22918-7

Praise for *Practice on Purpose* From Industry Leaders

This timely book addresses the changing landscape of financial services. It's where our industry is going. Gary, Phil, and Ed guide us toward the future by focusing on the present, and we're very fortunate that they have done so.

Daralee Barbera, CFP®, CMFC®, CLF®
Managing Principal, Waddell & Reed, and
GAMA International President, 2014–15

Practice on Purpose helps advisors and managers see the bigger picture. This book is inspirational, motivational, and educational—a must-read. *Practice on Purpose* will not only help people become better financial advisors; it will help financial advisors become better people.

Paul Blanco, LUTCF
Registered Principal, Barnum Financial Group, An Office of MetLife

Practice on Purpose is a must-read for financial advisors interested in growing their practices, as well as leaders responsible for developing others. This book provides best practices and thought-provoking exercises designed to help you bring clarity and purpose to your career. I encourage you to take the journey of personal and professional growth and discovery with these authors, learn from leaders in our industry, and discover your own potential!

Tom Burns, CLU®, ChFC®
Chief Distribution Officer, Allianz Life Insurance Company of North America

Many books have been written by successful financial advisors, but never before have three such successful people combined their wisdom and knowledge for the betterment of all who take the time to read this book. Each one of them could deliver a master class on achieving lasting success in our business, but put the three together and the wisdom just pours off the pages. It is uncomplicated and easy to absorb. A must-read for those who are serious about our business.

Tony Gordon
Past President, Million Dollar Round Table

May I suggest that you set aside what you thought was important for you to be doing right now and read this book cover to cover? It has taken me decades to learn and implement what this book can help you do in hours. My journey in our profession has taken me all over the world. Along the way, I've been fortunate enough to know personally the icons of our time. Included in this amazing journey is my friendship with the authors of *Practice on Purpose*. I can attest to their passion, professionalism, and pride in what we do to help people achieve financial dignity. This book is not about fact finding; rather, it's about *fact facing*, and the authors freely share with you what you need to know to be the best you. Now, keep reading!

Philip E. Harriman, CLU®, ChFC®, RFC®
Founding Partner, Lebel & Harriman, LLP;
Past President, Million Dollar Round Table

Wow! You want a road map to success? This is it. I cannot imagine that advisors who sincerely want to be successful and are willing to be relentless in their pursuit of excellence could read this book and *not* accomplish all of their dreams. I wish I had had this when I came into the business!

Tom Hegna, CLU®, ChFC®, CASL®
President, TomHegna.com; Author of *Paychecks and Playchecks*;
International Speaker and Author

Practice on Purpose shows how intentional financial consulting benefits both the advisor and the client. It offers an ideal balance of step-by-step direction with thought-provoking, overarching guidance.

Christopher M. Hilger
President, Securian Financial Group; CEO, Allied Solutions

Practice on Purpose is the complete guide to success as a financial advisor. It starts with the most important thing: purpose. It's been said, "It is not your own strength that holds you to your purpose, but the strength of the purpose itself." This book builds on that point brilliantly. Great job!

Harry P. Hoopis, CLU®, ChFC®
Chief Executive Officer, Hoopis Performance Network

If you were placed in a community where you knew no one and your access to advice and support were severely limited, if all you had was a copy of *Practice on Purpose*, you could succeed personally and also build a successful financial services practice. It is the definitive "here's how" for people starting out. More importantly, it will save the careers of those struggling.

Joseph Jordan
Behavioral Finance Speaker; Author of *Living a Life of Significance*

When I first saw this great book, my reaction was "Wow! What talent, power, success, and knowledge, all combined to create this literary masterpiece—and they are sharing it freely with any aspiring or practicing advisor." But I am not surprised. Sharing is the common denominator of the three authors and should be the primary attribute of all sincere advisors. Anyone who wants to raise their own bar of effectiveness and success must read this book and pick the brains of these three superstars.

Norman Levine, CLU®, CHFC®, RFC®
Motivational Speaker; Past President, GAMA International, GAMA Foundation, LUTC, NAIFA

If this were the *only book* ever written about building a successful career in our profession, millions of people would benefit tremendously in so many ways!

Regretfully, it is obvious that almost all people who are charged with building highly productive and successful people in our life's work simply aren't very good at it. Frankly, we have generations moving forward in our career, starting about halfway through the preparation/foundation period. First things first! The "fundamentals" aren't about memorizing an approach talk. The "fundamentals" are deciding "On Purpose" your "Purpose." What are your values? Why are you coming into this profession? This is not about selling products to prospects; it's all about helping prospects/clients keep their promises, dreams, and commitments.

Obviously, if the professional practitioner has clarity in his/her intent and values, it only follows that clients will have an advocate who will guide them to the achievement of their goals for themselves, the people they love, and the causes they believe in. Beginning with the end in mind is what we need to be doing. This book is absolutely the one best "how to" on this subject I have ever read or seen!

Reginald N. Rabjohns, CLU®, ChFC®
Chairman and CEO, Secure Futures, Rabjohns Financial Group; President, Million Dollar Round Table, and 45-Year Member; Chairman, The American College Foundation Board of Trustees; Huebner Gold Medal Recipient, The American College; Chairman, GAMA Foundation

I met Gary, who has been a friend for more than twenty years, through an introduction by Phil Richards, whom I consider to be the premier agency builder of the past several decades and followed by Ed Deutschlander, who has been such a great leader at such a young age. One of my greatest joys is to observe their success over the years. As I read the draft of the book, I became more and more enthused about the content. It is an outstanding step-by-step process for bringing new people into our great business and providing for them the philosophy, the basics of building a successful business and serving the client with *wow!* service. We are inundated with ideas and material by our industry and outside of our business with supposed shortcuts and ideas for success. It is so refreshing to read material that is tried and proven—time and time again—by associates who have joined the North Star organization. I would suggest that every agency leader and home office executive read this very carefully. It will enable our industry to grow the career-agency business with profitability and provide associates with a gateway for their present and future success. To Gary, Phil, and Ed: My hat is off to you for this magnificent book.

Maury Stewart, CLU®, ChFC®, CLF®
Executive Consultant, The Penn Mutual Life Insurance Company

I personally worked with Gary Schwartz for more than a decade and came to respect him for his business knowledge and years of financial services executive expertise. He has worked with thousands of advisors and financial professionals to help them build more successful advice-based businesses. In this book, he and his colleagues take their collective wisdom and make it practical, actionable, and compelling. If you are a financial services professional who wants to make a difference for your clients, grow your business, and leave a lasting legacy for those you care about, then this book is a *must*-read. My advice: Read it cover to cover, complete the practical exercises, and then *just* execute. This book should be in every advisor's office.

Bill Williams, Executive Vice President
Advisors Franchise Group, Ameriprise Financial

I have worked with Gary for the past eighteen months. I am an advisor with six years of industry experience. The book is targeted to the advisor trying to take the next step. Gary's systems have transformed my practice into a sustainable, repeatable, valuable, and successful business. I must say the concepts that Gary has brought to me are the core of a Practice on Purpose. I regularly reflect on the principles of this book that have helped satisfy my goals as an advisor and grow as a person in the community. I highly recommend any advisor or practice manager to take the time to read and implement the strategies.

Will Zimmerman
Financial Advisor

Dedications

To my family, who matters more than they know. To Laura, who makes me better; our children, Hunter and Madison; and my son, Brian, his wife, Allison, and their children, Emerson and newly arrived Benjamin. Also to my parents, Pat and Hollis, who taught me responsibility, curiosity, a love of reading, and a respect for work.

This book is also dedicated to the many advisors who have given me the privilege of being part of their lives and part of their practices. I have learned as much from you as I hopefully have shared with you. Without you, this book would not have been possible or necessary.

Gary H Schwartz, CLU®, ChFC®, CRPC®
Senior Vice President, Advisor Growth and Development,
North Star Resource Group

* * * *

My contribution to this work is in honor of those "Miracle Merchants," those advisors, who have dedicated their lives to lightening the loads of others. With almost a half century of mentoring, observing, and growing those at North Star, I have been blessed to be a small part of their careers and their lives.

To our son, Scott, who devoted his life to their cause: We collectively hope that we have been a source of pride.

To agents and advisors around the world whom I have been blessed to address: I pray that this book serves as a guide enabling you to navigate the uncertain future before us, as we use advice to help others.

Phillip C. Richards, CFP®, CLU®, RHU®
Chairman of the Board, Chief Executive Officer,
North Star Resource Group

This book is dedicated to every current and future financial advisor who has elected to have a purposeful career that truly changes lives, forever. I firmly believe, as my mentor taught me, that perhaps other than the clergy, medicine, and education, no other career can be as impactful as that of a caring, courageous financial advisor. This career and industry possess some of the most generous, grateful, and serving people in the world. This career serves as a vessel for many in their pursuit of being better people and becoming what they are fully capable of becoming. What other profession allows one to have the Three I's—Impact, Independence, and Income—and truly do well by doing good?

I encourage others to pause occasionally and reflect on the following statement: "I cannot imagine my life without…" and from that exercise begin to write down all of the people and opportunities that have shaped their lives. Well, I cannot imagine my life without this calling I have chosen (actually, it chose me, and I am forever grateful). I also am so ever grateful for those select few who have the entrepreneurial spirit of the capitalist and the heart of the social worker and take the road less traveled to pursue this calling, which not only changes their lives but the lives of those they serve—their clients.

Edward G. Deutschlander, CLU®, CLF®
Chief Executive Officer Elect, North Star Resource Group

Table of Contents

Dedications vii

About the Authors xi

Foreword xv

Preface xvii

Acknowledgments xiv

Introduction xxi

Chapter 1: Your Purpose Defines Your Practice 1

Chapter 2: Creating an Exceptional Client Experience 23

Chapter 3: Financial Advice as Its Own Value 49

Chapter 4: Acquiring Clients—How to Invite People to
    Join Your Practice 75

Chapter 5: Practice Design—From a Job to a True Practice
    on Purpose 97

Chapter 6: The Inner Game of Financial Advising 113

Chapter 7: The Big Five: Five Traits Common Among the
    Most Successful Advisors 127

Chapter 8: Valuing Your Life's Work 143

Chapter 9: Where the World Is Going 167

Chapter 10: A Time to Review and Execute 177

Chapter 11: Leading and Coaching Advisors:
    An Encore Chapter 183

Appendix: Supporting Documents 199

Suggested Reading 225

About the Authors

All three authors are affiliated with North Star Resource Group, the largest independently owned financial planning firm in the world. The firm has more than $4 billion of client assets entrusted to its advisors, and its origins trace back to 1908 in the Twin Cities community. GAMA International has ranked North Star Resource Group as one of the three largest organizations of its kind in the world for the past five years. GAMA has awarded North Star the prestigious Master Firm Award every year since 1988. The firm's combined gross sales revenues exceed $50 million.

North Star's three hundred associates provide customized solutions to help families, professionals, physicians, and business owners reach their financial goals through a broad range of wealth management services, diverse financial expertise, and responsive service. This unique organizational structure serves as a powerful resource that advisors use to address their clients' total financial picture.

North Star's training program is featured in two *New York Times* best sellers: *What the Dog Saw* by Malcolm Gladwell and *Use Your Head to Get Your Foot in the Door* by Harvey Mackay.

Only 10 percent of the financial advisors who apply to work with North Star are offered contracts. Through a rigorous selection practice, North Star hires advisors whose goals align with the firm's values. Advisors receive extensive training to learn and exemplify North Star's values, practices, and vision, which is "Changing lives, forever."® The culture of North Star is composed of five cherished values: faith, integrity, growth, gratitude, and service.

InvestmentNews awarded North Star the Community Service Award in 2010, and the firm received the Better Business Bureau's Integrity Award in 2011. Many of the firm's advisors and team members are heavily involved with charities of their choice, an initiative the firm calls "Paying It Forward."

In 2004, North Star established the Scott Richards North Star Foundation to maximize its charitable contributions. North Star has made a commitment to donate 10 percent of its profits to the foundation. Based on personal experiences the North Star family has had, they chose five causes as the focus of the foundation: ataxia, Alzheimer's disease, breast cancer, cystic fibrosis, and myelofibrosis. In addition to strategic giving for organizations that are working to cure these five diseases, North Star is committed to recognizing and supporting its own employees' volunteerism and charitable donations through an internal matching-funds program. The firm has conducted and sponsored the "Bikes for Kids" program with the Minnesota Twins for the past ten years.

North Star Resource Group
2701 University Avenue S.E.
Minneapolis, MN 55414
www.northstarfinancial.com
612-617-6167

Gary H Schwartz, CLU®, ChFC®, CRPC®
Senior Vice President, Advisor Growth and Development, North Star Resource Group
612-617-6029
gary.schwartz@northstarfinancial.com

Gary Schwartz provides professional consulting services to advisors on developing teams and composite practices, succession planning, and executive leadership. He also specializes in providing experienced advisor coaching services and developing practice-management analytics designed to improve practice growth, productivity, and effectiveness.

He is an adjunct professor emeritus for the University of Saint Thomas Graduate School of Business, where he taught the course "Financial Services in the Twenty-First Century." He is currently on the advisory board for Bright Peak Financial, a Thrivent startup for modest-income Christian families, and he serves on the board of Shepherd of the Lake Lutheran Church in Prior Lake.

He is a past Chair of LIMRA International's Career Agency Building Committee, a Securian Ambassador, and a Diplomat to GAMA International. He has presented at GAMA International's LAMP meeting on the topic of coaching experienced advisors.

When Gary was with what is now known as Ameriprise Financial, his territory was perennially among the top five territories and was number one during three of his ten years there. Gary's team had an average advisor retention rate of 97 percent and average advisor productivity of more than $450,000. By 2011, he had developed sixteen practices that exceeded more than $1 million of gross revenue, after having only one exceed that amount in 2005. He accomplished this achievement through teaming, aggressive asset and client-acquisition strategies, succession planning, and practice branding.

Previously, as Vice President of Field Management and Development for the Securian Financial Network, the individual distribution system for Minnesota Mutual, Gary directed the field-management and sales-promotion functions for sixty regional firms and twelve hundred advisors. He developed the advisor and managing partner recruiting and selection system, initiated and drove the development of Securian University, partnered with Saint Thomas University to develop a Mini MBA in entrepreneurial excellence, and designed and implemented the successful advisor coaching program known as Breakthrough.

Phillip C. Richards, CFP®, CLU®, RHU®
Chairman of the Board, Chief Executive Officer, North Star Resource Group

612-617-6167
phil.richards@northstarfinancial.com

Phil Richards entered the insurance and financial services industry in 1962. He acquired North Star Resource Group in 1969.

A winner of numerous industry awards, Phil is the 2005 inductee into the GAMA International Hall of Fame, is a GAMA past president, and founded GAMA Thailand. He is the only firm leader in the world to have received the International Management Award from GAMA every year since the inception of that award in 1975. In 2007, Phil received the sixty-sixth annual John Newton Russell Memorial Award, the highest honor in the insurance industry, from The National Association of Insurance and Financial Advisors.

His first book, *Twenty-Five Secrets for Sustainable Success*, was published in 2007, and he donated more than $250,000 in proceeds to GAMA International. His second book, *The Sky Is Not the Limit: Discovering the True North for Your Life's Path*, was published in 2013. He donated the proceeds to five nonprofits that have enriched his career and life.

Phil is an adjunct professor emeritus for the Carlson School of Management at the University of Minnesota and a former adjunct professor at Central University of Finance and Economics in Beijing, China. He is a four-time Chairman of Securian's National Advisory Board, and in 2008, he was inducted as the nineteenth member of its Hall of Fame.

Phil currently serves on the Board of Trustees for The American College in Philadelphia and on the Mayo Clinic of Arizona Leadership Council. He is the treasurer of the Arizona Heart Foundation's Board of Trustees, and he chairs the Scott Richards North Star Charitable Foundation. In 2009, he was elected to the Board of Trustees of his alma mater, Temple University, and was inducted into the National Wrestling Hall of Fame.

He has been a featured speaker in more than a dozen countries on topics including strategic planning, leadership, and alternate distribution systems in the financial services industry in the twenty-first century. He has addressed the annual meetings of more than one hundred and fifty companies.

Edward G. Deutschlander, CLU®, CLF®

Chief Executive Officer Elect, North Star Resource Group

612-617-6103

ed@northstarfinancial.com

Ed Deutschlander is the CEO-Elect at North Star Resource Group. In 2002, he became the youngest Managing Partner nationally for Minnesota Mutual's Securian Advisor Network, which has more than forty advising firms throughout the country.

Ed is a past president of GAMA International. In 2001, at age twenty-nine, he became the youngest board member in the organization's fifty-year history. He has been published in numerous publications on the topics of recruiting, leadership, selection, training, and development of financial advisors. His "Recruiter's Creed" is often used and cited at industry meetings and events.

Ed is recognized as one of the premier recruiters in the financial services industry, and he has educated tens of thousands of managers and advisors. He is the creator of "Recruiting University" and "Do Well by Doing Good." These two products have educated thousands of financial services leaders.

Since 1998, Ed has been a consultant to many of the largest insurance companies in the world, leading them to improve their recruitment, training, and leadership-development programs. Ed has been asked to present in China, Thailand, Singapore, South America, and Canada.

Foreword

Financial advisors who are "right" for the business have the minds of capitalists and the hearts of social workers, and they "Practice on Purpose." These financial advisors earn their living making a difference, and *Practice on Purpose* is for them and for leaders who support and develop them.

In my opinion, the human appetite for growth is insatiable, and in my experience, most financial advisors value growth…growth for their clients, for their practices, and for themselves. Gary Schwartz with Edward Deutschlander and Phillip Richards recognize that you have a big appetite for growth. Their goal in sharing their insights with you is to contribute to your personal and professional growth. When you grow, you help your clients grow, and you grow your number of clients. And when your clients grow, your practice grows with them.

When I started in this industry in the first half of the 1970s, growth was about more transaction fees (commissions) this year than last year. Much has changed in these past five decades, and much will continue to change. Products have been commoditized. Regulators and the public are becoming less and less tolerant of high product and transaction fees. Indeed, there is no evidence that if one gets to pay more for a product, it will perform better than a less expensive product. Consumers are wary of wolves on both Wall Street and Main Street. Data show that financial products and investments work better than investors, and that is often true because the wolf advisors and the wolf companies sell to their clients what is emotionally easy to get them to buy. Unfortunately, what is emotionally easy to get people to do is often irrational, and irrational decision making trumps high IQ every time.

Consumers are seeking simplicity and transparency from an industry known for neither. So what's the future? The future is advice. The future is behavioral advice (closing the gap between product/investment performance), and investor performance requires the focus to be on advisor and client behavior. Behavioral advice is anchored in values-based financial planning. The future is transparent pricing. Expect continued pricing pressure on products. Expect product margins to narrow. Expect that you will need to generate more revenues from the advice and the financial-planning support you provide. "Advice-based fees" will replace "fee-based advice" because consumers have figured out that the fee associated with "fee-based advice" is based on the amount of assets invested rather than the advice.

I've known Gary Schwartz for a number of years. I know that Gary knows that financial advice itself is valuable and that advisors should be paid for it. He also knows that client service is valuable and should be charged for. Your winning hand will necessitate that your cards include the Ace of Advice and the Ace of Client Service. Gary cares about this industry. He cares about you, and he is extremely well qualified to provide you guidance as you continue to grow, develop, and take your practice to the next level.

Doug Lennick, CFP®
CEO and Founder
Think2Perform

Preface

We wrote this book to capture what we have learned from the best advisors we know and to offer a blend of practical advice and thought leadership. This book is for advisors who want to achieve the practice of their dreams, as well as anyone who coaches or leads advisors. We have gathered our collective knowledge spanning multiple decades in this business to reveal the strategies, philosophies, and processes we use to coach and develop advisors to grow their practices. We enjoy coaching advisors who have been in the business for eight or ten years and who make $300,000 to $400,000 of gross revenue to reach or exceed the $1 million milestone. That is really the Holy Grail in our business, the ultimate goal: to have a million-dollar practice.

We have seen thousands of advisors fail in this business, and we have seen fewer succeed. Those who succeed are typically committed, hard-working, goal-oriented, and coachable. They are also passionate about changing their clients' lives. But there is another key characteristic of winning advisors—they are *intentional* about building their practices. They typically build what we call a "Practice on Purpose." That term suggests a double meaning of the word "purpose"—you build your practice around your personal *purpose*, and you build it in an intentional way, on *purpose*. Advisors who live their lives and run their financial advisory practices on purpose are more likely to experience a relevant and meaningful life journey than those who simply go through the motions, with no real focus, aim, or overarching purpose.

As you read this book, contemplate your personal purpose in life. Define and articulate who you are, first as a person, then as a financial advisor. Then you can build a practice that aligns with your purpose and deliver value to your clients through quality financial advice. The result is that you will build a legacy of leading clients to financial results they would not have achieved on their own.

It's a door only you, the advisor, can go through.

Our goal for this book is to lead you to break through your performance plateau and achieve extraordinary personal and professional growth. We want you to build a million-dollar Practice on Purpose that you want and your clients deserve. Your clients deserve to work with an advisor who is helping people on purpose and using financial advice as a model. Financial advice is the catalyst for clients to take action.

To use financial advice as a model, you first have to experience a breakthrough in your thinking, then in your systems, your structure, your practice design, and the mission of your practice. The thinking that helped you survive this business is not the same thinking that will help you build the phenomenal practice you can have and your clients deserve. We cannot teach smarts or work ethic. No book can do that. What we are striving for in this book is to propel you to grasp a new mindset and to see that you can achieve so much more than you expected.

It may be surprising to some people in the insurance and financial services industry that North Star Resource Group, a "legacy" firm that has been in business since 1908, would adopt and propose a fee-only model. As we discuss in Chapter 9, "Where the World Is Going," we believe this country is headed toward a fee-only financial services model. Like many others in the industry, we believe product compensation will eventually become obsolete—both due to federal regulations and consumer preference. If that happens, this will be the only way advisors can do business. So not only is ongoing financial advice a superior way to help your clients achieve their financial goals; it is the direction our industry is headed.

With Congress's 8 percent approval rating, Obamacare, and regulations like Sarbanes–Oxley changing our regulatory landscape and consumer marketplace, it is hard to predict where the legality of commissions on financial products will lead. Our hope is that advisors will be prepared for whatever the future holds and will continue to protect the dreams and future of Americans with risk-based products like life insurance, income replacement, long-term care, and annuities. Advisors will be able to do so only if they are prepared for legal and regulatory events. This book is intended to accomplish just that.

We want to stress that we are firm and committed believers in The Miracle of Life Insurance. It is the critical foundation and starting point for a secure financial future.

We hope the advice in this book helps you grow, both personally and professionally. Most advisors will grow even if they never meet us. Our challenge is to bend their growth curve upward by intervening in their practices in a positive way. As leaders, we think it is our responsibility to change the trajectory of our advisors' growth. That is what we attempt to do every day, and that is the focus of this book.

The advisor vignettes at the end of the chapters illustrate how some of our top North Star advisors are applying the concepts to achieve growth in their practices.

We like this quote by German playwright, poet, and novelist Johann Wolfgang von Goethe: "If I accept you as you are, I will make you worse; however, if I treat you as though you are what you are capable of becoming, I help you become that." This book is our way of treating you as though you are what you are capable of becoming. We want you to recognize that you have so much more inside of you than you ever realized. If you have succeeded in the career past those first four crucial years, then you are already a champion. And, with a simple change in your mindset and the desire to grow personally and professionally, you can reach a level of achievement you only dreamed of in the past. This book is our contribution to your discovering the power that is within you.

Acknowledgments

To my many mentors: Phil Richards, Terry Sullivan, Keith Campbell, Doug Lennick, Jody Johnson, Bill Williams, John McConneloug, John Greiber, and too many others to mention. You can see farther when you stand on the shoulders of the leaders before you.

To all of the fine people at North Star Resource Group, and in particular my co-authors, Phil Richards and Ed Deutschlander. Everything I have done in the past has prepared me for what I am doing at North Star today. I appreciate the opportunity.

This book has been on my bucket list and would not be possible without the advice and counsel of Lacey Struckman, Chialia Yang, Jacci Umphress, and our New Mexico editor, Libbye Morris. I am blessed with a sea of talent around me.

Finally, to the Seaview Terrace at the Grand Hyatt Kauai, where a good share of this book was completed. There is something about being up at four in the morning waiting for the sun to rise, listening to the cacophony of tropical birds' songs and hearing the ocean in the distance that just makes you want to write.

Gary H Schwartz, CLU®, ChFC®, CRPC®
Senior Vice President, Advisor Growth and Development,
North Star Resource Group

* * * *

My contribution to this book was made possible only with the support of my partner, Sue; our children, Kip, Michelle, and Christina; the advisors and leaders of North Star who have done the heavy lifting in my career; Libbye Morris, Lacey Struckman, and Jacci Umphress; and my co-authors and team members, Gary Schwartz and Ed Deutschlander.

Unbridled thanks must also go to the mentors and friends in my life: Maury Stewart, Dr. Larry Barton, Al Granum, Coley Bloomfield, Bob Senkler, Bonnie Godsman, Luis Chiappy, Norm Levine, Phil Harriman, Tom Burns, Eileen McDonald, Charlie Smith, Dave Porter, Joe Jordan, Conk Buckley, Paul Blanco, Bob Ferraro, Robert Rizzolino, Harry Hoopis, Bob Savage, Lewis Katz, Bob Kerzner, and the other members of both of my study groups, GAS and The Group. You have served as a band of sisters and brothers who have made all the difference. I am grateful!

Phillip C. Richards, CFP®, CLU®, RHU®
Chairman of the Board, Chief Executive Officer, North Star Resource Group

* * * *

I would like to acknowledge those who are part of this industry who have made me better:

All of the advisors of North Star Resource Group.

The Servant Leadership Steering Committee: Dave Vasos, Diane Yohn, Shaun McDuffee, Mark Bonnett, Don Schoeller, my co-author, Gary Schwartz, and my mentor, Phil Richards.

My study-group members: John Natoli, Howard Cowan, Chris Noonan, Daralee Barbera, Dave Karr, Jeff Golan, John Dixon, Kurt Jonson, Leo Tucker, Sal Durso, Tim Schmidt, William Grub, Athan Vorilas, Hugo Castro, John Becker, Brian Ferguson, David Pasciak, Terry Wold, Mike Condrey, Steve Earhart, Wayne Swenson, Harry Hoopis, Phil Richards.

The past presidents of GAMA whom I have served with: Charles A. Smith, Richard R. McCloskey, Gary L. Simpson, Conkling Buckley, Jr., William D. Pollakov, Phillip C. Richards, Michael R. White, James H. Krueger, Robert H. Baccigalupi, Timothy P. Murray, R. Michael Condrey, Linda L. Witham, Kenneth G. Gallacher, Luis G. Chiappy, Howard J. Elias, Daralee S. Barbera.

The GAMA Foundation Executive Committee: Richard Cleary, Reginald Rabjohns, Mark Rooney, Athan Vorilas, Kathryn Kellam.

John Nichols, Phil Harriman, Marv Feldman, David Woods, Bob Kerzner, Joe Jordan, Mickey Straub, Marshall Gifford, Jeff Jarnes, Larry Altman, Jim Quandt, Gaylen Harms, Paul Leighton, Chuck Housner, Todd Bramson, Doug Weisenberger, Brian Hensen, Tom Haunty, Dave Johnson, Dick McCloskey, Norm Levine, Tom Burns, Joe RoosEvans, Anna Marie Bonham, Libbye Morris, Lacey Struckman, Chialia Yang, Maury Stewart, Bob Savage, Bonnie Godsman, Bob Ferraro; and my sister, Catherine Deutschlander.

Those who have gone before us: Al Granum, Jim Krueger, Ross Borzin, Dave Nelson, Norb Winter, Brian Early, Scott Richards.

And my family: Toni, my wife, who changed my life forever, and our children: Ashley, Jake, Hannah, and Will.

Edward G. Deutschlander, CLU®, CLF®
Chief Executive Officer Elect, North Star Resource Group

Introduction

It's frustrating when people engage you in a business conversation and they leverage the phrase "back in the day." I've never understood it because there really was no single day, and we often capture select memories that have been clouded more positively than we probably should.

"Back in the day" was when insurance agents were primarily captive to one company and roamed weekly from client to client to pick up cash premiums—in cities as well as on farms. That same "day" is when agents were less captive and began to write business through several carriers, maximizing their ability to serve several masters and often capturing better pricing for clients.

Another "day" was when agents began to transform themselves into financial advisors, seeking to invest the often significant, noninsurance assets of clients. Along the way, those good old days were filled with incentive trips, long-tailed commissions, and industry meetings in which mostly older white men in suits lectured and motivated each other, followed by trophies and chicken dinners. They joined GAMA and aimed for MDRT status, earning a CLU® designation from The American College if they wanted a competitive edge and a dose of peer and client respect.

On balance, "back in the day" was very rewarding for agents and their clients. But there were swindles, ineffective regulators, some undercapitalized companies, and the introduction of products such as stranger-owned life insurance (SOLI) that soiled the wonderful work done by many ethical agents. I'm much more enamored with today.

In *Practice on Purpose*, you are exposed to some of the most challenging and important opportunities facing agents and financial advisors. A fee-only practice is feasible and exciting for many who have looked at the landscape already paved in much of Europe and Australia and have recognized that the days of commissions may not be totally gone, but that fee-only has tremendous appeal and some simplicity attached to it. For others, a hybrid of commissioned and fee-only services and products is a superb balance, allowing you to be a true navigator for your clients. I'm in that camp, believing that what the founder of The American College, Dr. Solomon S. Huebner, envisioned, was spot on in 1927 and even more so today—namely, that every financial advisor should place the interest of the client always, and only, above his or her own. Sometimes that may be fee-only, and sometimes not. But restricting your practice to one or the other misses profound opportunities for the client.

The industry you represent directly influences clients' quality of life in a more profound way than any other—medicine, aeronautics, the arts and sciences. Why? Without financial security, no one can afford health care, travel, or the perpetuation of museums, galleries, and education. Without the blessing of life insurance, there is no way to provide the only guaranteed product that lifts the quality of life for loved ones and charities. Without annuities and other retirement vehicles, there is a high likelihood that the fruit of a lifetime of work could be followed by the fall of a client's years challenged by inflation, health woes, and family debacles.

I'm ready for today.

The insurance and financial industry is indeed changing and evolving. The banks are sniffing around, globally, ready to invade space that has been previously firewalled to them in many markets. Many brokerage companies, if the truth is told, have never been very good at understanding, let alone embracing, life insurance. Several publicly traded companies have never been more aggressive about understanding that selling term insurance and treating each client as a six-decade prospect makes total sense. And the handful of thriving mutual companies that have prospered over the past century remain remarkably solvent because of superb, conservative management. But they, too, have their challenges. They must seriously ponder the fee-only space with an open mind, seeking answers.

I can't think of a more exciting and important time for you to grow your practice and support the financial and insurance needs of your clients. Forget about "back in the day." Taking the sound insight and incredibly perceptive thoughts from the pages that follow will make you proud to be part of the one industry that can help families...business...society...without peer. This is a journey worthy of your time.

Dr. Larry Barton, CAP®
Chancellor and O. Alfred Granum Chair in Management
The American College of Financial Services

Your Purpose Defines Your Practice

CHAPTER 1

Why are you here? To some extent, people are constantly contemplating their entire future—sometimes with a bold reality and sometimes more subtly, in their peripheral thinking. But most of us don't really face this critical question until we are in the throes of a life-changing situation or event. We typically don't think about it until we see our children growing up, notice our parents aging, swerve to avoid a traffic accident, receive a sobering medical diagnosis, get called into an unexpected meeting with our boss, or sit quietly in a religious setting.

Until you know what your purpose in life is, you cannot build a Practice on Purpose.

The definition of "purpose" is resolve, perseverance, an intention, the reason for which something is done or created or for which something exists. Your overarching personal purpose in life—the reason you are doing what you do—will shape and define your practice. Your personal purpose is larger than the purpose of your practice and encompasses the many facets of your personal life. People sometimes confuse their personal values with their values in the workplace. Although there is overlap between the various aspects of your personal life and your work life, as shown in the diagrams below, you are not your job.

> "The two most important days of your life are the day you are born ... and the day you find out why."
>
> **—Mark Twain**

To give you an idea of how an advisor might articulate his or her purpose, here is an example of one advisor's purpose statement for his financial advisory practice:

> ### Sample Purpose Statement
>
> The purpose of my practice is to provide individuals and families with an important measure of financial choice and dignity. We will achieve this by providing leadership through comprehensive advice that covers all areas of financial planning, including income allocation, risk management, investing for wealth accumulation, tax planning, retirement planning, and estate planning. We will create an exceptional client experience that serves the interests and goals of our clients. We will strive for integrity and will respect and align our values with the best interests of our clients. We will provide an attractive value proposition that will enable us to attract and retain those clients best suited for the services we provide. We will have contingency plans in place for a successful practice continuation that serves the interests of our clients and our advisors' families.

Sister Giovanni Gourhan was a community leader and nun of the School Sisters of Notre Dame. She ran a school in a financially poor section of St. Paul for kids whose public schools didn't want them. One time, she said, "We tell our students they are each a gift. God had a choice about their existence, and they were born."

Each of us has a purpose. There is a reason you are here. If you are an advisor, there is a good chance that your purpose in life is to help people achieve financial dignity.

Many people go to work each day without having a bigger purpose in mind. In his book *The Power of Purpose*, coach, leadership legend, and vitality expert Dick Leider says, "Working on purpose gives us a sense of direction. Without purpose, we eventually lose our way. We live without the true joy in life and work. Until we make peace with our purpose, we will never discover fulfillment in our work or contentment with what we have. Purpose is a way of life—a discipline to be practiced day in and day out. It requires a steady new commitment to face every new workday with the question, 'Why do I get up in the morning?' The wisdom to ask and the courage to answer this simple question is the essence of working on purpose."[1]

---

1. Richard J. Leider, *The Power of Purpose: Creating Meaning in Your Life and Work* (San Francisco, CA: Berrett–Koehler Publishers, Inc., 2010), 4, paperback version.

One of my favorite illustrations about a strong and clear sense of purpose is the story of the *Carpathia*. Just about everybody knows about the *Titanic*, but few people know about the *Carpathia*. It was a transatlantic passenger steamship that became famous for rescuing 705 survivors of the *Titanic* after the *Titanic* hit an iceberg and sank on April 15, 1912.

Around midnight, the *Carpathia*'s wireless operator sent a message to the *Titanic* crew. He received the *Titanic*'s distress signal in reply. The operator woke up the *Carpathia*'s captain, Arthur Henry Rostron, who immediately set a course at maximum speed to the *Titanic*'s last known position, approximately 58 miles away. He ordered the ship's heating and hot water cut off to make as much steam as possible available for the engines. But by the time the *Carpathia* reached the *Titanic* four hours later, it had already sunk.

When the *Carpathia* arrived on that horrific scene at 4 a.m., its crew members began lowering lifeboats and throwing life jackets out to people who were in the ocean. Their sense of purpose was incredibly strong and clear because they knew every life preserver and every boat they could get into the water would save lives.

Dr. Csaba Sziklai, a noted industry consultant, did significant work with us at Securian. His promotional literature used to feature an image of a life preserver. That's because I shared with him the *Carpathia* story, and we agreed that every time a person becomes a client of an advisor, we are saving a financial life. Our best advisors have a strong, urgent sense of purpose about their work because they know they are saving financial lives.

Personal Growth Leads to Practice Growth

We see many advisors who, mechanically speaking, run efficient practices. Yet their overbearing or pessimistic personalities and their tendency to think small limit the size of their practices. Many advisors see being a financial advisor primarily as a way to make money. Their practices are not closely aligned with a larger sense of why they are here. We don't see those practices getting large or thriving. It is notable to want to make a good living. However, the truly successful advisor has the mind of a capitalist *and* the heart of a social worker.

If you think small and are suspicious of the world, then your practice is going to reflect that mindset. Most importantly, an advisor who has high self-worth, high self-esteem, and an engaging personality that reflects his or her confidence is going to be much more effective at developing rapport and trust among clients than someone with an inferiority complex or a poor self-image.

You cannot outperform your self-image. If you think you can operate only at a certain level, that is going to be your optimum level of performance. Henry Ford said it well: "Whether you think you can or can't, you're right." It is rare for someone who is a small thinker and fearful of the world to be an awesome performer. Once in a while, we see an awesome performer who has another issue, which we call the "imposter syndrome." Advisors who have this attitude think, *Boy, if everybody knew me well, they would realize I really don't know as much as they give me credit for.* They believe they are not as good as people think they are. That worries us. Plato said, "We can easily forgive a child who is afraid of the dark. The real tragedy of life is when men are afraid of the light." Fear of success holds a lot of people back, just as fear of failure does. That is a hurdle an individual advisor must overcome—it is a door only the advisor can go through.

Do you happen to the world, or does the world happen to you? In the field of personality psychology, the term "locus of control" refers to the extent to which individuals believe they can control events that affect them. A person's "locus" (Latin for "location") is considered to be either internal, meaning that he believes he can control his life through his own actions, or external, meaning that he believes he has no control over his life. If a person has an external locus of control, he believes other people should receive credit when something good happens to him and blame when something bad happens to him.

> When you know your purpose, your best years are always ahead of you.

If you have an internal locus of control, you will feel that you are happening to the world and to your practice. As a result, you will be better able to create what you want than someone who has an external locus of control. If you feel you are a victim of the environment and that the world is happening to you, then no matter how good you are at what you do or how hard you try, you won't quite seem to get it done. That type of thinking is extremely limiting. When you strive to achieve personal and professional growth, you are more likely to have an internal locus of control, to perceive that you are making your own success happen.

At some point, most successful practices stall, and it is usually related to the advisor stalling as a person. Before you can grow your practice, you must go through a significant amount of personal development. When you grow as a person—as a human being, in society, in the community, in your faith, whatever it is—your practice is more likely to grow, too.

Wouldn't you rather enjoy what you're doing every day and focus on the positive impact you're making on people's lives instead of just counting dials, setting appointments, and trying to make your numbers? On his death bed, the last words of the noble economist John Maynard Keynes were, "I wish I'd drunk more champagne." If you enjoy the journey to success, you will drink more champagne along the way. If you have an articulated sense of purpose for your life and are engaged in personal growth, your practice will be more likely to grow as well.

Austrian neurologist and psychiatrist Viktor Frankl, MD, PhD, a Holocaust survivor, believed people find meaning in life by creating something or doing a deed, by experiencing something or encountering someone, and by the attitude we take toward unavoidable suffering. Be intentional about your work with your clients, and have a positive mindset that is focused on making the most of your circumstances.

When you know your purpose, your best years are always ahead of you.

Lifelong Learning Ensures Continued Growth

One of the most valuable investments you can make in your own personal growth is to build your knowledge base while acquiring designations and/or degrees. For nine decades, The American College of Financial Services (www.theamericancollege.edu) has produced and delivered the industry's foremost educational content. Its courses are taught by more than twenty-five of the nation's top thought leaders who serve as resident faculty. The curricula for designations and degrees cover a wide range of financial services practice and management topics, including success skills, financial planning, retirement, wealth transfer, leadership, and management.

Surveys conducted by The American College show that its sales training programs can help boost advisor production by up to 40 percent. Those who hold The American College financial planning designations increase their sales by 27 to 51 percent. And students who prepare for the CFP Board's exam with The American College have a 30 percent better chance of passing, compared with the average pass rates of other providers.

Here is a list of designations awarded by The American College:

- Chartered Advisor in Philanthropy® (CAP®)
- Chartered Advisor for Senior Living® (CASL®)
- Certified Financial Planner® (CFP®)
- Chartered Financial Consultant® (ChFC®)
- Chartered Healthcare Consultant® (ChHC®)
- Chartered Leadership Fellow® (CLF®)
- Chartered Life Underwriter® (CLU®)
- Financial Services Certified Professional™ (FSCP™)
- Registered Employee Benefits Consultant® (REBC®)
- Registered Health Underwriter® (RHU®)
- Retirement Income Certified Professional® (RICP®)

The American College also offers the following degrees:
- Master of Science in Financial Services (MSFS)
- Master of Science in Management (MSM)
- PhD in Financial Services and Retirement Planning

We believe lifelong learning not only facilitates personal growth but also enables advisors to remain knowledgeable as regulations and tax laws change—and they are always changing. It also gives advisors an extra level of credibility. Collectively, the three authors of this book have eight designations:
- Gary H. Schwartz, CLU®, ChFC®, CRPC®
- Phillip C. Richards, CFP®, CLU®, RHU®
- Edward G. Deutschlander, CLU®, CLF®

My Chartered Retirement Planning Counselor (CRPC®) designation is from the College for Financial Planning.

What a Practice on Purpose Looks Like

About 20 percent of tho advisors we see exemplify the ideal—a Practice on Purpose. This rather rare advisor comes into the career and enjoys helping people make sound financial decisions because doing so aligns with who he is as a person. He decides who he is, first as a person, and then as an advisor, and he defines and articulates his overarching personal purpose in life. Then he runs his practice effectively, efficiently, and on purpose. Everything he does—scheduling appointments, delivering client service, providing financial advice—reflects his purpose and values. As his practice grows, he starts bringing in other advisors who share his purpose and values, and they build out his practice, helping it grow steadily. Together, they deliver value for many years, essentially growing up with their clients. Then, as the advisor approaches his fifties, he begins transitioning the practice to junior associates. They take over the advisor's relationships and serve not only his clients but the children of his clients and continue his legacy. Then he might select a group of fifty clients he really likes and begin to spend more time with them and with his family. Finally, he enjoys a comfortable retirement that mirrors the one he has led so many other people to create. Or he rewires himself and devotes whatever time he chooses to guide the decisions of his reduced clientele.

We have an advisor we'll call Randy who manages a Practice on Purpose. Randy is in his forties. He grew up in a rural setting, came to the big city, and got a business degree. He came from a family of tremendous values. His parents believed in their children and instilled that belief in him. He has such a sense of purpose about working with clients that it's refreshing to sit and talk with him. He is so excited about their success. The fact that *he* is incredibly successful is secondary to him. Randy's entire aura is about helping his clients do really good things and make sound decisions. He knows which client gets which service. He knows their hobbies. He knows what gets them excited. We saw him at a kids' soccer game one day, and it wasn't his child playing on the field; it was the child of one of his clients.

He has a real sense of purpose. He prebooks his appointments—like a dentist, his clients know when they're going to see him next. He prepares agendas for his meetings. He follows a marketing plan. Everything he does is intentional—he does everything with purpose, on purpose. But when he is home with his lovely wife and three children, he is so home. There is no e-mail, and there are no work-related phone calls. Nothing. He is home with his family. And when he's at work, his family doesn't call him from home unless it's really serious. He has that clarity to "be where you are," which we think is important. Randy makes it fun to be a part of his practice. He puts together receptions, dinners, seminars, and social events.

He started out in this business like everyone else. He got on the phone and started calling people and going to see them. But he never took himself too seriously, so if things didn't go his way, he had such a personal belief in himself, he could shrug off discouragement and keep making phone calls. What happened later on is that people started liking him, and then they started recommending him more. He also had a couple of advisors sell their practices to him. They saw how he treated his clients, and they wanted him to treat their clients the same way. So he picked up two additional practices.

That's what a Practice on Purpose looks like.

The "Why" Is the Big Picture

People don't buy what you do or how you do it; they buy *why* you do it. Existential philosopher Friedrich Nietzsche said, "If you know the *why*, you can live any *how*." The "how" is the big picture, not the mundane details involved in your daily routine. Steve Jobs was known for creating aesthetically pleasing designs for Apple computers. But building attractive computers wasn't his mission; he wanted to *change the world*. That's much more compelling. It's motivational, and it catches people's attention.

> People don't buy what you do or how you do it; they buy *why* you do it.

When you speak with clients, do you talk about the advantages of asset allocation, dollar-cost averaging, and the Rule of 72? Or do you get clients excited about their future by talking about creating a comfortable retirement, making work an option, having the money work harder for them than they are working for their money, having their children go to any college that will take them, and leaving a legacy in a scholarship or foundation? Talk about the big picture. It will motivate your clients and capture their attention.

In developing advisors, one of our most important jobs is to find out *why* someone is an advisor.

We work with an advisor who is a big, burly, gruff guy. His clients love him, but he is rough and tough, and he is actually hard to get to know. One time we asked him, 'Tim, why did you become an advisor?"

He paused, and tears welled up in his eyes. Here is how he replied:

> Well, this is kind of a hard story for me to tell. It's really personal.
>
> I grew up in a rural community in Minnesota. We were farmers. I grew up in a farmhouse with two siblings and my mom and dad. We kids didn't know if we had money or not; we just had family. When I was ten, my dad was killed in a tractor accident. A lot of people came by with hot meals for a while after he died, and people showed up around the holidays. I noticed that my mom would serve us kids our lunch or dinner, but she wasn't eating with us. Then I realized why—there wasn't enough food for all of us. In fact, most days, my mom did not eat with us because there was not enough food. This went on for a long, long time.
>
> It made me really sad as a little boy. Eventually my mother remarried, and my stepdad was a wonderful man. Things got a lot better for our family. But there were a number of years there when things were really hard. We had no new clothes, and we didn't have many presents at Christmas time. We didn't quite know it at the time, but I realized later on just how hard that was for my mother.
>
> I became an advisor because I never want any of my clients to go through what my mother went through.

When you know the *why*, you can handle any *how*.

Where Skills, Personal Wealth, and Passion Intersect

A Venn diagram shows possible logical relationships among a collection of elements. A Venn diagram we use to depict the ideal career contains three circles that intersect. Inside those circles are three important elements of a successful career: a strong skill set, the ability to generate personal wealth, and a passion about doing work that employs those skills. A good way to tell if you are suited to a career as a financial advisor is to ask yourself if you have all three of those components.

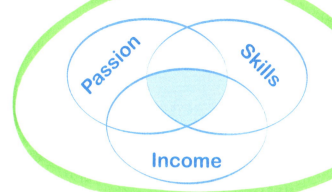

In the first circle is a skill in which you are competitive, where you can go toe to toe with the world. You are really good at those skills. You have an obligation to yourself to keep building that skill set. Each one of us can gather skills throughout our lifetimes; we can be getting better at our skills all the time. It could be an ability to work with other people, do mathematics, or work with technology. As financial advisors, we need to have skills like learning about financial products, making effective product presentations, building rapport with clients, persevering through rejection, being coachable, setting and achieving specific production goals, delegating tasks to administrative team members, and running a business.

In the second circle is the ability to generate wealth by using those skills to earn money. If you have a skill set that makes you competitive in society, you will receive financial rewards for using those skills. Your skills have monetary value in society, and the marketplace will pay you for them. It's important to note, though, that a motivation for money alone is incongruent with building a Practice on Purpose. In decades of doing quarterly reviews, we have seen plenty of advisors whose main motivation was to make a lot of money. They are not typically the advisors whose practices grow into thriving businesses that leave a positive legacy of helping people. When we do speaking engagements in Asia, the managers enjoy hearing about *purpose* because they tend to have a predominant focus on making money, and the concept of an overarching purpose is somewhat foreign to them. When exposed to the impact they can and should have on their clients, the epiphany they experience is heartwarming.

In the third circle is passion. Where do you get your juice? In your career, what do you *get* to do today versus what you *have* to do today? If your passion is to help other people with risk-based management, to help widows and orphans maintain a quality lifestyle when their breadwinner dies or becomes disabled, to help elderly people maintain financial dignity and a confident retirement, to be responsible for businesses being spared or jobs being saved, then that passion becomes your purpose.

If you can get those three elements to intersect in a career—you have competitive skills, you can generate wealth by using those skills to earn income, and you enjoy the work—then you are likely to have a fulfilling career that will more than sustain you for life.

Now let's look at those three overlapping circles again, but cover up the passion circle. Let's say you don't have passion for what you do, but you have great skills and you're generating wealth. If we go downtown at the noon hour, we can watch people with good careers making a lot of money walk by us. They look tired. They're hunched over, and they look older than they are. They're swimming against the current, and each day is labor. It's because they lack passion.

Now let's cover up only the money circle. You've got passion and skills, but you can't really make enough money doing that kind of work. That's called a hobby. You might like woodworking, and you can build beautiful cabinets in your garage. That's fun. It's a hobby. But you're not going to become a big-box home-improvement retailer doing that. You probably can't make a living at it. But you have a lot of passion for it. We often see people who have a hobby, and they try to make it into a career. It typically doesn't work out.

Finally, if you cover up only the skills circle, you are left with passion and a dream to make money. It's really not possible to create a fulfilling career without skills. Try to name something. Even a ditch digger has skills.

Before we flew around the country in airplanes, passenger trains were the latest mode of travel. The hub and spoke system of airports is built on the chassis of a great era of passenger rail transportation. Before our time, advisors and their leaders rode these rails. With this as a context, Harold Cummings, who led Minnesota Mutual Life to a position among the top ten mutual insurance companies in America, had a great phrase that may be lost in time but is still true: "No steam engine ever ran on lukewarm water. If you want to move forward, you have to get your water hot!" It's about passion.

The financial advisor who has the right skills, the ability to generate personal wealth, and passion for helping people most likely has the ability to succeed in the career. Do you have all three?

Are You an Entrepreneur, a Manager, or a Technician?

Here's a quick acid test to discover who and what you are. In his much-quoted book, *The E-Myth Revisited*, Michael Gerber says that when you start out in business, you're an entrepreneur, a manager, and a technician (artist/workman/carpenter/somebody who can bake pies). You have to be all three of them because you can't afford to hire anybody else yet. Gerber says the typical small-business owner is 10 percent entrepreneur, 20 percent manager, and 70 percent technician.[2]

If you are honest with yourself about which of those roles describes you best, then you will know who you are, what you enjoy doing, and what types of people you need to build your practice. We have advisors at North Star who, unfortunately, still don't know who they are. They don't know they're horrible managers, for example. And that's really the part of their practice they should be filling out.

We know a highly successful seventy-two-year-old business owner. He's a multi-multi-multi-millionaire. He has given almost $20 million to colleges, and he owns a $50 million company as big as North Star. One day at lunch, he said, "I'm a salesman. That's what I do." He knows himself—he is, in Gerber's words, a technician. And that's OK because when he was building his company, he knew the types of people he needed to hire to complement his own skill set—entrepreneurs and managers.

If you're an entrepreneur, you need people to manage your business, and you need technicians to execute the vital functions of your operation and keep everything organized. If you're a manager, you need to work with an entrepreneur who will be the visionary and big thinker to position your company and help you see the big picture, as well as technicians. If you're a technician, you need to team up with entrepreneurs and managers.

When we meet someone who says, "I'm going to go into this business," our first question is "Who are you? Which of those three are you?" We start asking them questions, and many times, they have no idea which of those roles fits them best. Being able to answer this fundamental question is a prerequisite for building a Practice on Purpose. A defining characteristic of a Practice on Purpose is that it is highly integrated and has a team in place that represents all of those roles in an optimal way. Every team member knows who he or she is, and they are all growing as people.

The Values Exercise

At North Star, we use an activity with our advisors called the values exercise. We learned about this incredibly revealing activity from its co-creator, Doug Lennick, the CEO and co-founder of Think2Perform.[3]

---

2. Michael E. Gerber, *The E-Myth Revisited: Why Most Small Businesses Don't Work and What to Do About It* (New York: HarperCollins Publishers, 2001), 29.

3. Doug Lennick is the CEO and co-founder of Think2Perform. He is legendary for his innovative approaches to developing high performance in individuals and organizations and is an expert at developing practical applications of the art and science of human behavior, financial and otherwise. Before founding Think2Perform, Doug, a certified financial planner (CFP®), was Executive Vice President – Advice and Retail Distribution for American Express Financial Advisors (now Ameriprise Financial). In that role, he led an organization of 17,000 field and corporate associates to unprecedented success.

Using a deck of fifty cards with a value and its definition printed on each one, we ask an advisor to select his or her top five values. It is quite difficult to narrow the choices down to five. When you select your top five values, that does not mean you have no regard for the other values; it just means those are your primary values. Some of them can be values we aspire to. For example, health may be one of my top values, but I may need to become more physically fit. Even though I'm not where I need to be, it is still one of my values. We are constantly striving to realize our values fully.

Once we know your top five values, our ability to coach you in alignment with your values improves significantly. We want what you want. If we know your values, we will understand what is important to you. Once we know those values, we can coach you to make decisions that align with your values and contribute to your getting exactly what you want. We will know what you will and will not agree to. We want you to know yourself that well, too—to know what you will and will not agree to, what you will fight for, what motivates you, what defines you. Once you know that, values become simply a matter of execution.

The same is true of your clients. If you know what your clients value in life, you can tailor your financial advice in a way that leads them to achieve and preserve those values.

If we were to look at your calendar, we could determine what your values are. You cannot manage time. We all have the same amount of time; it goes by at the same rate for all of us. But we *can* manage our priorities. Better said, we can manage our values. Where you spend your time should match your values and reflect who you are as a person. If you leave at two o'clock so that you can be with your daughter at her dental appointment, we already know a lot about you. A Practice on Purpose from a tactical standpoint is that you build your calendar around the priorities you have established.

We coach advisors to build their calendars beginning with setting time aside for their families and time away from the practice to go on vacation and rejuvenate themselves. Certain days of the week are your prep days (typically Monday and Friday), and certain days are your game days, your high-energy days when you will be more effective with clients (typically Tuesday, Wednesday, and Thursday). Then you decide which clients you are going to see on which days. That is one of the ways you build a Practice on Purpose.

The advisor who comes to work and reacts to new e-mails, phone calls, and questions is not building a Practice on Purpose. We have advisors who have no prebooked appointments. They are just showing up. Their clients are driving their practice. They react to the whims of anyone who comes along.

They are unable to distinguish between urgent and important matters. They are not happening to the practice; the practice is happening to them.

Stephen Covey, the author of *7 Habits of Highly Effective People*, does an exercise on stage during some of his presentations to demonstrate how to prioritize what's important. He has two big Plexiglass bowls on a table. In one bowl, he places a whole bunch of small beans. Next to that, he has three large rocks. He gets a participant from the audience and asks her, "What are the most important things in your life?" The participant might say, "Family, faith, and career." He explains to the audience that the beans represent all of the little chores in life like getting your laundry done, grocery shopping, paying your taxes, mowing your lawn, and calling your parents.

Then he tells the participant, "I want you to take the three big rocks and put them into the bowl with all of the little beans. But you can't have them sticking out over the top of the bowl because the bowl represents the amount of time you have in your life." The participant tries, but she cannot fit the big rocks in the bowl on top of all the beans.

Then he has the audience member put the three big rocks into an empty bowl first. Then she adds as many beans as she can fit into the bowl. There is enough space between the big rocks that all of the beans can fit. The moral of the story is if you don't take care of the big rocks, or priorities, first, you won't get to them. But if you put the big rocks in first, then you can fit in the little, less important priorities into your life.

> The advisor who has a Practice on Purpose takes care of the big priorities first.

The advisor who has a Practice on Purpose takes care of the big priorities first. An example is Kevin Brewer, one of our advisors in Atlanta. He goes to the gym to work out for an hour before work. Then, for the first four hours of his work day, Kevin is prospecting, calling leads, and marketing. He is doing the hardest work of his day in the first four hours. Then his day gets easier because he already has the big rocks in place. Your rocks are your values, which become your priorities.

The interesting thing about values is that you can ask a hundred different top-performing advisors, managing partners, physicians, attorneys, or anyone else what their values are. And even though they all share a high level of integrity, character, and passion for what they do, they can have widely varying values. For example, Phil, Ed, and I have done the "values card" exercise, and there is little overlap among our values:

Gary's Top Five Values
1. Achievement
2. Meaningful work
3. Family
4. Health
5. Leadership

Phil's Top Five Values
1. Religion
2. Family
3. Integrity
4. Independence
5. Leadership

Ed's Top Five Values
1. Integrity
2. Spirituality
3. Loyalty
4. Leadership
5. Excellence

The Importance of Self-Awareness

An important aspect of self-awareness is knowing what your top values are and what you are doing on a daily basis to honor and realize them. Self-awareness is about getting better every day. The advisor who has a Practice on Purpose is keenly self-aware and is always improving. We all have blind spots that are obstacles to becoming more self-aware. We can gain clarity and overcome those blind spots in several ways: by getting coaching, asking for feedback, being receptive to critiquing, and analyzing our progress.

Doug Lennick makes presentations frequently to clients and industry groups. He is a phenomenal speaker. One day a few years ago, he was speaking before a group of clients, and he was better than ever; he knocked the ball out of the park. Clients were on the edge of their chairs. Afterward, I commented about how he gets better and better. I told him I couldn't believe how he stayed so fresh and energized. His response was, "I really appreciate that. But think how much better I am going to be next year."

Doug was aware that he was getting better, and he was aware that he would be even better the next year. That's self-awareness. We remind our advisors how much better we can all get by next year by working together.

We have talked about the importance of knowing who you are, first as a person, then as an advisor; defining and articulating your overarching personal purpose; and knowing whether you are an entrepreneur, a manager, or a technician. Knowing these important facts about yourself requires self-awareness. The advisor who has a Practice on Purpose is keenly self-aware. If you want to create value, lead people to financial independence, and enjoy what you're doing, the first step is to know these fundamental facts about yourself. Before you attempt to grow your practice, take a hard look at yourself and decide who and what you are.

Once you have clarity about your role in your practice, we can work on developing your skills further, improving your self-image, and wordsmithing your presentation to clients. All of those tactical steps follow your conceptual work.

The problem with self-awareness is that if you don't have it, you don't know you don't have it, so you're not self-aware. But if you are self-aware, it's a powerful thing. Probably 20 percent of the advisors we've seen have the quality of self-awareness. In our meetings with advisors, we strive to increase their self-awareness and to lead them to be deliberate about the actions they're taking and the opportunity they have every day so it's not rote or routine.

> One way to increase your self-awareness is to seek out the advice of others, including your clients.

We coach our advisors to live with a sense of awareness and vitality. We want them to position their appointments as "Who do I get to meet with today? What can I learn about how their work is going and how their children are doing?" Too often, advisors focus on "What are the three appointments I have to complete today?" Advisors who have a strong sense of purpose are engaged and genuinely interested in their clients' lives. They provide financial leadership, which we define as taking someone to a place they would not have gone on their own. Leadership requires being a good listener and understanding each client's unique situation. If you know your client's resources are and what her values are, you can lead her to make prudent financial decisions.

One way to increase your self-awareness is to seek out the advice of others, including your clients. We recommend that you ask your clients, "What can I do to be a better advisor? What is one thing I should know to be a better advisor to you?" Even if your client can't think of any feedback for you at that moment, let her know you are open to hearing it at any time. It takes real courage to do that because most people don't like feedback. But in the end, feedback is the breakfast of champions.

Be Intentional in Everything You Do

When you are self-aware, you are intentional about everything you do. You have a purpose for every conversation, every action you take. Being intentional is closely related to having a Practice on Purpose—you are doing everything with a purpose, on purpose. Prepare for your conversations with clients. Be intentional in your conversations. Choose your language carefully.

Being intentional helps you make every moment in your life count for something, whether you are at work or at home. When I go home at the end of the day, the hour between five and six o'clock is a little chaotic because everyone is coming home, regrouping, looking for food, and moving on to the next thing for the evening. As I drive down my street, I am thinking, *I am going to be intentional. What is a compliment I can give somebody in my family? How can I reinforce something that went well today?* If I am more intentional during that period of time, the entire evening goes better.

Every year, Phil and Ed attend the Demontreville Jesuit Retreat in Lake Elmo, Minnesota, and are totally silent for three and a half days. It is a Catholic retreat. An important component is the sacrament of reconciliation, in which you confess your sins and shortcomings to a priest and commit to changing your ways. Then he shares his thoughts and says you are forgiven. Without declaring a commitment to change, the confession is meaningless. (The same is true of building a Practice on Purpose—unless you commit to changing your conceptual framework, intentions, strategies, and execution methods, you will not progress.)

One year at the retreat, Ed was talking with Father Ed Sthokal, a remarkable person, about how to connect better with family members. He said to Ed, "I want to share something that helped me a long time ago. Whenever I would wash my hands before dinner, I would always make it a point to think about what the conversation was going to be at dinner and what was the main theme. What did I want the result to be?"

Ever since then, when Ed washes his hands before dinner, it is an automatic thought for him: *What are we going to accomplish tonight at this meal? What do we want to have done? What do I want the outcome to be? What do I need to be sensitive to?*

It is a change in mindset, to do things intentionally and deliberately, with purpose, rather than just winging it and hoping for the best. Being intentional is part of the mindset that can propel an advisor from having a $300,000 practice to having a $1 million practice.

Your Vision

Once you have defined your purpose, it will be easy for you to decide on the vision for your practice—where you want to be in the future.

Purpose, goals, and vision are somewhat abstract concepts. They cannot make an impact in your practice until you combine them with action, execution.

Joel Barker is a futurist, author, and lecturer who has a great quote about that in his video on vision: "Vision without action is just a dream. Action without vision just passes the time. Vision with action can change the world."

As you can see in the vision statement below, which is an actual advisor's vision statement for his practice, a vision reflects the advisor's values.

> ### Sample Vision Statement
>
> As an advisor, I will make a significant and positive difference in the lives of our clients and their families by ensuring that, in my Practice on Purpose:
>
> - We prepare for the certainty of uncertainty.
> - Our clients are protected along the way in the event of disability, illness, or untimely death.
> - We ensure that our clients always have a safe and ready source of money if they need it for emergencies or opportunities.
> - We contribute to our clients' families having lives full of the things that matter to them—homes, travel, education, charitable giving, confident retirements, and estate creation.
> - Our clients are better off because they worked with our practice.
> - Our practice always aligns with my values, and we run it on purpose and with a purpose.
> - The practice becomes a significant asset for me in my retirement and that I leave a legacy and capable successors to continue providing quality advice to our clients and their children.

Your Personal Brand

Every professional, every advisor has a personal brand, which is essentially the thought that occurs to someone right after they hear your name. If you walk up someone and say, "Hey, have you ever met Jeff Lancaster?" a thought is going to pop into her head immediately. She might think, *Jeff is really talented and resourceful* or *He is a loyal friend*, for example.

When someone asks one of your clients about you, you want them to think, *He has been extremely helpful to us. He listens and understands our situation.*

What is the brand you are trying to build? It could be a reputational brand, a conversational brand, a print brand, your website brand, or your LinkedIn brand—any medium that causes an immediate thought. What is the adjective that pops into someone's head after they hear your name? That is your personal brand. Being a leader to your clients contributes to a strong personal brand.

You Are a Gift

In her best-selling book *A Return to Love*, Marianne Williamson wrote an inspiring passage that reminds us each of the inherent value we contribute to the world:

> Our deepest fear is not that we are inadequate. Our deepest fear is that we are powerful beyond measure. It is our light, not our darkness, that most frightens us. We ask ourselves, who am I to be brilliant, gorgeous, talented, fabulous? Actually, who are you not to be? You are a child of God. Your playing small doesn't serve the world. There's nothing enlightened about shrinking so that other people won't feel insecure around you. We are all meant to shine, as children do. We were born to make manifest the glory of God that is within us. It's not just in some of us; it's in everyone. And as we let our own light shine, we unconsciously give other people permission to do the same. As we're liberated from our own fear, our presence automatically liberates others.[4]

You are a gift. This is not a dress rehearsal; it is your real life. Offer your best and make your effort count in a big way. Have your purpose define your practice. Surveys of people on their deathbeds reveal that they are not afraid of dying; they are afraid their lives lacked meaning, significance, and relevance. They want to have mattered. As an advisor, if you leave a positive impact on people's families and give them dignity about their money, choices, honor—all the aspects of having money work for them rather than them working for money—you are, in our opinion, in the company of clergy members and surgeons. Who else makes a bigger impact on someone's life?

---

4. Marianne Williamson, *A Return to Love: Reflections on the Principles of "A Course in Miracles"* (New York: HarperCollins Publishers, 1992), 190. This quote is often attributed incorrectly to Nelson Mandela.

An American Indian quote says that a person is not truly gone until all that he or she has touched is gone. If the legacy you leave is significant enough, your impact can be felt forever.

> ### Marshall's Story: How My Purpose Drives My Practice
>
> Marshall W. Gifford, CLU®, ChFC®—Senior Partner and Founder, North Star Medical Division, North Star Resource Group
>
> My purpose is ingrained in everything I do. The reality is the vast majority of people need help planning, and unfortunately, too many don't even know it. My practice exists to help physicians and dentists make sound financial decisions, to first and foremost manage risk, followed by efficiently eliminating debt and accumulating and protecting wealth. I show them the most efficient ways to do these things, and if they want to follow my advice, they can. If they choose to not follow my advice, they can as well, but not under my watch and not within my practice.
>
> I've seen what happens when bad things occur and people haven't planned. Having the confidence to stand by your recommendations because they are right, regardless of whether or not the client likes them, is the key to having a lifelong practice built with people who share your values.

Applying the Concepts to *Your* Practice on Purpose

1. Why are you here? What is your purpose in life? It is important that you define your purpose clearly and articulate it. Your personal purpose is larger than your practice's purpose, and this is the most important element in building your Practice on Purpose.

_____
_____
_____
_____
_____
_____

2. Before you can grow your practice, you must go through a significant amount of personal development. When you grow as a person—as a human being, in society, in the community, in your faith, whatever it is—your practice is more likely to grow, too. What activities do you commit to doing in the next year to help you grow personally?

___

3. As you assess yourself honestly, to what extent do you think you have competitive skills, the ability to generate personal wealth, and the passion to build a highly successful financial advice practice?

___

4. Again, taking an honest look at your skill set and natural inclinations, would you say you are more of an entrepreneur, a manager, or a technician? To what extent have you surrounded yourself and populated your practice with the two roles in which you do not excel as much? What will you do to backfill those roles in your practice so that you can concentrate on what you do best?

___

5. What are your top five values? How will you build your Practice on Purpose around them?

6. How self-aware are you? To what extent do you recognize your strengths and weaknesses? To what extent do you know who you are—first as a person, and then as an advisor? If you don't think you are as self-aware as you should be, what steps can you take to increase your self-awareness?

7. To increase your self-awareness, to what extent do you seek out the advice of others, including your clients? Consider asking your clients, "What can I do to be a better advisor? What is one thing I should know to be a better advisor to you?" How will you word this question when you meet with your clients in the future?

Creating an Exceptional Client Experience

CHAPTER

2

The typical mid-career financial advisor has somewhere between two hundred and three hundred clients. He is doing OK, making money, paying the bills. He likes the career and is committed to being in the industry, but something is lacking in his practice—it's the fact that he is not managing his Practice on Purpose. He reacts more than he prepares. As a result, his clients are probably experiencing inconsistent, unpredictable service.

How would I know if I am a top client in your practice?

This chapter explains how you can create an exceptional client experience by working more systematically, proactively, and deliberately. When you enhance the client experience, you will build loyalty, and your top clients will recognize how much you value them. They will, in turn, value the relationship with you and are more likely to become an advocate for you.

> "Quality in a service or product is not what you put into it. It is what the client or customer gets out of it."
>
> —**Peter Drucker**
> Management Consultant, Educator, and Author

Take Inventory

Many advisors walk around without a good idea of what is going on in their practice. The leader of any retail or professional services firm, whether it's an Apple store, a CPA firm, a doctor's office, or a car-repair garage, should know who his or her clients are. When we begin working with an advisor, we want to get a clear picture of what's really going on in his practice, so we will request a suite of reports. The data we get will reveal how many households the advisor is servicing, which clients have which assets or products, the clients' ages, and how long the advisor has worked with each client. Often we'll rank the clients by revenue, from the highest-revenue client down to the lowest. Or we will rank the clients by assets or simply list them alphabetically by last name. There are different ways of organizing your client list. The important point is that the organization should take place.

We show their "colors" to them and make them shine—like the old Bob Dylan song "Lay, Lady, Lay." It says, "Whatever colors you have in your mind, I'll show them to you and you'll see them shine." We show them the numbers and say, "Here's what's in your practice. What do you think?" Often, it's a revelation for advisors, and they will say, "I didn't know I had that many households." Or "I didn't realize so many of my clients have just one product with me. They've done nothing else with me." Or "I met them a long time ago when I was just trying to survive in the business, and I haven't followed up with them." Or "I didn't realize that 80 percent of my revenue is coming from the top 20 percent of my clients." They are often surprised at what they discover.

In fact, it's quite common for advisors to find that the top 20 percent of their clients generate 80 percent of their revenue. It's the 80-20 rule, also called Pareto's Principle. It originated with the Italian economist Vilfredo Pareto, who proposed this theory in 1906. It suggests that 20 percent of something is always responsible for 80 percent of the results. We wish it were different, but it's not. This rule has stood the test of time.

We often have our advisors categorize their clients into deciles, or tenths. If you have 100 clients, for example, you can analyze them ten at a time. So, when you get to client number 30, you are three deciles into your client base, and that portion of your clientele will probably represent 90 percent of your revenue.

We see this consistently. It can be awakening to realize that 70 percent of your clients generate only 10 percent of your revenue. An important question to ask yourself is, "Why am I keeping these clients?" Chances are, you are not providing consistent, reliable service to them anyway. This would be a good time to enlist the help of a more junior advisor to provide service to these clients. Using our North Star succession planning techniques, the senior advisor can maintain control at the same time he or she is receiving revenue because of the efforts of others.

Another good rule of thumb is that your top 30 percent—the top three deciles of your client list—should be in an investment/advisory or planning relationship with you.

Segment Your Clients

The next step we take is to segment the advisor's clients into categories. There are various philosophies about how to do this. Some advisors categorize their clients into A, B, and C categories, while others color-code them—for example, as platinum, gold, or silver clients. At North Star, we often use the categories of AAA, AA, and A so that if a client sees her file, she won't be disappointed to see that she is a "C" client. All clients are important; they are just not equally important.

It's important for advisors to choose how they want to segment their clients. We will ask them, "Who do you think your top clients are, and why?" That decision can be based on revenue or assets, or they could be people you like or people who are going somewhere in their careers. Maybe someone otherwise would be lower in the ranking, but because they're related to one of your top clients, that elevates them into a higher category. Or maybe they are large centers of influence; they introduce you to a lot of other clients and market you well. So you may raise them to a higher category because of their contribution to your practice.

> All clients are important; they are just not equally important.

Identify Your Client Advocates

We do an exercise with advisors in which we look at their top fifty clients—one at a time—to determine how the advisor came to know them. It is a meticulous process. I ask the advisor, "How did you meet that client?" We identify the sources of all fifty clients—were they a recommendation, and if so, who recommended them to the advisor? Did the advisor meet the client at a seminar? Did he acquire that client from a list he purchased? What happened? What caused that client to join the practice? In the process of doing that, we start seeing themes. It is often an awakening for the advisor to look at the sources of his top fifty clients—the most important people in his practice. If they are almost all from recommendations, the moral of the story is the advisor probably should get even better at asking for recommendations. Advisors tend to get more clients using that approach than they do by purchasing a list or meeting people at seminars or dinners.

When we realize that one or two clients referred people they know to the advisor, I will circle those clients' names and then draw lines to the names of people they referred to the advisor. I call that the "spider diagram" because at some point it begins to look like a spider web.

Usually an advisor's top fifty clients are at the top because of the amount of assets they have invested or the amount of revenue they generate for the advisor. However, I often challenge advisors to rethink their definition of who their top clients are. A client who recommends three or more people to the advisor over the years is a valuable client, even if she may not have the amount of assets or income another client has. She is an advocate for your practice and should be treated as a top client.

Build Your Calendar around Your Clients

Once you have placed all of your clients in appropriate segments, you can plan which clients you will see and when. In Chapter 1, we talked about how we work with advisors to build their calendars first around their family time and then around their client meetings. We call it "time blocking," and it's about managing advisors' energy and time. Every Monday morning, you can review who you're seeing that week, but more importantly, you can review who you're going to see in the week that follows. If you're working at least two weeks ahead, that cuts down on the fire drills, and you're much more prepared. If you're getting ready for a Tuesday appointment on Monday, it's too late. If you are preparing for a meeting while the client is in the lobby, it's definitely too late. We know it happens.

We tell our advisors we want them to come in on the first day of January with fifty appointments already booked—with the right people. If they get off to a good first quarter, they are likely to have a good first half of the year. If they have a good first half of the year, they are likely to have a good year. So that first quarter is critical to having high client engagement and a good, fast start. Otherwise, you have a "feast and famine" situation going on. You might get really busy and put off booking the next group of appointments. Then June comes, and you have nothing going on because you spent the second quarter trying to clean up the work you did in the first quarter.

When we share this strategy with advisors, their eyes really light up. It's a game changer.

Be Attentive to File Construction

Once you have completed your client segmentation, you can devise a system that lets you and your team know which clients belong in which segments. Color coding works well in this respect because it provides an immediate visual cue about the client's status. You might use platinum-colored folders for your platinum-level clients, for example. So when a team member interacts with that client and grabs the folder, the client's category will be apparent immediately. If it's a top client, you and your team members will know you need to return that phone call quickly or do an extremely careful and thorough job of responding to requests.

A lot of people think this is funny, but we used to teach classes in file construction—the optimum way to construct a client's file. There is a science to it. Regardless of the system you use, your clients' files should be neat and organized in some kind of logical and predictable order—by topic or by date of contact, for example.

One strategy that works well is to use expanding folders with seven pockets. Label the pockets to represent the seven categories of financial advice as defined by the CFP® profession (financial planning, insurance planning and risk analysis, retirement planning, employee benefits, investment planning, tax and estate planning, and advanced financial planning). Staple the client's goals to the front cover. That way, the client's information is easy to reach every time she calls or sends you an e-mail. You can take a quick look at that front cover and say to the client, "Jennifer, I just want to confirm that retiring at age fifty-five is your top goal." Everything else you say after that point is helping her get to that goal. That enhances the client experience because she knows you are aware of key issues she has discussed with you before.

Take Advantage of CRM Programs

Most companies have customer relationship management (CRM) software available for their advisors, but many advisors do not take full advantage of this opportunity. You can use this tool to segment your clients, develop a contact strategy, keep track of your contacts with clients, take notes, document past meetings, and guide the agenda for future meetings.

We are fortunate that we have computers to handle these critical details now. Using a CRM system enables us to be more efficient, do a better job of documenting and chronicling our clients' needs and progress, and enable effective client service by multiple team members.

Present a Menu of Services

Having a menu of services to show your clients is an absolutely critical part of your Practice on Purpose. This is an important tool that will inform your decision about how to take care of each client's unique needs. It also will help you design your client-service model and give you a way to determine which clients belong in which segments. Then you can tailor the client experience for each segment.

There are typically three levels of service, or treatments, described below. Your menu of services will help you articulate each one to your clients. Some menus of services we use at North Star are shown in the appendix at the back of this book.

Three Levels of Service

The three primary levels of service are as follows:
1. **Comprehensive financial advice**—The top treatment is the comprehensive service model. We call it "full wealth management" or "comprehensive financial advice." It includes all seven areas of financial planning based on the CFP® exam mentioned earlier. This is the prestige treatment, and it is an ongoing advice relationship between you and your client. We discuss it in more detail in Chapter 3.

At this top level, you have context. You understand your clients' goals. After all, you're in the goal-achievement business. You understand the client's ultimate financial destination, and you are serving as the CFO of her household. Your leadership is about contributing to clients discovering or uncovering their true needs, wishes, and dreams—getting to the root of the matter.

At this level, you want to include only those clients who are fully engaged. They're cooperating, providing you with documents, and notifying you of any employer benefit changes. Engaging with your top-level clients is part of the fun of having a Practice on Purpose. You're working shoulder to shoulder with the client and looking at her financial situation with her—not sitting across the desk from her.

A big part of this model is conducting regular meetings with each client. You can determine how often you will meet with clients at this level of service. You might have two face-to-face meetings and two phone check-ins each year, for example. It is ideal for the top clients in your practice to know they are in this category based on the way you treat them and how frequently you contact them and meet with them.

2. **Investment advisory**—The second level of treatment is less comprehensive. You might provide this level of service to someone who is just starting out in her career, building net worth and income. Her financial concerns will be pretty basic, such as improving cash flow, protecting assets, or taking specific actions to leverage employer benefits. This level of service often relates to money management, a topic of advice we call "investment advisory," or IA.

    This level of service lacks context because you know a little about the client's financial situation, but you don't know the big picture. Your client might be putting some money aside every month and investing, but you don't know what her ultimate goal is. What is she going to do with that money? How much is enough? What kind of accounts does she want? How much risk is she willing to take?

3. **Transaction**—The third service category typically involves a product or transaction, typically in which the client transfers risk from herself to an insurance company. You will handle a significant amount of disability income and life insurance products at this level—specific client needs. For example, dentists who are just starting their practices need disability income insurance because if they become disabled after investing all that money and work to get educated and establish the business, they will be in big financial trouble. That is a transaction—the dentist will buy a disability income product from you. At the transaction level of service, you probably don't know much about what else is going on in your client's life.

When to Present the Menu of Services

You can present the menu of services when you meet with clients or prospects to discuss what's important to them. You may say, "There are three ways we can work together." Then you will present the three options and let the client choose the level of service that meets her needs at that time. When she tells you what her most pressing financial concern is, you will know which level of service is appropriate. She might say she just needs some life insurance, and that would be the third, or transactional, level of service. Or she might say she knows she should be saving some money. That's where the second level of service comes in. If she says she is worried about whether or not her kids can go to college, when she can retire, or what will happen if her husband is unable to work for a while, she is probably a candidate for the top level of service.

Often, when advisors are reaching their tenth year in the business and we sit down to work with them, we discover that they have never presented a menu of services to some of their clients. We encourage them to approach each client to determine the level of service each one needs. Then they can segment their client list.

Pricing Services Appropriately

Nordstrom's customer service is legendary. It is the epitome of high service and high quality. They have a liberal return policy, and their employees make an effort to connect with customers and to provide impeccable customer service. Folklore has it that they have been known to allow returns of products they don't even sell. But they're not cheap.

> Part of the problem with many advisors' practices is they don't charge appropriately for the level of service they're providing.

Part of the problem with many advisors' practices is they don't charge appropriately for the level of service they're providing. We have a lot of advisors who are providing Nordstrom service at the transactional level of pricing. Understandably, people want the Mercedes–Benz or Audi but want to pay a Chevrolet price. And, left on their own, many advisors allow that to happen. Their clients will ask for a lot of advice, and often, they provide it but don't charge for it. As a result, many advisors are underpaid for what they're doing.

The other side of inappropriate pricing can happen, too. An advisor may have a top client who's paying him a lot of revenue, but he isn't doing much. When that happens, the advisor is at risk of losing that client. Further, this is an area of exposure for an advisor if the regulators pursue their intention of examining the relationship of fees to deliverables. A primary reason advisors do not charge what they are worth for their time, knowledge, and discipline is the mindset we will discuss in Chapter 3—they are adult "elephants" still tied to the stake. They do not realize the incredible value they provide.

Be deliberate about deciding on the appropriate level of service for each client segment, then charge accordingly. Most advisors don't think this through. They're just taking an e-mail, making a phone call, and not being deliberate about making sure that the relationship is working for themselves and their clients. Make sure you're not shortchanging yourself by giving clients the Nordstrom treatment for a transaction price. Also make sure you're not ignoring an extremely valuable client.

How you charge is your business. But if you don't charge enough, you won't have a business! No one wins if that happens. When you are creating the fee structure for your practice, make sure you not only have a profitable practice today but also the ability to serve all of your clients well into the future. Take an inventory of your level of expertise. Think of the tens of thousands of hours you have invested in the discipline of financial advising. Think of all the hours of continuing education you have completed. Think of every seminar and every professional-development, summer, and winter summit meeting you have attended. Think of the professional designations you have earned. Think of all of the client cases you have worked on that have allowed you to diagnose, prescribe, and help your clients start and stay the course to financial security.

An exercise we often do with advisors is to divide the amount of money they think they should be taking home after business expenses by the 2,000 working hours in a year. Let's say, for example, that you would like to take home $250,000 net after business expenses and payout. When you divide $250,000 by 2,000 hours in a year, you get an hourly rate of $125. Next, we ask our advisors, regarding a specific client, "How many hours a year do you think you want to either meet with that client or prepare to meet with her?" If the advisor says ten hours, then we multiply that by the hourly rate of $125, which is $1,250. As a general rule, that is the amount of revenue the client is ideally producing for you, through either product compensation or an advice relationship.

An advisor who is a leader actually trains his clients by helping them acknowledge his worth. That takes courage, but it's a necessary step toward leading your clients to reach their goals and also to compensate you commensurately for the impact you are having on their lives. Again, it's a mindset issue. Learning to price your services appropriately requires coming to terms with yourself and acknowledging your value—it's a door only you can go through.

You have probably heard the old adage that there are three aspects to any service: cheap, good, and fast. In general, a client or customer can have any two of those three qualities in a service. He can have it cheap and good, but it won't be fast. He can have it cheap and fast, but it might not be as good as it could be. Or he can have it good and fast, but it won't be cheap. That could be another Venn diagram.

Keep that in mind with your clients. If they want superior advice provided in a timely manner, they can expect to compensate you appropriately. If they want really good advice and don't care when they get it, the cost might be a little lower. If they want cheap and fast advice, they cannot expect the best from you.

Appropriate pricing involves a delicate balance. We will lose clients if we charge inappropriately high fees, but our firm will lose advisors if our fees are inappropriately low. It's a dance advisors need to do. Most of the time, advisors are not compensated appropriately for the impact they have. Industry icon Norm Levine spoke to our advisors recently. He asked an important question: "Whose family benefits more when someone becomes your client—your family or the client's family?" The answer is the client's family. As the advisor, you certainly benefit a little bit, but nothing in proportion to that client's family. Who are you not to be paid appropriately?

The following diagram depicts this delicate balance:

1. If you provide low value at a low price, you are merely completing a transaction for your client.

2. If you provide low value at a high price, you will lose clients.

3. If you provide high value at a low price, you are in danger of losing your practice because you will be overworked and underpaid. This is where burnout originates, and advisors exhaust themselves and their resources by not charging appropriately for their service, expertise, and wisdom.

4. Of course, the ideal situation is in the upper right quadrant—providing high value for a high price. This is the hallmark of a Practice on Purpose—a mature practice that represents the exchange of your best effort for the client's compensation and trust.

Price & Value Matrix

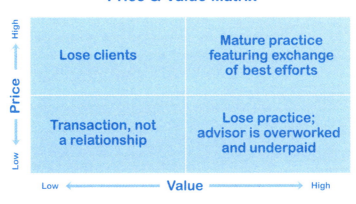

Recently, one of our North Star Resource Group Partners, Clarisa Hernandez, CFP®, asked me, "Gary, based on what you know about other practices, my practice, and the growth of practices, if you could give me only one piece of advice, what would it be?"

I thought about it for a few seconds, then said, "Clarisa, I think it is this: If you are giving Cadillac service to a Chevrolet client and the Chevrolet client is getting Cadillac service, it will literally tear apart your practice over time because you are not aligning what you are delivering for the right caliber of client."

Clarisa is twenty-eight years old and Hispanic. She is one of the few minority female advisors in our business who is in a field leadership role; she manages our Denver office. She is a perennial Million Dollar Round Table qualifier and is the first person in her family to be born in the United States; her parents came here from Mexico. She has been recognized with numerous awards in the industry. You can read more about Clarisa in the advisor vignette at the end of Chapter 10.

Emulate the Dentist-Office Model

Troy Korsgaden, an agent with Farmers Insurance Group of Companies, runs his office like a dental practice. One day, when he was in the lobby of his dentist office waiting for his appointment, he noticed that when the receptionist wasn't greeting clients or saying goodbye to them, she was on the phone scheduling people to come in to have their semi-annual checkups. She was an active and vital member of the team. He got the idea to run his agency the same way, and he has had tremendous success with this model. He doesn't schedule any of his appointments himself. He is now a motivational speaker and author, in addition to running his huge agency, and he has trained tens of thousands of agents in his model.

In his book, *Power Position Your Agency*, he says, "Call it an epiphany if you want. All I know is that I was suddenly struck by what a simple but powerful business strategy this was, because if the dentist did not have someone in his chair, he wouldn't have anything to bill out. The only things he would have were payments on his equipment and an unending stream of overhead costs. The person calling his clients was making sure that didn't happen. If it worked for him, I couldn't imagine why it couldn't work for me. It could, and it did."[5]

There are many parallels between how a dentist's office is run and how a Practice on Purpose should be run. Like Troy, we can learn from the dentist.

You probably know when your next dentist appointment is, even if it's six months from now. That's because most dentists have a really good service

---

5. Troy Korsgaden, *Power Position Your Agency: A Guide to Insurance Agency Success* (Amazon Digital Services, Inc., 1998), Kindle edition.

model. Before you leave an appointment, a staff member will schedule your next appointment. When that appointment approaches a few months later, you will receive a reminder post card, an e-mail, a text, and/or a phone call.

Once you arrive at the dentist's office, a dental hygienist preps you for the exam, and she cleans and polishes your teeth. The dentist isn't the one who walks you to the chair and does all of that. He doesn't come in until it's time for the detailed, high-knowledge work. Once he is done, he will shake your hand, give you a gleaming smile, and go into another exam room to do the high-level work with another patient. One of the team members will tidy you up, give you a little gift, walk you to the door, and tell you it's great to see you and that your teeth are looking good. You'll get some kind of positive reinforcement.

> Don't let a client leave your office without scheduling your next meeting.

We have seen advisor practices in which the client never goes in the advisor's office. The advisor is like the dentist, seeing each client for the high-knowledge work only. Clients will be in two or three different conference rooms, and the advisor will meet with them, one at a time. At the end of the meeting, the advisor's paraplanner or junior advisor will enter the room, and the advisor will recap the meeting. Everybody takes notes. The advisor is affirming with the client what just happened so that she can say, "No, that's not quite what I wanted" and clarify.

The objective of a dental practice is to get patients into the chairs. But the dentist did not book your appointment. He did not call to remind you about your appointment, nor did he send you a text. His office staff handled those details in a highly systematic way.

As an advisor, you can do the same. Start systematizing the appointments on your calendar with your clients so that they know when the next meeting is. Don't let a client leave your office without scheduling your next meeting. Then your team member will not have to do the cat-and-mouse routine and hunt the client down to try to get the next appointment scheduled. Administratively, it saves a lot of time. Everyone is busy. If your receptionist or assistant schedules the next meeting right then, your client will have it on her smartphone or device right away, and it's done.

Make Meetings Purposeful

Meeting with your clients regularly is critical. If you don't engage with them systematically in a structured, predictable way, they aren't likely to move forward with their financial goals, and your practice will be unable to move forward, too. Left on their own, most clients won't do anything. You cannot lead them if you do not see them.

Advisors are experts in the certainty of uncertainty. Of course you don't know what's going to happen in the future, but that doesn't mean you can't help your clients prepare.

Why do people go to McDonald's? Their food is not particularly culinary. But we go there because it's predictable. We know exactly what we're going to get. When you meet with your clients regularly, they will start seeing you as predictable, and they will grow accustomed to the repeatable experience you are creating for them. We have also found that advisors who meet with their clients regularly receive more recommendations. Clients know that if they recommend you to someone they know, you will provide a positive, predictable experience for them, too.

Prepare an Agenda

The advisor who manages a Practice on Purpose prepares for client meetings thoroughly. Too many advisors go to meetings without putting much thought into them. That is a missed opportunity because meetings are where the advisor's value proposition can be at its cutting edge. In a Practice on Purpose, you are using meetings to move the client ahead in her financial situation by engaging with her systematically and repeatedly in a purposeful way.

When you meet with a client, prepare an agenda in advance. An agenda typically covers the seven areas of financial advice. You can start out by saying, "How are things going with you? Has anything big happened in your life since the last time we met? Here's what I plan to cover with you today." Then hand her the agenda so that you can go through it together. Take notes on the agenda during the meeting. When the meeting ends, both you and the client will have some action items. Let your client know you will follow up with her about her progress on those tasks.

Your meetings need to start and end on time. Meetings shouldn't last longer than one hour. If you need more than an hour, schedule another meeting. Sometimes we hear of advisors having three-hour meetings. That is fatiguing and excessive.

Give Each Meeting a Theme

We recommend that advisors assign a theme to their meetings to provide a deep dive on important topics while keeping the broader goals in mind. If there is no theme, it's easy for both you and the client to get bored. The client is likely to disengage. Here are some ways you could assign a theme to each meeting:

1. The first meeting of the year might be a goal review. You can use your notes from your previous contacts with the client to find out if her goals have changed.
2. The second meeting could be a portfolio and investment review, particularly around taxes because by then, the client would have just completed them. During that meeting, you can review her tax returns to determine the tax implications of her investments and how well she has diversified her investments. You will keep those records as part of her client file.
3. The third meeting could be a protection review. Those meetings are often held in the early fall. Psychologically, that's a good time for a protection review because school is starting, winter's coming, and clients are focused on protecting themselves and their families.
4. If there is a fourth contact, we call it an "integration meeting." This is where the parts come together in a comprehensive plan—for example, planning a successful retirement. You want to find out if the client is getting closer to her goals since the last time you met. What has she accomplished? Does she feel good about the work she has done with your guidance? At this point, it might be the time to re-establish your advice fee if you are working with advice clients.

After you meet with the client, write her a follow-up note. If she is an advice client, document that advice. If you are affiliated with a company, it might require that you mail the client a letter. Sometimes an e-mail is acceptable.

In January 2014, I wrote an article for North Star's *Navigator* newsletter titled "Fifty Meetings with a Purpose." It discusses the benefits of conducting purposeful meetings with your top fifty clients. It is located in the appendix at the back of this book.

Fundamentally, the best advisors I know are strong leaders. They have notable personal leadership and are able to lead their clients as well. Clients and prospects are hungry for someone to take an interest in their financial future and an authentic interest in them. People are drowning in financial media and starved for specific knowledge and wisdom.

My definition of leadership is to take someone to a place they would not have gone on their own and leave them better than you found them. Your top fifty clients need this level of leadership, and they expect it as well. It will make your practice be *on* purpose, *with* a purpose, and it will leave your clients better at the end of this year than they are today. It is a door only you can go through.

Standardize, Then Customize, Your Meetings

A lot of advisors handle every client meeting differently. They invent every meeting from scratch. That is a really inefficient model. To a certain extent, there will be differences among client meetings, of course, because every client has different needs. But one of the hallmarks of a Practice on Purpose is that your meetings are standardized, for the most part. Your goal should not be to make each client meeting a one-of-a-kind experience. Your goal should be to standardize your meetings using a template that can be modified as needed.

We tell our advisors to standardize, then customize. When you go to the dentist's office, they do not customize your appointment. You may have a specific dental issue that they will customize, but that will happen after you've experienced the standardized treatment.

Set the Stage—Make the Pre-Call

A highly effective component of the client relationship is the pre-call. About two weeks before the client is scheduled to come in, the advisor (not a team member) calls the client. About 99 percent of the time, they have to leave a voice mail, and that's OK.

Here's the script: "Sharon, I just want to confirm that we're on to meet next Tuesday at two o'clock. We have been working on your portfolio and reviewing your files. I've noticed some things that we can work on, and I'm excited to get some ideas in front of you. We are excited to see you. I think we're going to have some fun things to talk about. If there's any problem with the appointment, just give me a quick call. But I'm looking forward to seeing you next week."

The pre-call accomplishes three important things:

1. You have confirmed the appointment.
2. Your client sees that you have been studying her situation. She knows you're not preparing for the meeting while she's sitting in the lobby, five minutes before the meeting.
3. It creates anticipation for the client that something is going to happen in that meeting. You can be specific about what you plan to discuss. You might say, "Sharon, I know you will be getting that bonus at work soon. Let's talk about that before you get that bonus in your checking account. Given these are your goals, what do you think would be a good treatment for that bonus?" Or "You got a raise. What would you like to do to change your savings rate?"

Choose Your Language Carefully

The language you use is a big part of how you present yourself. What if you walk up to someone and say, "Nice to meet you," but it turns out that you have already met that person but forgot, and they remember meeting you? That can be really awkward. Instead, just say, "It's nice to see you."

Language varies a lot by culture. In America, when we meet someone, we tend to ask, "What do you do?" In Asia, people are more likely to ask, "How is your family?" or they will say, "Tell me about your family." If you are in Scandinavia, apparently they ask, "What are your hobbies?"

In the end, language is the only tool we have as advisors. We can get credentials and software, but when it gets down to it, the only real tool we have is our language, the words we choose. When the words change, the conversations changes. And until the words change, the conversation does not change.

In your client meetings, try to phrase your recommendations in a way that reminds clients that you are partnering with them to help them get what they want. Be intentional about your language; choose your words and phrases carefully. Clients are meeting with you for what is in it for them. They do it for their reasons, not yours. They want to know what the expected outcome of an action is. They don't want a sales pitch. That is why a phrase like "We want to work with you on building a confident retirement" is preferable to saying, "You need an annuity." Focus the discussion on what they can accomplish by working with you. Maybe it is to send their child to any college that will take them or to buy a vacation home overseas. Here are some other terms we refer:

Try to Say This:	Instead of This:
Firm	Agency
Advisor	Agent
Team member	Employee
Advising, consulting, recommending	Selling
Selecting	Recruiting
Implementing	Selling
Recommendations	Referrals
Contribution	Fee
Investment	Cost

Also, two of our favorite conversation-starting phrases for advisors to use in client meetings are "I've noticed that …" and "If I could show you a way.…"

Here are four more phrases that can move your conversation along in a way that makes sense for the client:

1. **"Money is a wonderful servant and a terrible master."** You can build a conversation around this topic with your clients. It will allow

you to discuss with them how stressful it can be if money is their master. It's a concept that most people relate to and can grasp quickly.

2. **"We want to make that money work harder for you than you are working for the money."** When you use that language with your client, it means you might invest her money in American corporations that are deriving value for profit, and the client will benefit from that value through her investments. So while she is working hard, you are going to get her money to work hard, too. People like the notion of getting their money to work for them versus thinking it is in sitting in a dormant account.

3. **"Most people will earn a fortune in their lifetime. Without an advisor, few will have anything to show for it."** When many people look at their tax returns, they say, "Wow, where did the money go?" People who have an advisor typically know where the money went, and they still have some of it left. We all face the lure of relentless consumerism. Our society encourages us to purchase things all the time. If you are not disciplined about your money, you will succumb to that temptation to indulge—"I want it now, I want to have fun, and I want to live." People do some incredible rationalizing about frittering away their money. John Schubert, an advisor at Ameriprise and a well-known speaker, often says that advisors keep people from "spending money they don't have on things they don't need to impress people they don't like."

4. **"The right advice at the right time can make all the difference."** As advisors, we manage emotions more than we manage money. If you stay in close contact with your clients, you will know when they are facing major life changes that can cause them to experience a lot of emotions—either positive or negative—around their money. Being there to guide them during such challenging times can make a huge difference, both in earning clients' trust and in helping them make wise decisions when they might not be thinking clearly.

Create a Pleasant Physical Environment

At North Star Resource Group, we believe it is critical for advisors to pay close attention to the physical surroundings of their offices and the overall ambiance. Because we conduct all of our client meetings in our offices, we want our clients to feel comfortable and well taken care of from the moment they walk in the door until the moment they leave. The physical environment is a huge part of the exceptional client experience.

It begins with how a client is greeted. Someone should greet her promptly and in a genuinely friendly manner. Because we refer to the people we work with as "team members"—*not* "employees"—all of our receptionists in our various offices are given the title of" Director of First Impressions" because that is exactly what they are.

Notice what is in the lobby—what types of magazines are on display? How do the furniture, lighting, and carpet look? Are refreshments like water, soda, and coffee available? Often, an advisor will keep a small refrigerator in the office, filled with pop and water.

Many people who put their homes on the market will hire professional staging companies to make their homes looks as inviting as possible. Advisors can do the same. Some people don't care about this kind of thing; they would be happy to meet with you in a garage. But other people do care—and you don't know which clients are which. A client who has $1 million worth of assets with you probably expects to see a well-appointed office and to receive the Nordstrom treatment. When she walks in, she will want to see pictures on the wall of your family or a serene landscape and hear soft music.

Having a TV in the lobby is a nice touch, but we don't recommend that you have it tuned to a news station. A lot of advisors think they need to have financial-news programming on the TV to show clients what they're about. But it can scare people. That was particularly true back in 2008 and 2009, during the economic downturn. One financial consultant on TV is pretty dramatic. He talks about hog-belly futures in Argentina, and that has nothing to do with financial planning.

When the client leaves your office after a meeting, the way you say goodbye is important. At Nordstrom, they always walk around the cashier's station, hand your bag to you, and shake your hand. One day, we saw an advisor's team member execute the ideal goodbye. She walked the clients to the lobby, handed them a folder and a small gift, and said, "We really enjoyed seeing you today, and I want you to know you're two of our favorite clients. If you know of anyone else who would like the kind of experience you just had or wants to feel as confident as you feel right now, we'd like to meet them. Here are two of your advisor's business cards. It's been great seeing you!" When she walked them out the door, it was raining. She popped open an umbrella, held it over the clients' heads, walked them to their car, got them in their car, and scooted back into the office.

At North Star, we have a young woman with a fantastic personality in the front office. She just lights up a room. She makes people feel fantastic about being there. She always says to clients something like, "I'm really glad you're going to meet with Joe today. He's such a good advisor and is just great to work with."

That matters. It's part of the exceptional client experience.

When Two People Are in Your Office, They Are Both Clients

Too many times, when advisors work with couples, they tend to address the man more often than his wife. According to a 2012 Charles Schwab report, 70 percent of women change financial advisors within one year of their husband's death.[6] It's quite common for a woman to consider an advisor to be her husband's advisor, not hers. That is most likely because many advisors work harder at forming a bond with male clients than with those clients' wives.

We have a huge opportunity in this industry to make the client experience better for women. According to a Boston Consulting Group study, financial services is the industrial sector that is least sympathetic to women, based on responses from more than 12,000 women on how they were being served by businesses. In a 2009 book published by that group, the authors say, "Despite the huge importance of finances in most women's lives, despite the fact that women's income and economic power continue to grow, and despite the fact that women need and welcome financial advice, they are continually let down by and exasperated with the level and quality of advice and service they get from financial companies."[7]

An ongoing financial-advice relationship with an advisor helps allay women's anxiety about money. A 2014 Wells Fargo Financial Health study revealed that half of women consider it difficult to talk with others about personal finances, versus 38 percent of men. Women are also less confident about their investment knowledge. Only 29 percent of women said they know where to invest in today's market, compared to 42 percent of men. Almost half of women (45 percent) grade their financial literacy a "C" or below, while 65 percent of men assess their level of financial literacy as a "B" or higher.[8]

When widows change advisors, that tells us is that they were not in engaged advice relationships with their advisors, which is the topic of Chapter 3. A good advisor will engage everyone in the family in the conversation about financial health. He will even bring the client's children and parents into the picture, as well as the client's CPA and attorney. A good advisor takes a comprehensive view of a client's situation because they're in an advice relationship.

---

6. "Five Kinds of Women Investors: What Do They Need from an Advisor?" Charles Schwab website, http://content.schwab.com/email/as/advisornews/articles/Women_Investors_article_9-4-13.html.

7. Michael J. Silverstein and Kate Sayre, *Women Want More: How to Capture Your Share of the World's Largest, Fastest-Growing Market* (New York: The Boston Consulting Group, 2009), 181.

8. "Conversations about Personal Finances More Difficult than Religion or Politics, According to New Wells Fargo Survey," Wells Fargo press release, last modified February 20, 2014, https://www.wellsfargo.com/press/2014/20140220_financial-health.

A technique that is helpful in all client meetings is to think the people in front of you have invisible signs around their necks that say, "Make me feel important." All people, regardless of their occupation, education, net worth, dreams, and hopes, deserve to be treated with respect and dignity. This is doubly true when they have come to you and opened up about a subject that is so intimate and important to them and their families—their finances.

Nurture the Client Relationship

Nurturing client relationships is an area many advisors overlook today because of the "hunting" mindset so many of them bring into the career. We see too many missed opportunities for advisors to connect with clients and create an exceptional experience for them. This important aspect of an advisor's practice can be taken care of so easily with competent team members and the technology we have today. Your team members can send your clients timely, relevant information with a couple strokes of the computer keyboard. It's a matter of being aware that you should be highly visible to your clients and having a system in place to ensure that you "touch" your clients regularly with some type of communication.

One way to nurture a client relationship is to compliment your clients on their progress. Notice when they're doing something well, and give them "tough love" when they're not.

We often talk about the "richness" of communication. Face-to-face communication is rich and warm. You get to see your clients, shake hands with them, and communicate while you're both in the same environment. Handwritten notes are a fairly rich mode of communication. At the other end of the spectrum, the cold and unrich side, are the less personal modes of communication like e-mail. Having a team member call a client on your behalf is somewhere on that continuum.

To nurture client relationships, know what level of richness you need for what you're trying to accomplish. If you are confirming a meeting, an e-mail is fine. If you're trying to convince a client to save money or buy a range of insurance products, that needs to be rich, so it needs to be a face-to-face meeting.

The key is to "touch" your clients many times throughout the year, with all types of communication. You can send them holiday cards, pictures of your family, pictures of your team, handwritten notes, and links to online articles they might enjoy. Many of our advisors e-mail newsletters to their clients regularly. There are a lot of things you can do with technology and the Internet now, including e-mail updates.

We encourage advisors to have a "hot" list of clients who should receive a call when certain things happen, such as if the market drops 100 points in one day. Or, let's say something happens overseas that you know might affect a client. You can call him and say, "Hey, I know you have a lot of holdings in Greece. I'm calling to let you know that I'm aware of what's going on. I looked at your portfolio, and I don't recommend that you make any moves at this point. I'll let you know if that changes." When you make it a point to communicate with your clients at that level, you are developing a highly nurtured relationship.

It's important to know what each client likes. Some people enjoy getting candy baskets at Christmas. Others couldn't care less and think you're wasting your money. The better you know your clients, the better you can nurture your relationship with them.

One of our advisors calls each man in his practice about a week before that client's wedding anniversary to remind him that it's coming up.

If you know your clients have saved money to go on a nice trip, why not have a bottle of champagne waiting for them when they arrive at their hotel? You can attach a note to it that says, "Congratulations on your trip!"

Some advisors will send to a client a book they know will interest them. They will mail it with a note that says, "I saw this in a bookstore the other day and thought you might like it." There are rules about how much money you can spend on gifts, but you can do small things.

Each effort you make to connect with a client matters. These "touches" add up and contribute to an exceptional client experience, which, in turn, will result in client satisfaction and loyalty, more recommendations, greater personal satisfaction for you, and growth in your practice.

Ann's Story: How Segmenting My Clients Facilitates Client Service

Ann M. Wengronowitz, CFP®, Partner, North Star Resource Group

Segmenting our clients has allowed my associate and me to identify which clients we want to give the most attention to, versus which clients ask and require the most attention from us. Segmentation has allowed me to take more of an offensive role versus a defensive role.

Segmentation is based on income generated, amount of assets, and number of quality leads/recommendations I have received from the client.

(continued)

> ### Ann's Story: How Segmenting My Clients Facilitates Client Service (continued)
>
> We mail or e-mail annual review letters to all clients, whether they are at the A or AAA level. ("AAA"-level clients are our top-tier clients.) The letter asks them to complete and return to us a short questionnaire regarding their needs and concerns. If that form is not returned, A clients receive only the letter, AA clients receive the letter and one or two follow-up phone calls from me or my associate, and AAA clients receive two or three follow-up phone calls from me.
>
> We prepare agendas for all meetings. The agenda is on the first page of the review form. At the beginning of the appointment, I review with the client what I want to discuss and then ask if anything is missing that they want to add or discuss. When the meeting is over, we then review the agenda once again to make sure nothing was missed.
>
> AA and AAA clients receive a meeting summary via an e-mail or letter a few days after the appointment. The summary includes what we discussed, if there are any follow-up items, who is responsible for the items, and an updated net-worth statement.
>
> My administrative assistant sends an e-mail to the client 24 to 48 hours prior to each appointment to confirm the appointment. The e-mail asks the client to let us know if he or she needs to reschedule, and if so, the administrative assistant does it at that time.

Applying the Concepts to *Your* Practice on Purpose

1. How much do you know about your clientele? Do you know how many households you are servicing, which clients have which assets or products, and how long you have worked with each client? If you don't know this information, what will you do to get the details, and when?

   _____
   _____
   _____
   _____
   _____
   _____

2. Have you segmented your clients into categories? If so, how do you categorize them? If not, what criteria will you use to segment them and then decide how frequently to contact the clients in each segment?

3. How many appointments are prebooked on your calendar? Are you working at least a week in advance, or are you preparing for tomorrow's meetings today? How can you do a better job of building your calendar around your clients?

4. Do you present a menu of services to all clients to determine the level of service they want? If not, will you commit to developing and using one?

5. To what extent do you charge appropriately for the service you provide? Are you providing Nordstrom service and charging a transaction price for some clients? Are you ignoring any valuable clients? What can you do to make your pricing structure align better with the service you provide?

6. How much does your practice resemble the dentist-office model? Does your assistant book each client's next appointment before he or she leaves your office? How can you follow that model more closely?

7. Do you prepare for your client meetings in advance? Do you prepare an agenda for each meeting, assign it a theme, and use a standardized approach for your meetings? What can you do to make your meetings more purposeful?

8. Do you call all clients about two weeks before a scheduled meeting to touch base with them and remind them of their appointment? If you do not make use of this pre-call tool, will you commit to doing so?

9. How pleasant is the physical environment in your office? To what extent does it create an exceptional client experience in terms of what clients see, hear, smell, touch, and taste? What can you improve about your office furnishings, ambiance, and the way clients are greeted and told goodbye?

10. When working with couples, how effective are you at treating the female client with just as much focus and respect as the male respect? What can you do to improve in this area?

11. How good are you at nurturing your client relationships? Do you have a system that helps ensure that you "touch" each client a certain number of times a year via various modes of communication? What additional types of communication can you start using to create an exceptional client experience?

_____
_____
_____
_____
_____
_____

Financial Advice as Its Own Value

CHAPTER 3

When you evolve from the transactional and investment-related tiers of the service model we discussed in Chapter 2 and begin offering the top service level—an ongoing financial advice relationship—you will be providing your clients with the optimum level of service. As a result, you will be more likely to recognize the significant value you provide and to charge appropriately.

The advisors we have the most coaching success with in this area are the ones who are already building advice relationships with clients; we just get them to do it more. It's easier to get someone who has ten advice relationships already to go to twenty than it is to get someone who has zero to go to ten. They already get it. It's easier to get someone to press the accelerator a little harder than it is to get someone to go from stop to first gear.

Advisors' advice fees usually represent 10 to 20 percent of their overall revenue, at least in the early years of their practices. It isn't enough to drive the entire practice, but most advice-focused advisors are not in it for the fee revenue; they're in it for the client engagement. This is about what's right and good for clients. It's not about trying to get more money out of them.

But you can, and should, earn commissions on products that are implemented from the advice relationship. Here are some guidelines regarding fees and commissions: A $1,000 fee plan can generate $2,000 in commission, a $2,000 fee plan can generate a $4,000 commission, and a $3,000 fee plan can generate a $9,000 commission. There are several reasons for that:

1. The higher the fee, the more trust a client has placed in your advice.

"We must have perseverance and above all confidence in ourselves. We must believe that we are gifted for something and that this thing, at whatever cost, must be attained."

—**Marie Curie**
Polish Physicist and Chemist

2. The client who is able to pay a $3,000 fee versus a $1,000 fee obviously is more affluent and probably has more complex financial needs, which gives you more opportunities for applying value.

3. Clients who are in that top tier of your business—in an ongoing advice relationship with you—are much more engaged and therefore more likely to actually follow your recommendations and experience the value you provide.

Some of the advisors we work with are catalysts. When advisors see them having success with advice relationships, they get interested, and the momentum builds in their practices, too. They want to emulate that success. It's because most advisors are sensitive to comparisons. If they see someone else down the hallway doing something well, they tend to make more of an effort to match and exceed that performance.

> It is extremely difficult for those who do not have a positive self-image to succeed with the advice model because they don't feel worthy of charging appropriately.

Moving from a transactional or investment-based relationship to an advice relationship requires advisors to change their mindset and shift their focus. To build a million-dollar practice requires that you genuinely believe in the value you are providing to clients and charge appropriately for your services. The reluctance to charge what you're worth is a huge obstacle. There is a direct correlation between one's self-image and success in the advice area. It is extremely difficult for those who do not have a positive self-image to succeed with the advice model because they don't feel worthy of charging appropriately.

Without active intervention, such as the coaching we provide at North Star and the advice contained in this book, it is a steep incline, and most advisors do not overcome it. Being aware of this obstacle is the first step to conquering it.

Advisors' Biggest Obstacle: The Elephant and the Stake

Every business model has pros and cons.

The many advantages of hiring brand-new people right off of college campuses are limitless. They tend to fit well into our culture and are open to adopting and respecting our values. They generally go with the flow. They are like the liquid that takes the shape of whatever vessel it's poured into. If you pour it into a flask, it looks like a flask. If you pour it into a cup, it looks like a cup. The biggest disadvantage is the enormity of capital needed to hire and train twenty-two-year-olds off of college campuses. A second disadvantage is that, for the first two to four years of their careers, nobody wants to talk to them. That's not good for their self-esteem. It makes them feel like their knowledge is not valuable.

Then, after they get five or ten years of experience, when you're trying to get them to be paid for their very good advice, they still don't know how to ask for it because they never learned how to do so. It's like the baby elephant that is tied to a stake—he isn't strong enough to pull the stake out of the ground, so he stops trying. When he gets to be a big elephant, he could easily pull the stake out because it's the same stake that's always been there, and he is now much bigger and stronger. But his mind has been hardwired to think he can't pull the stake out of the ground, so he gives up.

Many new advisors have a similar mindset.

Many of the thirty-two-year-olds who started out in this business ten years earlier have a hard time telling a client, "The advice needed to answer your question is four thousand dollars. That's how much I'm going to charge you for my time." They're still tied to the stake. They still have the perception that nobody wants to talk to them, and nobody wants their advice. It creates an uphill battle when we are trying to develop advisors and coach them to provide clients with optimum service. Even after years of experience and obtaining hard-earned designations such as CLU®, ChFC®, and CFP®, many advisors struggle with their ability to charge for their valuable advice.

Firms that hire career changers don't tend to have this problem because they often hire people who have been in positions in which they were comfortable with charging an appropriate fee for their education, credentials, knowledge, wisdom, and experience.

For some reason, it's different for attorneys. An attorney who has just graduated from law school and gets hired into a firm might make $50 or $100 an hour. Somebody who's making $400 an hour has set that rate for the new attorney, who doesn't have a problem with that because someone else is charging the client. But for some reason, what is so natural for an attorney is unnatural for somebody who comes into the financial services business, especially at a young age.

We have noticed that even with team selling, when we pair a senior advisor with junior advisors who all have different areas of expertise to offer clients, many of the senior advisors on our teams exhibit that same elephant-and-stake mindset. We have an advisor named Ron who is teaming with a second-year advisor named Shannon. Intellectually, Shannon understands the concept of the advice fee, but Ron doesn't really get it. She is starting to push him to charge for his advice. As they bring in new clients, which is actually the easiest way to sell an advice relationship, she's helping him realize the value of the service they are providing.

> The number of families who are in ongoing advice relationships with advisors at North Star increased 44.3 percent from 2012 to 2013.

Once we recognized this uphill battle, we began to address the issue in our advisor-development process. As a result, the number of families who are in ongoing advice relationships with advisors at North Star increased 44.3 percent from 2012 to 2013. We achieved that increase one advisor at a time. We counseled advisors individually in weekly or biweekly meetings. In the next two to three years at North Star, we expect to see an even more significant lift in peer leadership and peer acceptance of financial advice as a viable and client-centered service.

Everyone benefits when advisors engage in ongoing advice relationships—the firm, the advisors, and especially the clients. Let's look at some of the many ways both you and your clients benefit.

The Impact of a Practice on Purpose

According to a 2013 study from Fidelity Investments, the average retirement savings for 11.8 million Americans' 401(k) balances is just $74,600.[9] When we see dismal life savings like that, we know a couple of things. First, that is not enough money. Second, we know that person did not have an advisor. Most people look at their year-end tax return and say, "Where did all that money go?" They have nothing left. But if they have an advisor, they actually know where the money went, and they still have some of it left.

One of our roles as advisors is to help our clients understand why they are spending or saving money. It is a key part of the advice we provide. It takes a lot of courage to bring this subject up with a client, but it can lead to an important discussion.

The diagram below shows how clients can build wealth by managing their cash flow (money in, money out). By teaching them sound money-management principles like using automatic bill payment to make their bill paying predictable and paying their credit cards off every month, you are teaching them to be the CFO of their own household.

---

9. "The Average Retirement Savings in America Are Not Nearly Enough," IRA vs. 401(k) Central website, last modified September 25, 2013, http://www.iravs401kcentral.com/average-retirement-savings-in-america/.

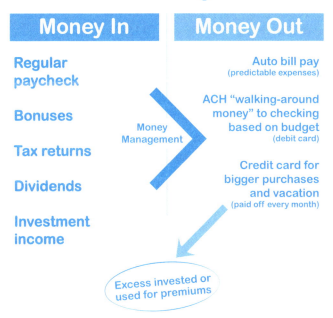

The financial advice you provide to your clients is paramount to helping them accumulate and manage their assets. If you understand the value of your advice, you can help your clients create wealth and great retirements. The impact we can have in this business is phenomenal. But it is predicated on advisors understanding who they are and the kind of impact they can have with busy, successful people.

How You Can Benefit from an Ongoing Advice Relationship

Marshall Gifford is one of North Star's top advisors. He specializes in serving physicians and dentists. Recently, he made the transition from transaction-based relationships to ongoing financial advice relationships with many of his clients. I asked him, "What do you notice when you start working on an advice basis?"

Marshall said, "Gary, I have much happier clients. They are more engaged, they feel better about their future, and they feel they have a sense of direction. It changes the quality and depth of the conversation."

Marshall's clients make a modest amount of money after going to school for a long time. Then, at some point in their careers, they experience a tremendous uptick in income. Marshall said, "When that uptick happens, they are ripe to make some poor decisions. Because we have a financial advice relationship, I am able to guide them as their income quadruples in twelve months and help them make good decisions around their money. We make sure those decisions align with their goals and values. I look forward to those client meetings much more than I do the meetings that are purely about a product solution."

We know that clients who are in an ongoing advice relationship are more loyal and engaged than clients who are not. Ameriprise Financial and the CFP organization have conducted research that reveals the following about advice clients—facts that benefit you, the advisor:

- They stay with the advisor longer.
- A firm's retention of advice clients is higher.
- Advice clients implement multiple solutions and strategies more readily.
- They're more fully engaged.
- They are more likely to recommend their advisor to people they know.
- They give their advisor higher ratings in client-satisfaction surveys.
- They generate four times the revenue of a non-advice client.
- Ongoing advice raises the value of your practice.
- Their goal attainment is two to three times higher than that of a client who is engaged in a transactional relationship.

This list is part of an article I wrote for North Star Resource Group's newsletter, *Navigator*, in October 2013. That newsletter is included in the Appendix.

Some of our advisors believe in the advice relationship so much that they will no longer accept clients who do not work with them on an advice basis. To do that takes courage and the conviction that the service you are providing has tremendous value.

How Your Clients Can Benefit from an Ongoing Advice Relationship

We live in complicated times. Trying to keep up with the ever-changing tax laws, navigate the volatile stock market, and understand all of the different types of investments can be overwhelming for most people. Selling a client a protection product and getting her into a couple of investments is not a sufficient strategy for helping her reach her ultimate financial goals.

Plus, financial plans are limiting and become outdated quickly, and they do not offer clients lasting value. Mitch Anthony,[10] the founder and president of Advisor Insights Inc., has been helping advisors connect with their clients for a decade. He refers to advisors who consider clients' ongoing financial needs as "return on life (ROL)" practitioners. Here is what he has to say about financial plans versus ongoing financial advice:

> Clients often view the task of creating a financial plan as a one-time event that easily becomes outdated. As a financial plan becomes outdated, clients begin to chafe at paying the same fee for what they perceive as less effort. The real value is in monitoring the plan—hinging on how personal, how frequent, and how synchronized the monitoring is to the client's life and circumstances.
>
> The return on life (ROL) practitioner perceives that for a financial plan to be a living, breathing instrument, it must be infused with aspects addressing individualized life needs in the context of money that basic data gathering, analysis, and projections alone cannot provide. The ultimate end of a financial plan is that it will comprehend a client's meaning as it relates to his or her means. The plan will articulate the why as well as the how. Why are we developing and monitoring this plan? This question must move beyond clichés like "So I can retire" or "So I can have enough to not worry anymore." It also must move beyond simple metrics that often are determined by factors and causes beyond your control.
>
> The value of the planning process must be felt as well as seen. Five core values need to be articulated for today's clients to earn a more privileged position in their lives. These values address real needs in their hearts and minds as they relate to their money:
>
> 1. **Organization**—Help bring order to your clients' lives.
> 2. **Objectivity**—Provide untainted perspectives that lead to suitable and rational money decisions.
> 3. **Proactivity**—Help clients anticipate life transitions and prepare financially.
> 4. **Accountability**—Help clients follow through on their commitments.
> 5. **Partnership**—Help clients make decisions that move them toward the best life possible with the money they have.

---

10. Mitch Anthony is the author of *From the Boiler Room to the Living Room*, *The New Retirementality*, *Your Clients for Life*, *The Cash in the Hat*, and *The Bean Is Not Green*. He is the co-author of *StorySelling for Financial Advisors*, *Defining Conversations*, and *Your Client's Story*. You can read more about him and his company, Advisor Insights, Inc., at http://www.mitchanthony.com/.

Providing clients with all of that support is priceless. When clients enter into an ongoing advice relationship with you, they are receiving more than just the benefit of your education and credentials. They also benefit from the wisdom, knowledge, discipline, and emotional competence you provide to them as they navigate market conditions and life events that are often challenging and can cause them to act out of pure emotion. Through this process, they get to know you, learn about your values, and appreciate who you are as a person.

Knowledge and Wisdom

Nick Murray,[11] a well-known author in the financial services industry, says this is the best time in the history of modern man to be in the financial services industry. He uses the acronym YOYO. He explains by saying, "I am not referring to that toy on the end of a string that you flip out from your fingers. I am referring to the fact that governments around the world have demonstrated conclusively they can no longer keep promises and commitments they have made. Consequently, You're On Your Own—YOYO."

The need for financial advice has never, ever been greater. Now, more than ever, people are dependent on someone to help them make good financial decisions. Increasingly, they must depend on their own resources and not on government resources. That means there is more opportunity than ever for you to make a positive impact in people's lives.

The 2014 Wells Fargo Financial Health study we mentioned earlier revealed that nearly half of Americans say the most challenging topic to discuss with others is personal finances (44 percent), whereas death (38 percent), politics (35 percent), religion (32 percent), taxes (21 percent), and personal health (20 percent) rank as less difficult. The study also revealed that for 39 percent of Americans, money is the biggest stress in their life, 39 percent say they are more stressed about finances now than they were last year, and one-third (33 percent) report losing sleep because they worry about money. Respondents also said that the hardest part of achieving financial health and saving money is "knowing the best approach" (35 percent) and "sticking to a

---

11. Nick Murray has been providing financial advice for forty-seven years. He is one of the financial services industry's premier speakers. He has written eleven books for financial services professionals. His book for clients, *Simple Wealth, Inevitable Wealth*, is among the most successful privately published books of the last dozen years. Nick also publishes a monthly newsletter and "spot coaching" service for advisors, *Nick Murray Interactive*. In 2007, he received the Malcolm S. Forbes Public Awareness Award for Excellence in Advancing Financial Understanding. You can read more about him at http://www.nickmurraynewsletters.com/public/main.cfm.

plan" (35 percent). Only a third (33 percent) described feeling that they are in good or great shape in their ability to retire comfortably.[12]

People need ongoing advice relationships with advisors. Their ability to save for retirement depends on your knowledge, wisdom, and expertise. Advice is knowledge in action.

Ed likes to tell the story about a woman who had a squeaky wood floor in her house. She hired a local handyman to come fix the squeak. The gentleman walked in the house, entered the room with the squeaky floor, took a few steps, and located the source of the squeak near a corner. He pulled out a nail and pounded it into the floor. The squeak was gone. The woman was very grateful and asked the man, "How much do I owe you?"

He said, "You owe me one hundred dollars."

Her jaw dropped. "One hundred dollars! You were here for only two minutes. Can you give me an itemized receipt for the hundred dollars?"

"No problem." He pulled out a piece of paper, and here's what he wrote:

Itemized Receipt	
$ 1:	The nail
99:	Knowing where to put the nail
$100	Total

Just like that handyman, you have a lifetime of cumulative experience that represents knowledge and wisdom to your clients. Those who engage in a financial-advice relationship with you can tap into that wealth of knowledge and wisdom at any time.

To visualize the different components of financial advice, picture a pyramid. Now let's slice it horizontally into four parts. The top of the pyramid is wisdom. The next section is knowledge, followed by information, then data. The bottom segment, data, makes up the largest part of the pyramid. That represents the wealth of data that's out there in the financial services realm. A lot of so-called experts, on the Internet and otherwise, are spewing data and information, but there isn't much

---

12. "Conversations about Personal Finances More Difficult than Religion or Politics, According to New Wells Fargo Survey," Wells Fargo press release, last modified February 20, 2014, https://www.wellsfargo.com/press/2014/20140220_financial-health.

knowledge to help guide people. Wisdom, the smallest section at the top of the pyramid, is the scarcest commodity. People are drowning in information and starved for wisdom.

When you go to a surgeon, you are not paying him just for what he's going to do during your surgery; you are really buying the two thousand other surgeries like yours that he has already performed. If you are an advisor with a large client base, your clients are buying your experience in providing advice to those two or three hundred other executives.

Authors like Malcolm Gladwell (*Outliers: The Story of Success*) and Matthew Syed (*Bounce: Mozart, Federer, Picasso, Beckham, and the Science of Success*) talk about the concept of 10,000 hours being required to excel in any endeavor. Probably the first author to quantify the number of hours required to master an activity was Earl Nightingale. He said, "One hour per day of study will put you at the top of your field within three years. Within five years you'll be a national authority. In seven years, you can be one of the best people in the world at what you do." There are 2,555 hours in seven years, so he was saying that you can be one of the best at what you do in that amount of time.

A valuable advisor is one who not only has education, designations, and licenses but one who has witnessed hundreds of client meetings and created solutions for myriad financial situations. Clients rely on your knowledge and wisdom, which they can't get anywhere else.

Discipline

You play a key role in helping your clients create a vision about their financial future, and you provide them with the discipline and knowledge to have something to show for their hard work. The average fifty-year-old in the United States has only $48,000 set aside for retirement. That is unacceptable.

Advisors are in the habit-formation and behavior-modification business, and both fall into the category of discipline. You can help your clients form proper habits so that they can stay the course to financial security. Left to their own devices, most people are their own worst enemy. Unless they have an ongoing advice relationship with an advisor, most clients will not implement financial advice, and they certainly won't do it consistently.

We see many clients who have the resources to achieve financial success, but they don't make good decisions, or they make decisions at the wrong time, or they base their decisions on emotion, or they don't stay with their game and follow a bigger vision for themselves. Most people have good intentions. They want to do the right thing, but they need a little coaching to actually follow through with it.

Just like a fitness instructor makes sure a client is at the gym at a certain time to exercise, you are making sure your clients do the work and follow through. You are helping them implement your financial advice. Part of your value is that month after month, year after year, you are making sure that your clients form the right habits, adopt the right behaviors, and make adjustments as needed, based on market conditions or life events.

Encouragement

It's important for advisors to let clients know when they're doing well and compliment them on having great careers. Providing encouragement is a valuable service you provide. It builds people's self-esteem and helps them reach their financial goals more quickly.

A lot of people go through their entire life wondering if they're doing anything right. We have watched advisors raise the self-esteem of their clients by complimenting them on their progress.

> We have watched advisors raise the self-esteem of their clients by complimenting them on their progress.

Emotional Competence

One of the biggest mistakes people make is letting their emotions influence their financial decisions. Emotions and money often intersect in people's lives during events like job changes, marital changes, and retirement. Emotions also run rampant when people try to "beat the market." The standard investment plan typically has a 10 percent rate of return, but investors earn, on average, only 4 percent. Why? Because when the market drops precipitously, investors bail out, and then they don't get back in low. If they were to put their money into their investments and leave it alone, they would be much better off. They're jumping in and out and missing those opportunities for a gain because they're not in the market at the right time.

We have plenty of statistics that show a consistently significant gap between investor returns and investment returns and a tendency among investors to bail out of investments too quickly. Jeff Landt, CFA®, CFP®, Vice President and Director of Investments for North Star Resource Group, sees reports that document these facts regularly. Here are some examples:

1. Investment consulting firm Cambridge Associates found that "the decision to switch [funds], often on the basis of short-term criteria, usually resulted in the destruction of value." It also says the interests of participants in investment funds "are best served by a process that focuses on considerably longer periods of time—at least ten years and, when practical, twenty or more."[13]

---

13. "Can Emphasis on Short-Term Results Generate Best-in-Class Fund Lineups?" American Funds, 2010.

2. The decade's best-performing US diversified stock mutual fund, the CGM Focus Fund, rose more than 18 percent annually. But the typical CGM Focus shareholder lost 11 percent annually in the ten years ending November 30, 2009, because many investors bought the fund after it had a strong run and sold as it hit bottom.[14]

3. A 2008 Dalbar, Inc., study revealed that a key finding uncovered in the company's first study, in 1994, remained true fourteen years later: "Investment return is far more dependent on investor behavior than on fund performance. Mutual fund investors who hold their investments typically earn higher returns over time than those who time the market." The report offers this advice: "Start early, keep contributing, and don't panic."[15]

4. A 2012 Munder report, referring to a less volatile market in 2012, said, "The fact that the average investor could not beat the market in the best of times indicates that behavioral factors continue to make market timing a bad idea. Fear cultivated from previous years caused investors to sell low while short-term rallies tempted investors to buy high. While investors attempted to maximize returns by guessing right, they in fact guessed wrong. Moreover, regardless of their investment time frames, many investors simply don't have the patience or discipline necessary to ride out the rough periods.... By helping investors stay the course, a financial advisor may have a major impact on the results that an investor achieves."[16]

> Managing clients' emotions and behavior can be even more valuable than managing their money.

This is another area in which you provide monumental value. As an advisor, you can hold the client's hand and say, "Now is the time when you want to buy more stocks because they are on sale right now. Prices just dropped." A lot of investors need an advisor who has the wisdom and "emotional competence" that come from having been through these cycles many times before. Those qualities go a long way toward calming the client's panic. You can help the client stay the course and assure her that the market will be back.

---

14. Eleanor Laise, "Best Stock Fund of the Decade: CGM Focus," *The Wall Street Journal* website, last modified December 31, 2009, http://online.wsj.com/news/articles/SB10001424052748704876804574628561609012716.
15. Russ Thornton, "Dalbar: The Measurement of Success," from "Quantitative Analysis of Investor Behavior 2008," Thornton Wealth Management, 2008.
16. "Mutual Fund Investor Behavior," Munder.

Managing clients' emotions and behavior can be even more valuable than managing their money. Doug Lennick, a behavioral finance expert we mentioned earlier, is the author of several books, including *Financial Intelligence*. He often says, "I'm always curious about why people behave the way they do about their money."

Our industry could do a better job of equipping advisors with skills related to coaching clients through the emotional aspects of money management. A lot of our credentials are based on tax laws, investment dynamics, and economics. The American College's CFP capstone course is designed to address the "soft" skills of persuasion, interpersonal communication, and building trust and rapport with clients. When an advisor has those skills, it makes an advice relationship come alive.

Better Physical Health

Another interesting ripple effect of working with a financial advisor is that it can improve people's physical health.

According to Scott Spiker, CEO of First Command Financial Services, Inc., "Even Americans with six-figure incomes are reporting problems with anxiety, sleep, and related issues. One key to decreasing stress appears to be increasing control over your finances. And one obvious way to take control is to seek help from a trusted financial professional, someone who can help you change your financial behaviors for the better."

A 2010 First Command study revealed that people who had a financial planner experienced finance-related stress symptoms to a significantly lower extent than those who did not have a planner. For example, 31 percent of people who did not have a financial planner felt increased feelings of anxiety, compared to only 24 percent of people who did have a planner. "People who put their trust in a financial coach are experiencing real benefits in both their physical and fiscal health," Spiker said.[17]

In 2013, Northwestern University studied 8,400 young adults ages twenty-four to thirty-two. While previous studies have found evidence that debt is associated with adverse psychological health, this is said to be the first study to look at physical health as well. The study revealed that a higher debt-to-asset ratio is associated with higher perceived stress and depression, worse self-reported general health, and higher diastolic blood pressure. Those with higher debt were found to have a 1.3 percent increase (relative to the mean) in diastolic blood pressure, which is clinically significant. For example, a two-point

---

17. "Financial Pros Offer Buffer against Stress-Related Health Issues," *Journey*, the Online Magazine for First Command Services, http://www.fcjourney.com/financial-pros-offer-buffer-against-stress-related-health-issues.

increase in diastolic blood pressure is associated with a 17 percent higher risk of hypertension and a 15 percent higher risk of stroke.[18]

A study by a Fortune 500 company that did not want to be named reported that migraines and other types of headaches occurred in 44 percent of people with high stress levels related to finances versus 15 percent with low levels of financial stress. For stomach ulcers, the comparisons were 27 percent versus 8 percent; and muscle tension, 51 percent versus 31 percent. The widest gap, for severe anxiety, was reported in 29 percent of those with high stress levels vs. 4 percent of those with low levels.[19]

And finally, a poll conducted by the Associated Press and AOL found that people with high stress levels related to debt were twice as likely to have a heart attack compared with those who do not worry about their financial situation. The study also revealed that ulcers and other digestive problems, headaches or migraines, depression, and muscle tension or lower back pain were much more prevalent among people who were worried about their financial situations than those who were not.

While that news is distressing, the good news is that people who take an active role in planning and learning about their finances are less stressed and more confident in their financial situations.[20] That is another important value advisors provide to their clients—a reduction in financial-related stress and resulting health problems.

How to Evolve from Protection to Financial Advice

As we stated in the Preface, we are committed to trumpeting the tremendous value of life insurance—what Phil's mentor, Maury Stewart, calls The Miracle of Life Insurance. When a breadwinner dies unexpectedly, life insurance can make the difference between a future of poverty and a future of financial comfort for the surviving family members. It is the foundation of a sound financial future.

When you get insurance in place as the first order of business with a new physician, veterinarian, or young family, you are transferring the risk of disability or death onto an insurance company and away from your client, and that is extremely important. Once protection is in place, evolve to encouraging

---

18. Erin White, "High Debt Could Be Hazardous to Your Health," Northwestern University website, last updated August 15, 2013, http://www.northwestern.edu/newscenter/stories/2013/08/high-debt-could-be-hazardous-to-your-health.html.

19. Kristen B. Frasch, "Financial Health Straining Physical Well-Being," Human Resources Executive Online, last updated February 20, 2012, http://www.hreonline.com/HRE/view/story.jhtml?id=533345193&ss=Financial+Health+Straining+Physical+Well-Being.

20. David Mielach, "How Worrying about Money Affects Your Health," BusinessNewsDaily website, last updated April 25, 2012, http://www.businessnewsdaily.com/2419-money-worry-health.html.

your clients to start peeling off a respectful portion of their earnings to invest in the future—for their children's college education, their own retirement, or whatever it might be. Help clients build wealth through accumulation by getting them into the investment business, whether it's mutual funds or money management.

Then eventually, bigger questions come up. Clients begin asking themselves, "Why am I working so hard? What am I going to do with this money I'm making? How much money is enough? What kind of money do I need? How much risk do I want to take? How do my investments work with my protection? Do I need a will or an estate plan?" When clients start asking bigger "life" questions, that is when the advice relationship can really begin. The advisors at North Star who are doing best on the advice side are people who realize that many clients have bigger questions than those that relate to just protection and investments. This diagram shows the three primary levels of services we discussed in Chapter 2:

If you have clients you've helped with protection and investment products, how do you persuade them to engage in an ongoing advice relationship with you? How do you evolve your practice to a financial advice practice or add advice as a service? It's one of the most problematic elements of building a Practice on Purpose, and it's the one obstacle that prevents many advisors from getting there.

We have a highly capable woman at North Star who has been an advisor for twenty-five years. She is arguably one of the finest advisors in the company and would be competitive as a top advisor in any company. But she cannot get her head around the idea that she should get paid well for her advice. Her thought is, "Why and how could I ever dare to say that now you're going to pay me for what I've been giving you for free all these years?"

It is a lot easier to establish an advice relationship with a brand-new client than an existing client. When you first acquire a new client, you can say, "This is how I work with clients. We have an ongoing advice relationship. Here is what you'll get, and we will meet this many times during the year. We will cover these topics. I am in the goal-achieving business. I'm going to provide you with good advice, and we're going to implement whatever products will help you take advantage of an opportunity or solve a problem." Of course you will take care of their protection needs right away, but you will engage in the advice relationship from the beginning.

But with your existing clients, it's an evolution. After you take care of their protection issues, then you can begin to help them put money aside, and then you can address those big life questions.

Let's look at some guidelines for evolving your practice to the financial-advice model with existing clients. A lot of it involves recognizing your value, which requires a mindset change.

Choose Your Mindset

It is up to you to see—or not see—the potential impact you can have in people's lives. Akio Morita, cofounder of SONY, told this great story that paints a vivid picture of how two different salespeople can perceive their opportunities in distinctly different ways: "Two shoe salesmen find themselves in a rustic backwater of Africa. The first salesman wires a note back to this head office: 'There is no prospect of sales. Natives do not wear shoes!' The other salesman wired this message: 'No one wears shoes here. We can dominate the market. Send all possible stock.'"

> Advisors and firms lose millions of dollars every year in lost fees because advisors do not charge appropriate prices for their advice.

It's a door that only the advisor can go through. Until you go through the door saying, "My knowledge and the discipline I can bring to someone's situation have value," you won't appreciate yourself enough to charge what your advice is worth. It requires a substantial mindset change for some advisors.

We recommend that advisors build a business model around the seven areas of the CFP curriculum (financial planning, insurance planning and risk analysis, retirement planning, employee benefits, investment planning, tax and estate planning, and advanced financial planning). Those who don't do that are, unfortunately, giving much of their advice away for free because they don't value it. Therefore, the client doesn't value it, so it cannot have its full impact. The stake stays in the ground.

A few years ago, we worked with an advisor who had about fifty advice relationships by the end of his second year in the business. We asked him, "How did you do that? You were brand new in the business. You hardly knew a mutual fund from a bond."

He replied, "I was one chapter ahead of my clients."

He knew his licensing and finance degree put him in a better position than his clients were to make sound financial recommendations. He got it into his head early on that he was providing a valuable service. In fact, if a client did not want to work on an advice basis, he would move on to someone who did.

He had a lot of courage, and it was refreshing. But he also had a clear sense of his vision and of his value. He pulled out the stake we discussed earlier.

Some advisors try to understand the basic concept, so they begin to charge some fees for financial advice, but they still rely heavily on the products to pay them. We see advisors who look at financial advice as a loss leader or as a placating revenue source, as something they do so they can get to the other stuff. As we discuss in Chapter 9, the regulators in countries like England and Australia are saying, "You are not going to get to the other stuff." So now what are you worth? What happens if product commissions are no longer allowed? Advisors and firms lose millions of dollars every year in lost fees because advisors do not charge appropriate prices for their advice.

We also see advisors actually lower their advice fees if a client buys more products from them. We absolutely dissuade advisors from doing that. If you gave a client $3,000 worth of advice, it was worth $3,000, regardless of whether or not they buy more products from you after that. It's like going to an internist who discovers a lump in your side and refers you to get an MRI and consult with a surgeon. When the surgeon removes the malignancy, you will still pay the internist, in addition to the surgeon. The internist isn't going to reduce his fee just because you went on to receive more medical service from the surgeon. Likewise, your advice fee has nothing to do with additional products a client might buy. Too many advisors confuse the analysis with the implementation. There are two parts to any plan: the analysis of the situation and the implementation of a program the analysis deems necessary.

Advisors who reduce their advice fees because a client buys more products still have the stake in the ground. They do not recognize the value they provide.

It's Not about the Plan; It's about the Advice

At the first-ever GAMA Asia conference, in February 2014, Phil's presentation on fee planning was extremely well received. He recapped North Star's thirty-two years in fee planning. One of his main points was that many firms, including North Star, have lost considerable amounts of profitability for several reasons. One is that for too many years, we offered a product—a financial plan. The product was the plan, and we did not price it accordingly. North Star alone lost a quarter of a million dollars every year for twenty years because we were being manufacturers instead of distributors. We would have been better off if we had distributed other companies' products, put a price on them, and made profit.

It is not about the financial plan. We can't say that too many times. Few clients will ever read that inch-thick book (financial plan). They will sit still and wait for you to review the executive summary with them. That is all they are interested in. But when you evolve from a focus on plans and engage them in an ongoing advice relationship, the moment they make a check out to you is what we call the "proof of commitment." From that point forward, your client has proved her commitment to your process.

At this top level of your service tier, you are not preparing a financial plan. Advisors sometimes say, "I will do a plan for you and charge you for it." A financial plan is a document that an advisor prepares "behind the curtain," then hands it to the client and says, "Here's your plan. You owe me a thousand dollars." A plan doesn't paint the whole picture. Clients want to know what they're supposed to do to get to their goals. There was a time when advisors focused heavily on creating financial plans. But they rarely followed up with their clients to find out if they were implementing their recommendations. Implementation was not part of the equation, but it is a critical part of the formula for helping clients achieve their financial goals.

The plan is more for you than your client. It provides the road map for you to make recommendations and guide your clients and moves them closer to their goals.

Again, it takes a shift in your mindset to get away from the idea that you're going to produce a paper document and that is where your value exists. The value you provide to clients is not the document. Financial plans are tools—"guardrails"—for advisors. Financial software programs like eMoney Advisor and MoneyEdge are designed for advisors to use with clients to determine what actions they need to take to achieve their financial goals. Financial plans are similar tools for advisors.

You can hand your client a document, but most people don't know what to do with it. They don't know how to execute it without your wisdom and guidance. A great example of this concept is a story Phil tells about the 1998 "merger of equals" of Norwest and Wells Fargo. As the merger was under way, it was reported that Norwest chairman Dick Kovacevich left a valuable strategic planning document containing details of the merger on an airplane. He said to someone, "I just left our strategic plan on the airplane."

His colleague said, "Well, aren't you going to call and get the plan back? You'd better find that document."

Kovacevich said, "I don't have to worry about it. Nobody can execute it like we can."

Another story that illustrates the point that a mere document is void of wisdom is about Knute Rockne, who was the head football coach at Notre Dame from 1918 to 1930. One season, as the Fighting Irish prepared to play their long-time rival, the Army Black Knights football team of the US Military Academy, Army's coach wrote Coach Rockne a letter and said, "Hey, we're going to play you later in the season. Why don't we do this? Instead of sending our assistant coaches to one another's schools, which will cause them to miss some games, why don't we just keep our assistants at our own games to help us? Why don't you just send us your plays, and we'll send you our plays? Then we don't have to go and scout you."

Rockne sent a letter back to Army, and here's what it said:

> Dear Coach,
>
> Attached are the eleven offensive plays Notre Dame will be using this year. We will be at all of your games.
>
> P.S. You'll never know when we're going to use them.

Discover Your Clients' Values

In Chapter 1, we mentioned a deck of values cards we use to discover what drives people in life. Our advisors sometimes do that values exercise with clients.

Once you know a client's values, you are on your way to helping her achieve the kind of life she is striving for. If she tells you that financial security, travel, and adventure are her values, then you can say, "If I could show you a way you could do more of that, would you be interested?" You are connecting with her on a personal level about her values and what she wants to achieve. No product is involved. You're having a conversation about what she wants to do with her life and how she can use her money to get the kind of life she has always wanted. And that can help you start the conversation about the value of an ongoing advice relationship.

Envision It Differently

Years ago, it was common for the advisor to sit across a table or desk from the client, closing a transaction. In the financial-advice model, the visual image is a lot different. The client is sitting shoulder to shoulder with the advisor on the same side of the table. They're looking at the client's financial situation together. The client brings her hard work, earnings, and revenue to the picture, and you bring knowledge, wisdom, and discipline. It's a partnership.

How You Can Benefit from a Script

When we coach advisors in adopting the financial-advice model, it helps them to have a script to follow with existing clients, at least in the beginning. Here is one you can use to get started.

Advice Relationship Discussion

(Sample Script)

I'd like to visit with you about the way we can work together as we move ahead. The reason is that I have a good portion of my clients asking for more services, asking more questions, and bringing me more complex situations. While I'm complimented by these requests, there are only so many hours in the week. I'm finding that their lives have evolved to being more complex, and therefore, my practice needs to evolve to provide these services.

I want to determine what level of service interests you and matches your situation. We have three options: a service model based on work we have already done, a foundation advice relationship for the basics, or a comprehensive advice relationship that integrates all aspects of your financial world and drives us to reach your goals. Most people at your level of wealth and complexity engage in a comprehensive relationship where we cover the following topics (show the menu of services). The decision is yours. In any case, you will remain part of our practice. Fortunately, I have an excellent team who will respond to those clients who have service requests. Clients in an advice relationship will continue to work with me and meet with me. We will have a defined service model and experience during the year.

I have found that clients who work with me in an advice relationship consider me the CFO of their household and the guardian of their financial future. With me, you are benefiting from literally thousands of client meetings, in which I have seen both smart and not-so-smart decisions regarding finances. My value to you is that I bring both knowledge and discipline to your financial situation to help you reach your goals. Most people will make a fortune in their lifetime. Without an advisor, few have anything to show for it in the end. Working in an advice relationship will mean that you will have something to show for it, and that money will be your servant, not your master.

How would you like to move forward?

It is a subtle pivot. You're not taking anything away from your existing clients. You're just adding value to those who want to work with you on an advice basis.

Advice Is Leadership

Advice is leadership because it allows you to lead clients where they would likely not go on their own. When you provide your clients with ongoing advice, support, and encouragement, it ignites a spark in them that fuels their desire to do better. As Ed Deutschlander and Rich Campe stress in their 2013 book *Be the First Believer*, you can help your clients by believing in their potential to achieve the life they have always imagined: "Everyone needs someone in their life to expect greatness from them. You can be that one for many, and in doing so, you will see how many will expect greatness from you."[21]

> Advice is leadership because it allows you to lead clients where they would likely not go on their own.

A common question we ask clients is, "What is important to you about money? What are your goals?" They typically know the types of financial goals that drive them—a college education for their children, a vacation home, a comfortable retirement. But often our clients don't know what they need. They can't see it, but an advisor can. As an advisor, you are providing a valuable service to your clients when you tell them they really should have an emergency fund or that they probably should get some risks like disability off the table and fund a life insurance contract. Younger clients don't always understand why they need to worry about saving for retirement now. You can educate them about the miracle of compound interest. Because of your knowledge and experience, you are helping people, through leadership, to see and appreciate what they don't know yet. We sell a lot of life insurance at North Star, but most people do not walk in saying, "I want to buy life insurance." They do not realize they need it until an advisor shares the facts with them.

Some clients are reluctant to engage in a planning relationship because they think you are going to take away all their fun. Some people like shiny things, and they want them now. I often hear from advisors that in couples, one spouse is a spender and one a saver. One is stepping on the gas and the other on the brake. This is where leadership from the advisor enters the picture. The phrase "delayed spending" sometimes helps, as do many other pearls of thought leadership. The right advice at the right time can make a tremendous difference in their financial health and personal future.

---

21. Ed Deutschlander and Rich Campe, *Be the First Believer: Leadership Life Lessons* (Bloomington, MN: Bethany Press International, 2013), 36.

Be an Advocate for Life Insurance

We have talked a lot about evolving from engaging in purely transactional relationships with clients to establishing ongoing financial advice relationships with clients. We want to emphasize that this does not mean you should move away from a focus on life insurance. Our advisors in the career system are probably the last vestige of people who have the courage to put life insurance in place. There was a time when firms and agencies believed in leading with life insurance, but fewer of us are doing this now than ten years ago.

> We should use the financial advice process as a catalyst for the sale of life insurance.

A strong financial advice relationship with an engaged client can lead to their getting more protection in place. We should use the financial advice process as a catalyst for the sale of life insurance. It is one of the first things advisors include in a financial plan, to get risk transferred away from the client.

We can make a huge impact in people's lives through the coverage we have in place. Life insurance is an important part of the ongoing financial advice relationship. It has helped many families avoid financial hardship when the primary breadwinner in the family dies unexpectedly. And that will not change in the future. People buy life insurance not because *they* believe in it but because *you* believe in it. Be passionate about its power and value, and that passion will be contagious.

The Rule, Not the Exception

It is a challenge to lead advisors to change their mindsets enough to consider evolving from transactional relationships to ongoing advice relationships with clients. When we finally see progress in this area, most advisors think of this top tier of service as an additional service to offer as a sideline to a few selected clients. The goal is to offer ongoing financial advice as a pervasive way of life for the vast majority of your practice.

We want to encourage you to think big on advice relationships. We need to envision our practices providing 150 to 200 advice deliverables each year, with appropriate fees of $150,00 to $250,000. When I discuss this level of advice planning, most advisors gasp and say, "There is no way I could provide that many advice relationships!"

My response is, "I don't expect *you* to do that; I expect *your practice* to do that." It requires a mind shift, and again, it's a door only you, the advisor, can go through. If advice is good for your top clients because of the complexity of their situation, why wouldn't it also be good for the middle tier of your clients who also want a successful retirement? It's not as in-depth a relationship, nor is it at the same fee level. But advisors can and should think about this business model in a bigger way.

* * * *

People asked Steve Jobs what market research he did when developing the iPad. He laughed and said, "Zero. I didn't do any market research. I just knew that people would need this and want this." He was right. I have an iPad, and I can't leave the house without it now. I didn't know I needed it, but now that I know what it can do, it is important to me.

Much earlier, the great automaker Henry Ford developed and manufactured the first automobile that many middle-class Americans could afford. It was certainly a novelty at the time. He was quoted as saying, "If I had asked my customers what they wanted, they would have said a faster horse." Now, of course, it would be difficult to imagine life without automobiles.

The same can and should be said of clients who are engaged in an ongoing advice relationship. They may not realize they need your help, but once they have it, they will wonder how they ever lived without it.

What Happens when Advice Is the Total Value Proposition?

Dave Johnson is a perennial leading advisor at North Star. He is also remarkable for the leadership he brings to, and the vision he has for, his practice. He wants to be the best financial advisor in the country that money can buy, as measured by the value delivered to the client, not personal "production." This value is captured in providing comprehensive advice to high-net-worth clients, where advice is the total value. Instead of having the client be the center of the relationship among protection subject-matter experts (SMEs), attorneys, CPAs, investment experts, and other key parties, the advisor serves this integrating role. Dave and his staff coordinate all advice from an entire team of SMEs who have dedicated their entire professional lives to their narrow field of expertise. The most important role Dave plays is holding clients accountable to implement the advice. If they follow the advice, they have the highest probability of achieving every financial goal they set for themselves, for the reasons that are important to them.

By working on a comprehensive, fee-only basis, and by having a single point of contact, clients are free to focus on their families, careers, and whatever else contributes to their happiness.

Dave has developed a systematic and well-defined process that captures virtually every contingency and opportunity clients and their families will face. Over an eighteen-month period, he and his team moved the client to this platform. Over the initial fifteen months of the client relationship, Dave and his team work to get the client's financial house in perfect order. Then they release the client into a three-meetings-per-year cycle to keep it that way. The fee he charges is considerable yet is still a value to clients because of the impact it will make on their goals and financial future. He has total conviction when he says, "We want to overpromise and overdeliver." He admits he has had to scrub his sales language to focus on advice around execution, action steps, and measuring progress toward clients' goals.

The transition to this model has not been without some risk. It has taken courage as well as a significant investment of time and money. In the end, Dave is convinced that it will be a better practice model for that level of client, and it provides transparency, which in turn contributes to a high level of trust between the client and his or her team.

Dave has a clear sense of the quality of life he wants for himself and for his family. While he provides a remarkable level of value for his clients, the practice is built to serve his values and to allow him to spend time on the hobbies, travel, and interests that give his life full meaning. It's truly a Practice on Purpose.

Erik's Story: How Ongoing Financial Advice Benefits All of Us

Erik R. Andrews, CFP®, Partner and Senior Financial Consultant, North Star Resource Group

About a decade ago, I made the decision to build my practice around comprehensive financial planning. Clients benefit from a higher level of service and attention to detail that they come to expect, it enhances the overall client experience, and it deepens the relationship for them and for me. Engaging in a comprehensive planning relationship allows me to take a holistic approach to financial well-being and provide purely objective, proactive, and ongoing comprehensive advice. Just as important as financial discussions and strategies are the clients' personal emotions, philosophies, and values.

It is extremely liberating to be able to speak candidly to clients about all facets of their financial lives (even when it has nothing to do with a particular product), as sometimes I feel I am more of a financial therapist than a planner at times! Engaging in a financial planning relationship ensures that we are on the same page and connected, and our discussions are not limited to just talking about a product. This is precisely the reason I chose to get into this wonderful career and to earn my CFP® designation: to be an advocate for my clients and help them ensure they accomplish their personal financial wishes.

Applying the Concepts to *Your* Practice on Purpose

1. Are you engaged in an ongoing advice relationship with any of your existing clients? If not, will you commit to evolving to this model? What steps do you need to take to convert existing clients to this type of relationship? What is your timeline for making the transition?

   _____
   _____
   _____
   _____
   _____

2. What steps will you take to begin encouraging new clients to engage in an ongoing advice relationship with you?

   _____
   _____
   _____
   _____
   _____

3. To what extent are you an advocate for life insurance? Is transferring risk away from clients your first priority in working with clients? If not, what will you do to ensure that the focus on life insurance becomes more prominent in your practice?

   _____
   _____
   _____
   _____
   _____

Acquiring Clients—How to Invite People to Join Your Practice

CHAPTER 4

> "The question isn't who is going to let me; it's who is going to stop me."
>
> **—Ayn Rand**
> American Novelist, Philosopher, Playwright, and Screenwriter

There is no room for cowardice when building your clientele. The advisors who are more tenacious about seeking out clients and more inclined to strike up a conversation with strangers tend to acquire more clients. Ayn Rand's quote on this page captures the spirit of getting out there and meeting as many people as possible. If you have a clear purpose and a passion for helping people, who is going to stop you?

The goal isn't to seek out just anyone to be your client, however. In a Practice on Purpose, the clients are more similar than different and are categorized by their similarities—for example, in terms of household income, type of occupation, or life goals. That is by design. If everyone is your potential client, it means you have not figured out who your ideal client is, and you are serving whomever you come across. In this chapter, we look at how an advisor with an established practice can determine which type of clients to serve and how to attract them.

But before we can talk about how to attract clients to your practice, we first need to discuss *your* pivotal role in your practice.

The Advisor Is the Core of the Practice

A practice is a reflection of the advisor. Advisors' clients usually reflect their views, values, and demographics. So the first step, as we discussed earlier, is to define your values. The second step is to find clients with similar values.

The diagram below shows five concentric circles. The smallest circle is in the middle of the diagram, and it represents the advisor. Each circle that radiates out from it is a little bigger than the previous one. The second ring represents your physical office space and how you "touch" your clients. The third circle represents client recommendations and client service meetings. The fourth one represents social media and your website, and the fifth and last ring represents your centers of influence, seminars, events, and advertising to the public. The diagram illustrates how you communicate your value proposition.

As the advisor, you are the core, the center, of the entire process. Your value proposition starts with who you are as a person, and you communicate your value through those mechanisms.

Marketing Begins with You

If you have a weak value proposition and cannot communicate it well, it really doesn't matter what else happens. If that first circle, the core, is weak, the other activities cannot salvage your practice.

We have an advisor who received low client satisfaction scores on a survey. She was constantly late to meetings, had a disheveled appearance, kept a messy office, and did not greet her clients in a warm, professional manner. When we met with her about her low scores, she said—with a straight face—"I just don't understand why I don't get recommendations."

An advisor who lacks self-awareness at that level most likely has a weak value proposition. Neither attractive advertising nor a professional website will attract clients to the practice of an advisor whose value proposition is weak.

Another situation we see is that we will plan an event and get clients and guests there. The advisor will show up but is too terrified to speak in front of the audience. Not only that, the advisor lacks the social skills to go around the room and greet people. The ideal situation is for the advisor to act like a honeybee, going around to pollinate flowers, to connect with people. Some advisors are gifted in this area; they buzz about the room and hook people together with common interests. They greet people when they first walk in the door, and they don't let anybody stand by themselves too long.

We once hired an etiquette coach to meet with our advisors who were hosting seminars. The coach provided tips on how to behave in a room and introduce people to each other. It helped a lot.

The stronger your social skills, confidence, and ability to communicate your value, the better you will be at attracting the right clients. In the last chapter, we asked, "Whose family benefits more by becoming your client? Does the advisor's family benefit more, or does the client's family?" You will benefit a little, but your clients will benefit much more. Acknowledging that fact, having that conviction, will arm you with a strong value proposition.

> The stronger your social skills, confidence, and ability to communicate your value, the better you will be at attracting the right clients.

Dan Sullivan, who has coached thousands of financial advisors for forty years, wrote a book called *The Good That Financial Advisors Do*.[22] In it, he lists compelling benefits advisors provide to clients in the twenty-first century. If you need a good reminder about the value you bring to the table, spend some time reading what he has to say.

Once you determine who you are as a person first and then as an advisor—in other words, once you define your value proposition—you will begin to attract like-minded people who have similar political or life philosophies. Your practice will reflect your central purpose in life and the purpose of your practice.

Now that we have established that you are at the core of your practice, let's examine some effective ways to build a clientele that reflects your personal and professional values.

---

22. Dan Sullivan, *The Good That Advisors Do* (Toronto, Ontario: The Strategic Coach, Inc., 2010), Kindle edition.

Three Types of Clients

Not everyone is your ideal client. It's important to determine what type of client you want to serve and then focus on that market.

We have identified three categories, or types, of clients and have separated them into three different household-income levels. The next diagram shows nine different groups of clients. Let's take a look at these groups and discuss whether or not each group is an ideal fit for your practice.

We want our advisors to seek out clients who fall into the four categories in the lower right-hand corner of the table shown below. Your ideal clients (noted in blue) have sufficient income and complex issues, and they are open and receptive to your advice.

Would They Be Ideal Clients for You?

		Household Income		
		$50,000	$150,000	$300,000+
Client Type	Self-Directed	No	No	No
	Opinion-Seeking	No	Yes	Yes
	Dependent	No	Yes	Yes

1. **Self-Directed Clients**—These are people who have more time than money. They read financial self-help books, watch investment shows on TV, read financial-advice magazines, invest using online brokerage services, and listen to advice from their neighbors or their barber. They buy the stocks that so-called experts recommend. In essence, they are doing their own brain surgery. They get a little bit of knowledge from various sources and feel equipped to do it all themselves. Worse, they meet with a broker to get good ideas and say, "You know, I think I'm just going to do this myself. I appreciate your advice." The reality is, they are weak in implementation, and they typically don't address the complex topics of protection, tax implications, and coordination of legal and tax advisors. They value advice but either get incorrect advice or are reluctant to pay for quality advice. The very worst thing is that many of these people are in our advisors' practices. You may have clients like this. They are a drain on your practice. They want to have you provide them with answers but are not necessarily willing to pay you for your wisdom.

If a self-directed person had a leaky sink, he would watch a video, go to a home-improvement store to buy some parts, and attempt to fix the leak himself. Professional plumbers love these guys because they make a lot of money cleaning up after them.

Here is a story that might help you understand how to communicate effectively with self-directed clients.

One of my coached advisors had a grandfather who was in declining health. He was referred to a land attorney to discuss how to transfer ownership of the grandfather's assets. He called her up and said, "This is my situation, this is who I am, and I have a few questions."

She replied, "I don't do a few questions." (She probably perceived him as a self-directed client.)

He said, "Oh, OK. So how can I work with you?"

"I charge five hundred dollars an hour. I will be glad to meet with you, and I have no doubt I can help your situation." She was only twenty-eight years old but highly confident about the value she could provide.

When he went to meet with her, he took his checkbook with him. She said, "You will need to pay me in advance for today's meeting." He was a little irritated but wrote her a $500 check and set it on her desk. She didn't touch it.

She asked him to describe the situation. He went through it. She drew a couple of pictures and asked him a dozen questions. Then she said, "Here is how we can structure this." She described a strategy, then said, "It will take two more meetings, and you will have what you need."

When the grandfather died, he owned nothing, which is exactly what he had wanted. He did not own a car or his farm anymore; all he owned was his clothes. It was all given away the way he wanted it done, and his survivors saved hundreds of thousands of dollars on estate taxes. All for only $1,500.

The attorney knew her value, and she was not going to let her client self-direct her. She was not going to let him pick her brain and then walk out of there without paying her anything. It might be difficult to do this at first, but it gets easier, especially if you are convinced of the value you provide.

2. **Opinion-Seeking Clients**—These are typically busy, successful people who have more money than time. They are too busy to do financial planning themselves. They invest in the best efforts of others. They know they need advice. They recognize they need someone to help them with implementation, discipline, and follow-through.

3. **Dependent Clients**—For clients in this category, money is a foreign language. They are somewhat intimidated by money. They could be working in valuable occupations—as veterinarians or teachers, for example—but their work is not related to business. They tend to hand the reins over to somebody else. Unfortunately, they are quite vulnerable to bad advice. They want and value advice and know they cannot handle their own financial planning, nor do they want to do it themselves. They are not self-directed. They say, "I need help, but I don't even know what questions to ask."

Now let's look at each type of client in each income category. The guidelines we are about to share are extremely accurate.

A **self-directed client** with a household income of about $50,000 is not the ideal client for our advisors. She might be a good client for another company that markets to that segment of the population.

Self-directed clients in the $150,000 and $300,000 income categories are not ideal clients for our advisors, either. Why? Because they want to do it all themselves. They are not likely to engage in an ongoing financial advice relationship with an advisor. It is fatiguing trying to get clients like this to provide documents, agree to a financial strategy, and follow recommendations.

> Opinion-seeking clients who earn $150,000 and $300,000 and above in annual household income typically make fantastic clients for us.

It is possible that some **opinion-seeking clients** who have about $50,000 in household income might be good prospects for our advisors because they value our services and expertise, especially if they are vertically mobile in their careers. You have to be careful with this category, though, because our services might be expensive for them. In many cases, they have high demands and expectations, but they are never going to make a lot of household income. There are probably better companies for them to work with.

Opinion-seeking clients who earn $150,000 and $300,000 and above in annual household income typically make fantastic clients for us. These are the people with sufficient household income, their issues are typically complex, they are busy people, and they don't have time to do their own financial planning. They need help. They need knowledge and discipline, and they are great candidates for financial advice. They will fit into your practice very well.

Dependent clients who are making about $50,000 a year need help, and many of our advisors give them pro bono advice just because they want to. But you have to be careful that you don't end up balancing their checkbook for them. We often refer them to a bank to establish a relationship, and sometimes that is all they need.

Dependent clients who earn $150,000 and $300,000 make fantastic clients because they tend to value advice and benefit from it.

Prune Your Client List Regularly

To manage a Practice on Purpose requires a constant "pruning" of your client list, just as a tree needs to be pruned to keep its branches strong and growing. On a regular basis, determine which clients fit your practice best and which ones should either work with a junior partner or maybe work with another firm.

If you have self-directed clients who want piecemeal advice, you can suggest they look for another representative who will work on more of a transactional basis with them. You can say something like, "I will be helpful in any way I can, but we're not going to be able to work together anymore. I appreciate all we have done together."

How to Fire a Client

While we are on the topic of acquiring clients, it might be helpful to discuss the opposite—how to quit working with clients who are annoying or abusive or just don't fit into the demographic you want to focus on. We have known of clients who were actually destructive to an advisor's practice. We hear of this happening more often than you might expect. Clients will ask for a lot more service than they want to pay for, or they treat an advisor or team member with disrespect.

We have an advisor in Iowa named Bill. He had a client who was extremely demanding and rude to Bill's team members. Bill asked the client to behave more professionally, but he did not. Eventually Bill got up the courage to let the client know he could not work with him anymore. Then we found out that Bill got the client as a recommendation from another advisor who had gotten tired of working with him.

If you have a prospect you do not wish to work with, for whatever reason, a tactful way to handle that is simply to say, "My practice is not taking new clients right now." Exiting a relationship with an established client might take a little more courage. You are not obligated to give a specific reason. You could say something like, "I am narrowing the focus of my practice and have decided to serve only (fill in the blank—e.g., "those in the medical profession" or "high-net-worth individuals").

Asking for Recommendations

Asking for referrals—which we prefer to call "recommendations"—and the language we use in doing so is analogous to learning and knowing a foreign language. If we reach a certain level of fluency, let's say in German, we gain confidence the more we speak the language. On the other hand, if we don't speak German frequently, we lose confidence and become timid, and then we get worried about making a mistake and embarrassing ourselves, so we speak it less and less. Soon enough, we don't speak the new language at all. That is also the way it is with the language we use to request recommendations.

Some advisors who start asking for recommendations are often quickly discouraged when they don't get immediate success, so they stop asking. If a Major League baseball player is hitting .300, that means he gets a hit only three of every ten times he is up to bat. He strikes out seven out of ten times. Babe Ruth, the legendary hitter, said, "Every strike brings me closer to the next homerun." Shrug off discouragement and move on to the next opportunity. The more you ask for recommendations, the more you will receive.

> Asking for recommendations when you are meeting with your best clients is one of the best return-on-investment strategies you can incorporate into your practice.

The best recommendations are likely to come from your top clients. Once you have established relationships with the specific type of clients you want to work with, you can grow your practice exponentially by asking them to refer people they know to your practice. Chances are, they will know people who are like them in terms of demographics and income. Asking for recommendations when you are meeting with your best clients is one of the best return-on-investment strategies you can incorporate into your practice.

Keep in mind, though, that many people recommend downward. In other words, they will give you the names of people they know who make less money than they do. In that segment, you are a "*deal*" for them, but they are not *ideal* for you. Be aware of this, and try to encourage your clients to recommend you to people who are in a similar demographic group as they are. It helps to describe your menu of services and explain that you can do the most for clients who value what you do in the top service tier.

The Life Event Recommendation Talk

A good way to position your request for a recommendation is to pivot into it right after your client gives you a compliment about how much she appreciates what you are doing for her. We call it the "Life Event Recommendation talk." It goes something like this:

You know, I have been giving a lot of thought to my practice over the past year, and I have come to a conclusion I would like to share with you. I have watched many clients go through three types of significant life events. The first one is a job change like a promotion or a layoff. The second one is a change in marital status—they are getting married or divorced. The third one is retirement. I have found that when clients are going through any of those three events, I can do the most good for them because during those events, money and emotions intersect. When money and emotions come together, there is a prime opportunity for unwise decisions to be made. I feel good when I can interact with my clients and be there for them to help them make better decisions during those critical times. I just wanted to share that with you.

I am going to ask you, then, who in your social circle is going through a job change, a marital change, or considering retirement? Maybe we can help them together. Sometimes people will call you and say, "I'm having trouble at work." We all want to help, but we don't know what to do. I can suggest that if you recommend me to them, that is something good we can do for them. Of course I can help them, too. It is a way we can create value and happiness and good things for people in a difficult situation. So I would like for you, over the next couple of days, to think about people you know in your social circle who might be going through any of those three events. If I can get your permission to call you Monday afternoon, I will check in with you quickly and see if you have thought of anyone. Then I am going to ask you for a way I could meet them that is respectful of your relationship with them. Would that be OK with you?

Following My Doctor's Lead

Every spring, I used to get a horrific cold. Then one day, a buddy of mine said, "It might not be a cold. You might have allergies."

I thought, *I'm rough and tough, and I'm a guy. I don't have allergies.* But I asked my general practitioner to refer me to an allergist, just in case. When I went to see her, she gave me a scratch test. She exposed the skin on my back to a wide variety of allergens, such as mold, pollen, and plants, to see if I had a reaction to any of them. She found out that I was allergic to several things and gave me a prescription for an allergy medication.

When she was finished, she asked me, "Has this been a good appointment for you? Do you think we got to the root of your problem?"

I said, "Yes, I think we did."

"You know, a lot of people walk around with allergies, and they have no idea that is what they have," she said. "I am new at this clinic and am establishing my practice. I would like to give you three business cards to carry in your wallet to give to people who may have symptoms similar to yours. You just said this has been helpful, and I can probably help some other people you know who have similar issues. Please carry these three business cards around and give them to people you know so that they can come see me. Better yet, if you let me know who they are, I will call them."

Think about that for a minute. This is a medical doctor. She worked extremely hard to get through med school, is very professional, and asked me to carry three of her business cards around. She was prospecting. I had a good appointment with her, so I was fine with recommending her. I thought, *If she can do it, why can't we do it?*

We can. Once you determine that a client is happy with your service, that is the perfect time to ask for a recommendation. It makes perfect sense to do so.

Three Reasons Advisors Don't Get More Recommendations

There are three primary reasons advisors get fewer recommendations than they could:

1. **They don't ask.** Remember, as Wayne Gretzky said, you miss 100 percent of the shots you don't take. I tell advisors to say to their clients, "I can't help people I don't meet."

2. **They don't believe in themselves or in the value they provide.** Remember, when the advisor grows, the practice grows. As you gain confidence that you are delivering value, you will feel more comfortable about asking for referrals. Believe that you have something of value because your client's family is going to benefit from your value more than yours will. That's a critical part of your belief system, and it should help you have the courage to ask people to join your practice.

3. **They lack preparation.** They just haven't thought it through. They haven't practiced the language. They don't quite know when to ask for a recommendation, how to set the stage, or how to pivot in a way that is comfortable for the client.

The Art of Turning Casual Conversations into Appointments

You don't have to acquire all of your clients through formal means. Sometimes you can meet new clients in social situations that start out with casual conversation. There is an art to creating an appointment from that kind of a situation. I call it "the lost art of conversation."

If you are not a natural conversationalist who is gifted in this area, write out scripts that will help you anticipate how conversations might start and then steer those conversations into discussions about how you can help people. I have been an advisor for a long time, and I still write scripts. If I have an important conversation coming up, I write it out and practice it until it is second nature. Then, when I have the conversation, I am comfortable enough with the script that my mind is freed up to get to a higher order of thinking versus worrying about the words I am going to use. I can focus on strategizing as we are having the conversation.

Wherever you are, keep your "antennae" up, and be aware that the person you just met at a holiday party, baseball game, or church function could be your next client.

Norb Winter was a general agent whose family had been with Minnesota Life and Securian since the 1920s. Norb had the uncanny ability to go to any lunch, any event, and walk out with a handful of appointments. People wanted to meet him. He was positive, fun, kind, and respectful. He always said, "A stranger is a friend I have yet to meet." Norb was renowned for having social confidence, a sense of humor, and the ability to compliment people easily but genuinely; it wasn't contrived. He was as authentic as you could imagine, and he enjoyed meeting new people. He had a high level of emotional competence. He knew who he was as a person and was keenly aware of the good he could do for others. He had the attitude that it was OK if someone didn't like him, but there was nobody he didn't like. He was amazing at converting casual conversations into appointments. Many readers may have encountered Norb at MDRT or LAMP, where he was a main-platform speaker and became known as "the suitcase man."

The Red-Car Story

I like to share my "red-car story" with advisors because it is a good example of how an opportunity like that can arise.

One gorgeous spring day, I was in a little town in central Minnesota visiting an advisor at his office. I parked diagonally on the street because their streets are not designed for parallel parking. A man in his late fifties pulled up in a brand new, red Thunderbird convertible. He looked at me, and I looked at him and said, "Hey, nice car."

He said, "Yeah, I got this for retirement."

I replied, "That's quite the company you work for that you got a car like this for retirement."

He said, "Yeah" and laughed a little.

Then I asked him, "How did you know you could retire?"

His facial expression changed, and he said, "I got retired."

I sensed that I needed to rescue him. I could tell he wasn't feeling good about where we were in the conversation. So I said, "There is a lot of that going around. It happens. But this is a really nice car."

He said, "My wife always wanted me to get a Thunderbird because I had a Thunderbird as a kid. I always looked up to them as a kid, and Ford started coming out with them again."

Then we talked about cars for a minute. I said, "You mentioned that you 'got retired.' How do you know you can stay retired? I appreciate the car; it is great. But how do you know you can really retire?"

"Well, I really don't," he said.

I asked him, "Would you like to feel better about that decision? I work with financial advisors, and this is the kind of work we do. In fact, I just walked out of Mike's office. He is standing there in the lobby; I can see him."

The guy said, "I kind of know Mike."

"I want to introduce you to Mike," I said. "Would that be OK with you?"

I walked him in and introduced him to Mike, and we all engaged in some small talk. I said, "Hey, I love your car, but I am getting out of here." And I left.

About a week later, I got a call from the advisor. He said, "Hey, that was a three hundred thousand dollar rollover. The guy is actually in far better financial shape than he thought he was. It was great to meet him."

It all started with, "Hey, nice car." I didn't know where that conversation was going to go, but I am always aware that anyone I meet is a potential client for one of my advisors. If you approach every situation with that frame of mind, you can get good at turning those conversations into appointments. Look for busy, successful people who are starved for time and want wisdom. Remember the ideal clients we talked about who are in the four quadrants of that table—the opinion-seeking and dependent clients who earn more than $150,000 of household income or are going to have this level of income. You deserve each other.

Engage in Napkin Talks

Related to the subject of turning casual conversations into appointments is the subject of "napkin talks." Sometimes those casual conversations we enter into are a little more involved, and you begin discussing the critical topic of mitigating risk with a potential client at a social gathering. You can grab a napkin or anything else handy to write on and sketch out a diagram that helps explain what advisors do. In five minutes, you can show people how advance preparation can help them offset the financial risks of becoming disabled, outliving their savings, or dying unexpectedly.

We often talk about "time diversification." We all know about tax diversification and asset diversification. Time diversification is nature's way of making sure everything doesn't happen at once.

The four diagrams below depict four stages of the napkin talk. You can draw a rudimentary version of these diagrams on a napkin or piece of paper as you are describing how you can help people manage major risks. In all four diagrams, we represent a person's life using a horizontal line that represents a timeline of major events—birth, childhood, high school, college, and retirement. Of course we don't know how long a person will live, but according to 2010 actuary tables, the average woman in America will live to be 80.8 years old, and the average man in America will live to be 75.7 years old.[23]

In all four diagrams, the squiggly line that looks like a bell curve is the money line. It increases and decreases throughout a person's adult life as he or she begins a career, advances in that career, accumulates assets, and experiences market volatility. Around age sixty-five, about when the typical person retires, the money line peaks and then declines. Ideally, the money line should intersect to the right of where the person's actuarial life expectancy line is.

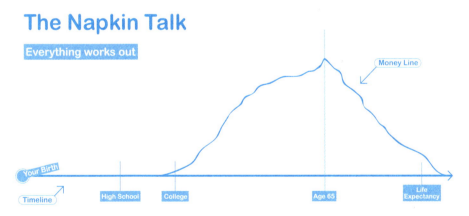

Part of an advisor's job is to make sure a client's money line is longer than her life line. We all have risk in our lives. One risk is that we might get sick or disabled and can't work. On the horizontal life line in the second diagram, I have shown a short gap. That represents a year when the client can't work,

---

23. "Retirees Underestimate Life Expectancy, Risk Underfunding Retirement," press release, Society of Actuaries, last modified July 30, 2012, http://www.soa.org/News-and-Publications/Newsroom/Press-Releases/2012-07-30-retirees-under.aspx.

so her money line is interrupted. As an advisor, you can transfer that risk to an insurance company for pennies on the dollar and get it off the table.

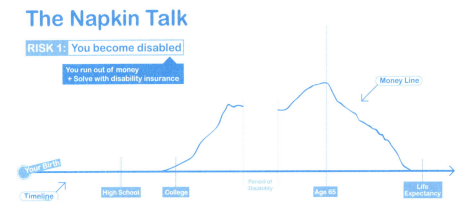

The vertical line that is perpendicular to the horizontal life line represents the age at which the person dies. As shown in the third diagram, that's where the money line stops—the day that person doesn't make it home, for whatever reason. That breadwinner's family thought the money line was going to keep going. That is the risk of premature death, and of course we can transfer that risk to an insurance company, too.

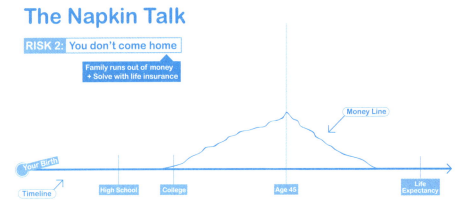

The fourth diagram depicts a third risk everyone faces: outliving accumulated assets. When that happens, the money line ends up being shorter than the life line. We can transfer that risk to an insurance company as well, through an annuity. We always want to make sure clients will never outlive their money line.

The Napkin Talk

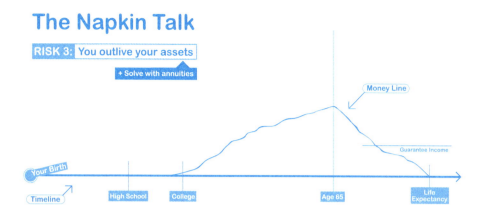

Our job is to address all of these risks for our clients and make their money work harder for them than they are working for the money. We want money to be our clients' servant, not their master.

You can modify this discussion in a way that's comfortable for you and makes sense in the conversation you're having. It's a great way to get people engaged and lead them to understand the value you offer them. The next step is to secure an appointment in your office to go deeper with the discussion.

Tap into Social Media to Meet and Serve Clients

The 2014 GAMA LAMP conference in Nashville was an outstanding meeting. One of the overriding themes was the use of social media to both market to the right clients and serve current clients. This is becoming an industry in itself, and it appears to be ready to explode. Resources like LinkedIn, Facebook, and Twitter are our new marketplaces, our new store fronts.

When I returned from the conference, a Yellow Pages directory was lying on my door stoop. It went right into the recycle bin next to my rotary wall phone.

Some advisors are quite adept at using social media to meet people; others haven't tapped into the medium yet. LinkedIn is a powerful tool. We have team members at North Star who will review and audit advisors' LinkedIn sites and help them build them in a way that is searchable and that creates the right image. When people visit your LinkedIn site, you want them to be able to get a good idea of who you are as a person and the value you can provide to them. Our North Star website works in concert with our individual advisors' websites.

LinkedIn is also a valuable tool for discovering more about clients you might be meeting with soon, as well as people they are linked to on the site. We recommend that you visit a specific client's site and identify two or three busy, successful people who are doing something good with their careers and appear to be in those four categories we talked about. Print the pages from their LinkedIn sites that describe their occupations. Then, when you meet with your client to go through her goals and progress, you can say at the end of the meeting, "Can I get your advice on something? I visited your LinkedIn site. I think you have such a great career going. I wanted to find out more about who you are. While I was visiting your site, I came across some people you know. You are really fortunate; you have a great network of people who are connected with you. Good going, really nice job. Three people who are linked to you kind of stood out to me. I printed out their profiles here. How do you know them, and do you think they would be good people for me to work with? And do you have any advice regarding a good way to meet them that respects your relationship with them?"

This strategy allows you to assign specific names to the prospecting activity. That tends to be more effective than asking, "Hey, who do you know who could benefit from the work I do?" Most people don't have a clue and can't think of a name. If you show them a name and a picture, they can react to that specific person. Chances are, your client will be honest with you and tell you how much potential that person has as a prospect for you. We have seen some advisors make great use of LinkedIn for referrals.

Probably the most powerful LinkedIn feature is LinkedIn Maps. This feature uses a color-coded diagram to "map" your contacts—in other words, to show how you know your contacts and how your contacts know one another. You do not have to be a premium member of LinkedIn to use this feature. First, you select colors to represent how you know some of your contacts—for example, you might choose green to represent people you know from the university where you earned your undergraduate degree, red for the university where you earned your master's degree, blue for the people you met during an overseas assignment, orange for the people you know through your volunteer work, and green for your current clients. This is an illuminating exercise because you might discover, for example, that one of your fellow advisors attended the same school you did, although you did not know her at the time. Or you might discover that one of your contacts knows one hundred of your clients. If that happens, you will know it is definitely a relationship you need to cultivate. It tells you who your potential advocates are. Your clients don't know prospects; they know people. There is a big difference. How you make those connections is critical, and LinkedIn Maps reveals how you are doing so.

Facebook can be another valuable social media resource, depending on your company's policy regarding Facebook. If you are able to connect with clients on Facebook, it can be valuable in keeping you up to date on people's life events that have an impact on the work you do. If your clients have reported a marriage, the birth of a child, vacation plans, the purchase of a new home, a new job, or a college graduation, all of these events have financial-advice implications, and you should know about them before your next client meeting.

Host Unique Events

Another great way to meet new clients is to create a social experience, an event. Invite your clients, and encourage them to bring family members, friends, and coworkers. Events are a way to create a social accident where people meet you and are curious to learn more. You pique their interest.

I am on the advisory board of a company called MOMENTUM Meetings & Events, LLC. They are experts in the planning and management of meetings and events for corporate clients. The company's founder, Paula Carlson, has planned and hosted more than one thousand client events. Her business card says, "Anybody can throw a party; few people can throw a successful event." You can read more about Paula and her company at http://www.momentum-test.com/about.html.

MOMENTUM's philosophy is similar to our philosophy of the importance of creating a "Practice on Purpose"—they refer to their events as "Parties with a Purpose." Paula wishes she had a dollar for every time she heard someone say, "Oh yeah, our receptionist in the office plans our events. She can do that." Or, "We did a wine tasting a couple years ago but never got anything out of it." Most people who host events fail to achieve the desired number of attendees, introductions, or new clients because they are not Parties with a Purpose. Paula's tips for hosting a Party with a Purpose are in this book's appendix.

It takes some skill to put together an event. The details are critical. They include whom you invite, which hotel to use, what the invitations will look like, which speakers to hire, what kind of food to serve, and how you will follow up with the attendees afterward. We have hosted educational seminars, cooking demonstrations, and English teas in old mansions.

One of our female advisors had a client who enjoyed fly fishing. She put together a trout-fishing trip with a group of five clients and five guests. She hired a fishing guide to take the group on a guided fishing tour in a nearby stream. She also had a guy who built fishing rods share his expertise on the trip. The group fished all morning. When they returned to shore, they ate lunch outdoors that a professional chef prepared. Within the next sixty days, three of those five guests were clients.

There are a thousand different things you can do. As you build relationships with your clients, learn what they like to do, and then build events around those preferences.

Use the Family Tree Worksheet

When I was a new advisor in Seattle, I had a client whom I had worked with for about two years. He wanted to come by my office with a $2,000 IRA check, his annual deposit. He said, "I want to bring my daughter. We would like to see your office." Because I was a junior advisor, my office was on the drab parking-lot side of the building, not on the gorgeous Puget Sound side. That was good because I saw him pull up in a van. When the side door opened, a young girl got out, and she was in a wheelchair. Of course, I rallied pretty quickly and rushed to the front door to help them in. I gave her a nice tour of our office; she was an absolutely delightful young lady. He told me that she had cerebral palsy. It bothered me a lot that I had known this client for two years, yet I never knew he had a daughter in a wheelchair. I thought, *I just can't let that happen to me again.* A month later, I came across a family tree document, and I decided I would use it with all of the important people I worked with. The family tree worksheet we now use at North Star is shown in the appendix of this book.

I am natively curious about people's families. It makes the job more interesting. Knowing about a client's family not only gives you better insight into the client's life and priorities; it also provides you with potential new business and helps you understand your clients' situations better. Numerous studies have revealed that one of the top reasons clients select a new advisor is because they felt their former advisor did not understand their situation. Using the family tree worksheet will help you understand your clients' situations much better.

The script goes something like this: "When you leave my office, you enter a world of people who are important to you. To be the best financial advisor I can for you, I would do a better job for you if I understood the world you go to after you leave my office. If you would, before our next meeting, complete this family tree diagram. It will be very helpful." Or you can mail it out before the next meeting. Once you see the completed worksheet, you will know if the client's parents are still living and if so, how old they are, as well as and who their siblings are and what they do for a living.

Once you have that information, you can ask questions like, "Who are your beneficiaries? Do your parents want to set up a 529 plan for your children?" There are many business implications of knowing the client's family and her relationships within her family. If your client says, "My sister works at 3M, and she just got promoted," you might circle back later and say, "You mentioned your sister. Is she working with an advisor? Would this type of conversation be helpful for her?" Or if your client's parents are aging, maybe one of them is struggling with memory issues. You might ask her if her parents should be meeting with her and her siblings. The discussion can go in a lot of directions.

We have seen people build almost their entire practice from knowing their key clients' family trees.

Shrug Off Rejection—Keep Your Perspective!

We started this chapter off with a quote by Ayn Rand that says, "The question isn't who is going to let me; it's who is going to stop me." It reminds me of a story that has been circulating in our business as far back as the 1920s. It goes like this.

A sales manager kept a gallon-sized glass jar full of dried lima beans on his desk. One day he asked one of his advisors, "Who are you going to go see today?"

The advisor gave him three names.

"Great," the manager said. "Now, I want you to take these three beans out of the jar and put them in your left pocket. When you are done with each meeting, move a bean over from your left pocket to your right pocket. Then come back at the end of the day and tell me how it went."

When the day was over, the manager asked the advisor what happened.

"Well, I had a nice conversation with the first person I met with about some financial goals he had and some things he could do. We were having such a good conversation that we ran out of time. We agreed that we need to meet again. It went pretty well. And the third person I went to see was just super. This guy just got a new position in his job, and he and his wife have a new baby. They know they need some coverage, and we have started the underwriting process. It just clicked. It was really good."

The manager said, 'Wait a minute. That was the third call. What happened to the second call?"

"It didn't go so well," the advisor replied. "When I went to see the guy, it was like he forgot we had an appointment. What really put me off was that he made me sit in the lobby for a long time. When he finally let me in, it was obvious that he wasn't going to give me much time. He started getting upset at me for bothering him, taking up his time, and being yet another salesperson he had to deal with."

"So what did you do?"

"Well, I took that bean out of my left pocket, held it up to him, and said, 'Listen, buddy. I've got to tell you something. In my life, you are just one little bean, and I have a gallon jar full of you back at my office.' Then I moved the bean to my right pocket and went on to my third call."

The lesson here is that there are lots of beans in the jar. If one call doesn't work out, just move on. That is still the case today, just like it was a hundred years ago, when that story originated. When you are acquiring clients, you win some and you don't win some, but you keep going. It's a numbers game. The better you are at shrugging off rejection, the more successful you will be.

* * * *

When everyone is your potential client, building a practice is difficult. When you define your ideal client, attracting clients becomes easier because you are laser-focused. As you nourish your relationships with your ideal clients, they will be a valuable source of recommendations to other ideal clients. Then you will be well on your way to building a Practice on Purpose, full of clients you want to work with who recognize and respect the value you provide.

> ### Brett's Story: How I Ensured I Was Getting in Front of the Right People
>
> Brett T. Vander Bloemen, Financial Consultant/Partner,
> North Star Resource Group
>
> The biggest obstacle advisors need to overcome when trying to get in front of the right people is *asking*!
>
> A while back in my career, it dawned on me that clients aren't afraid to refer the right people to me. I was afraid to ask. Obviously, there is an appropriate time to approach the client, and it's important to understand how to position yourself or a more specialized advisor. I started getting in front of high-profile clients because I learned how to ask, I leveraged my social networks, and I wasn't afraid to do joint work when I was in over my head.
>
> Your network of prospective clients is right in front of you—and this book will give you the tools you need to get in front of them.

Applying the Concepts to *Your* Practice on Purpose

1. To what extent have you defined your ideal client? What are the characteristics of your ideal client?

   _____
   _____
   _____
   _____
   _____
   _____

2. How often do you ask you clients for recommendations? Prepare a script for asking for them, and use it every time you meet with a client.

3. How adept are you at turning casual conversation into an appointment? How can you improve on this skill? The first step is to keep your "antennae" up and realize that every person you meet could be a potential client.

4. Do you have a LinkedIn profile? To what extent does it communicate who you are as a person and how you can help people? How well do you use it to meet new clients? How can you improve?

5. How well do you know what your clients like? What kinds of events can you plan and host that your top clients will enjoy? Plan these events, and ask your clients to bring guests.

_____
_____
_____
_____
_____

Practice Design—From a Job to a True Practice on Purpose

CHAPTER 5

> "I have been impressed with the urgency of doing. Knowing is not enough; we must apply. Being willing is not enough; we must do."
>
> —**Leonardo da Vinci**

Transitioning from a job to a Practice on Purpose requires thoughtful practice design, effective practice operations, and timely practice execution. We have talked about the conceptual framework that lays the foundation for a Practice on Purpose—determining your vision, values, and purpose. But that is only part of the equation; execution is just as critical.

I am working with an early-career advisor who is doing well with translating his purpose into execution. He has established a model week and is committed to having four appointments with prospects each week. He segments his day so that he gets specific tasks done at certain times. First thing in the morning, he prospects because it is the most important activity. In the afternoon, he does urgent but not important work. We coach advisors to structure their weeks in a way that ensures completion of the work that needs to be done.

Financial Advisory Practices Are Highly Scalable

It is possible that you actually have the infrastructure to support a much bigger practice than you have now because a unique feature of financial advisory practices is they are quite scalable.

Once you build the infrastructure of your Practice on Purpose, you can expand your business without a significant investment in further resources. For many advisors, that next growth curve is almost pure margin. They already have the fixed cost of the practice at $100,000 more than their current practice. So that next $100,000 in revenue will be almost pure profit. Once you have team members and staff in place, you can sustain 20 to 25 percent more growth without adding a lot more cost. Most practices could grow another 25 percent without incurring a significant expense.

That means it might be easier for you to reach the million-dollar mark than you had imagined. At the end of 2013, North Star Resource Group had eleven advisors with million-dollar practices, as measured by revenue. These are the advisors who manage Practices on Purpose. They are the best of the best. They have a vision for the future, and they know exactly what they need to do to realize that vision. They are also open to receiving coaching and have a high level of self-awareness.

A Job vs. a Revenue Stream

We see too many advisors leave this business because they don't understand why they are here. One advisor who left North Star recently was a technician who thought he was an entrepreneur. He came out of college, we provided him with a salary (which we call a "scholarship" at North Star), and he survived. God bless him for making it. But he's going to learn a lot about himself when he goes out there into the world.

A lot of advisors are making money, but one day they realize they're not having any fun. Their work is drudgery. And then they reach a mature age, and they want to talk not about business continuation but about successorship. They want somebody to buy their practice. They think their practice is worth fifty times more than an individual would be willing to pay for it. But they don't have a practice. They don't have a business. They have a job! They have a job that they have to come to every day, and if they don't come to that job, there's no business. No money is made that day. Who wants to buy a job? We want to buy a revenue stream. When we coach advisors to build a Practice on Purpose, we teach them to create a sustainable value proposition with recurring revenue—even when they're vacationing in Bermuda. Last January, one of our advisors vacationed in Florida for two weeks and led our entire company in results that month as a result of having systems in place and a staff who worked when he didn't. That's a business—not a job!

Focus and Work

Most overnight successes take ten years. All of the ideas in this book are worthless without one thing: work! Ideas are a dime a dozen. Those who implement them are priceless.

When Nicolai Tesla, the famous inventor, needed to complete a task, he would work uninterrupted for hours, sometimes overnight, to get it done. He was legendary because of his focus and intensity. Top advisors we know work harder and longer than everyone else. There is no shortcut. We have seen practices change in a year when an advisor regularly works on Saturday mornings or in the evenings. Some growth can happen from 8 a.m. to 5 p.m., but the big growth happens from 5 p.m. to 8 a.m.

Work and family balance is important. We often get stuck in the tyranny of the "or"—focusing on either work or family—instead of the abundance of "and." Todd Bramson, one of the perennial top North Star advisors, has a phrase: "You can have it all: Work less, earn more money, have more fun." While it can be done, it cannot be done without a foundation of work.

> Some growth can happen from 8 a.m. to 5 p.m., but the big growth happens from 5 p.m. to 8 a.m.

To transition from a job to a true Practice on Purpose takes work. Industry legend Harold Cummings had a timeless phrase: "If you want to leave your footprints on the sands of time, wear work shoes."

The Solo Practitioner's Inevitable Plateau

If you are a solo practitioner, at some point you will reach limitations—probably around the $250,000 revenue level. There is a limit to how many clients you can service and how many hours you can work each week. Pretty soon, you will reach your "ceiling of complexity," to use strategic coach Dan Sullivan's phrase.

If you don't change or grow at that point, eventually your practice becomes static. To get to the $500,000 and $750,000 range of revenue—the CEO level—requires that you reinvent the way you think about your practice and examine who does the work in the practice.

This is where organization design comes in. To design your practice deliberately—on purpose—determine what your first staff person can do, then your first junior advisor, and so on. Recognize that you cannot do it all and that you can accomplish more by building a team. Everyone on your team will have a specific role and set of responsibilities.

In *The Sky Is Not the Limit: Discovering the True North for Your Life's Calling*, Phil Richards suggests a simple but highly effective technique for ensuring that you and your team members' skills complement one another. He recommends that you list twenty-one activities that are a part of your daily life. Then rank them, with number 1 being the task you enjoy doing the most and number 21 being the one you enjoy doing the least. Then, when you are ready to hire a team member, recruit someone who loves doing the things at the bottom of your list—the things you hate doing. That way, you can backfill into your team the things you would rather not do and may not be as good at as someone else.

Building the strongest team possible is critical to your success. If you compare an athlete who runs 800 meters by himself to four athletes who each run 200 meters in a relay, the relay team will have a faster time than the solo runner. The individual cannot perform at a level that is comparable to what a team can do. That is true in our business, too. Everyone on the team runs the race together, and when we get to the end, we have better overall performance and are not as fatigued as we would be if we had run the race alone.

One advisor cannot possibly be an expert in every aspect of providing and implementing financial advice. When several people work together, each one is likely to have expertise in a different area, such as investments, risk management, or retirement planning. Plus, everyone needs to be out of the office at times, taking care of personal business, going on vacation, or taking classes. In a team setting, other advisors can serve clients when one advisor is away.

Mentoring junior advisors can pay off huge dividends in the future. Enlisting the help of junior advisors who have great potential can free up some of your time to concentrate on seeing more clients. In *The Sky Is Not the Limit*, Phil says this about mentoring:

> We don't remember the headliners of yesterday—even though they are the best in their fields. The applause dies. Awards tarnish. Achievements are forgotten. Accolades and certificates are buried with their owners. The people who make a difference in your life are not the ones with the most credentials, the most money, or the most awards. They are the coaches, teachers, and mentors who care. Mentors change lives forever, and it's usually someone other than a parent, although parents often serve this role as well.[24]

Thoughtful practice design allows your practice to continue to grow beyond the personal capabilities of the original founder—you. Most businesses die with the founder. Our goal is to lead advisors to build Practices on Purpose that allow them to manage successful businesses for as long as they want, give them significant value for what they have built, and continue serving their top clients even after they retire, if they so choose.

Know Your Critical Number

When advisors enter the insurance and financial services industry, their training is all about metrics. They're trying to make their numbers every year, quarter, month, week, and day. If they don't make their numbers, they aren't likely to survive in the career. But once they've been in the business for eight to ten years, they're not quite as focused on those numbers anymore. When

---

24. Richards, *The Sky Is Not the Limit*, 92.

we work with our mid-career advisors, we get them to focus on those metrics again. There aren't many successful businesses that don't have a clue about what their metrics are.

So we encourage advisors to begin focusing on the numbers again. Metrics are not meant to be punishment; they are meant to be helpful diagnostic tools. You can't manage what you don't measure.

We have an associate on our team. Every week, we go through his pipeline of potential candidates. He bristles. He does not like this conversation. We remind him that we are here to help. We tell him, "If the numbers indicate that we are not putting enough resources into your practice, or that maybe we could do a better job of getting new clients in the pipeline, it could have nothing to do with you except that it affects your end result." If you look at the metrics as punishment or a personal insult, they lose their ability to serve you in a positive way.

Some advisors also bristle at the word "accountability," so we use the phrase, "We're going to take a keen interest in your practice."

Metrics and accountability are a big part of North Star's culture. The more experience you get as an advisor, the more important it is for you to know that critical number that will make your practice work well. The advisors who gross a million dollars have a strong sense of metrics. It might be net flow of assets, number of appointments a week, or life cases—some quantifiable activity that will tell them if they're on track or not. If you're watching, inspecting, and measuring that one key metric, it causes you to build your practice so that it's predictable. Everything seems to fall into place if you reach that metric.

Our top advisors typically translate that critical number into what they need to do weekly in terms of activity because it creates a sense of urgency. It might be a certain number of first appointments you hold on a weekly basis. It might be a certain number of total appointments on your books over the next month, a certain number of marketing events you need to conduct, or a certain number of introductions or recommendations you need to get each week.

As the advisor, you are the one who will choose what that critical number is for your Practice on Purpose. Having a critical number and focusing on it is a career maker. Not doing so is a career breaker.

Terry Sullivan, my mentor for many years, ran the career agency system for Minnesota Life and is a close friend to Phil, Ed, and me. He used to say, "Everything you do today is preparing you for something in the future. You don't know what that is, so pay attention!"

Two CEO Models

The CEO role of a financial-planning practice can take two forms. One is the "Frank Sinatra" model, where you do nothing but conduct financial-planning meetings with clients. You have team members who handle all of your other work, including setting appointments and completing paperwork.

In the second CEO model, you manage the entire process and still see clients. You focus on a select group of top clients and manage a number of junior or even senior advisors who have smaller financial-planning practices within your larger practice. You are running a company. You are a personal producer within the company, but you are focusing only on a selected group of your best clients.

An advisor I knew at Ameriprise named John maintained relationships with fifty $1 million clients. That was his minimum—he would not work with clients unless they had at least $1 million in assets to invest. John had three junior advisors, and each one had one hundred clients. So John had a total of 350 clients in the practice. The three juniors split their compensation with John. He gave them a base salary, plus bonuses. The junior advisors got to keep any business that originated from recommendations from the clients they served. That was their incentive to grow the practice underneath the senior advisor, John.

We like that model a lot because it provides a functional mentoring model. It results in the growth of others and a better experience for clients who have the added benefit of having John's experience as another outcome.

Are Advisor Partnerships Viable?

At North Star, a few of our advisors team up to serve the same clients. They are equal partners. They split compensation and share the cost of speakers, presenters, and coaches. That is a matrix practice. In that kind of model, the advisors can pursue their own strategies for acquiring and serving clients, and they can take recommendations for themselves. It is almost a free-agency, open-architecture CEO model.

We do not see many practices like this. It can become problematic to have more than one advisor working with a client. Clients often build trust in one advisor and do not feel comfortable sharing personal information—frustration with a spouse's spending habits, for example—with more than one advisor. It can get complicated when two advisors try to take the lead role in maintaining a close personal relationship with a client.

We have seen situations in which two advisors would work with a husband and wife. The wife would align herself with one advisor, and the husband would align himself with the other advisor, and they ultimately started having "camps." They ended up somewhat opposing one another instead of working together. That is totally dysfunctional.

A much more viable model is the true CEO model, with one person leading the firm, building a culture of teamwork, sharing, and optimizing the various team members' competencies. The CEO is like the conductor of an orchestra, leading each individual on the team to contribute a unique skill set, resulting in a harmonious and productive effort. The CEO model relies on a cohesive team to serve clients together.

The Stages of an Advisor's Practice

For this discussion, we will categorize advisors into categories of practice development: those whose practices generate $250,000 in annual revenue and those at revenue of $250,000, $500,000, and $1 million and above. Each of these stages has a distinct practice design. The thinking and strategies that help you get to the first stage will not necessarily help you get to the next stage. You reinvent yourself at each stage.

As we discuss stages of an advisor practice, it is appropriate to make a comment on adding team members. A good rule of thumb is to have one full-time team member for each $250,000 of gross revenue. The advisor may take a short-term reduction in revenue to gain a higher margin later. This is difficult for some advisors to execute because they are more focused on managing costs than on leading revenue.

Why do dentists and attorneys refer to their businesses as "practices"? The Oxford English Dictionary defines "practice" as follows: "To be currently proficient in a particular activity or skill as a result of repeated exercise or performance or as a practitioner; to practice a profession or to execute a profession." Compare that definition with that of a job: "A piece of work; *esp.* a small and discrete piece of work done as part of one's regular occupation or profession." In a job, someone else tells you what to do.

Early on, the job of advisor defines your roles and responsibilities. After a few years, you start pulling alongside the job, and finally you transition to this being a career and to having a Practice on Purpose. At this last stage, you lead the practice and define its role in your life, how it aligns with your values, and how it will be an engine for bigger goals in your life.

Let's look at a visual representation of this process. When you are a new advisor, the job—the tasks and activities your supervisor defines as being required for you to complete in that job—are predominant. The job actually defines you, so it comes before you.

You will be at that stage until you reach about $250,000 in annual revenue. As you grow in the profession, you will pull up alongside that box so that you and the job now are horizontal with each other. At this stage, you will be making about $500,000, and the job is no longer driving you; you are driving it to an equal extent. You and the job are aligned beside one another.

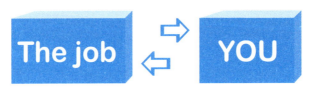

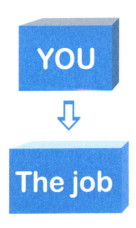

When you get to the $750,000 to $1 million stage, you actually pull ahead of the job. Now you are telling the job what to do because you have knowledge, discretion, and experience. You are able to discern, prioritize, and leverage your knowledge to define what your practice looks like and how your clients will be served.

In the early stage, you are learning the technical aspects of how to be an advisor. You are learning how insurance works, what a mutual fund is, and how the Rule of 72 works. But that is not what makes a successful million-dollar advisor. Advisors who run million-dollar practices are fully bloomed in what we call the "mental stages."

The Mental Stages of Practice Building

We have an advisor at North Star who has a $250,000 practice. It is not clear what is keeping him from being a $500,000-a-year producer because he has all of the skills he needs to perform at that level. To get him there, we are leading him to change how he thinks about his practice. Is he delegating the $9-an-hour work to someone else so that he can get in front of more clients? Is he meeting his team members every Monday and teeing up the week? Is he running his business like a Practice on Purpose, or is he just showing up to see what e-mails he has received? Is he running the practice, or is the practice running him?

We also have to decide what that practice needs to look like. What does the next team member he hires need to do? What does the team member after that need to do? Has he segmented his clients? It's likely that his current client base will not get him to the next level, so we need to change who is in his practice.

Learning how to run a business and be an entrepreneur requires an entirely different skill set than learning the technical aspects of the career. At this point, you begin working *on* the business, not *in* the business. This requires you to get outside of your own head and get out of your own way so that you can run the business. Getting outside of yourself is important because it allows you to see the big picture—the future of your practice—instead of the details.

One of the challenges of coaching advisors is there are almost as many kinds of advisors as there are people, so the advisor career or profession is as unique as the people in it. Advisors all have different personalities, and the way an advisor builds a practice reflects his or her personality. The transition from a job to a true Practice on Purpose is a mental and emotional progression as much as it is a progression in business strategy. It is important to allow the practice to evolve beyond being only a reflection of the advisor's personality.

In Chapter 6, we talk more about how critical an advisor's mindset, or mental focus, is to practice development.

Anticipating and Conquering Plateaus

We know at least two things about practices: They are scalable, and costs will increase over time. Your only option is to grow if your goal is to build wealth in your practice and have a sustainable model that will continue into the next generation. When the advisor grows, the practice grows. Investing in personal growth, people, and marketing can help you break a plateau. We have known many advisors who reached a plateau but had enough take-home revenue to be OK for a while. But eventually, their business passed them by. Later, they wished they had invested money into their practices back when they could have.

The most successful advisors have a way of anticipating and navigating plateaus. They know how to invest in their practices and navigate their way out of a plateau. They can see the plateau coming and "shed their skin," or reinvent themselves to continue growing. They take action to make growth happen before the decline begins. A Chinese proverb says, "The person who says it cannot be done should not interrupt the person doing it."

Take a look at the two graphs below. The first one is the typical growth curve, with the advisor's revenue increasing steadily through different stages of growth and then declining once the advisor quits investing in the practice:

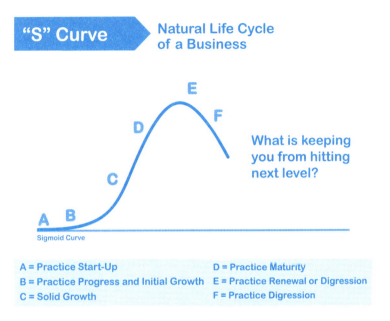

A = Practice Start-Up
B = Practice Progress and Initial Growth
C = Solid Growth
D = Practice Maturity
E = Practice Renewal or Digression
F = Practice Digression

The second graph, below, depicts what happens when an advisor invests in personal growth, people, and marketing to break out of a plateau:

A = Practice Start-Up (subsequent jump-starts)
B = Practice Progress and Initial Growth
C = Solid Growth
D = Practice Maturity
E = Practice Renewal or Digression
F = Practice Digression

The letter "E" is the maximum value the advisor's practice would have achieved if he or she had stopped investing in the practice.

Growth requires an investment. For example, it will cost money to bring on a junior associate, but having that junior associate can enable you to address the needs of more than one generation—your clients and their children.

So initially, you will reduce your personal margin to increase your margin later. You are making these changes to achieve growth that will not result unless you make that investment. If you are truly an entrepreneur and a business owner, you will invest in your practice for the long term, even if you experience a temporary decline in revenue. Clearly it is the best investment you can make!

When practices reach maturity (noted by the letter "E" on the curves shown above), advisors often begin to take success for granted. They stop being innovative and creative, and they stop demonstrating the leadership they exhibited early on, when they had no money and were highly motivated to get their start-up companies off the ground. At that point, their revenue begins going downhill. That's when a practice needs a new shot of adrenaline—an infusion of leadership, resources, and forward thinking. Once the practice receives that infusion of support, growth begins again, and the "S" curve resumes its upward ascent. It is a continuous process.

Advisors with purpose and foresight know that their practices will get to "C" and that, eventually, they will reach "E." Their practices will mature. Before maturity occurs, they begin at "A" again—they infuse new energy into the practice and begin growing again. This is a hallmark of a mature advisor who manages a Practice on Purpose. This is when the advisor's personal growth translates into the practice's growth.

Why Clients Like Team Practices

In his book *The Ensemble Practice: A Team-Based Approach*, Phil Palaveev describes the power of what he calls "ensemble practices." He defines the concept this way: "The ensemble practice is a team of financial advisory professionals that relies on the team rather than an individual to service and manage client relationships. The ensemble practice involves multiple professionals who often have specialized roles and bring different skills and knowledge. Ensembles also employ different levels of professionals, combining the enthusiasm, energy, and lower cost of less experienced advisors with the experience, wisdom, relationships, and network of highly experienced team principals—a process we will call *leverage*."[25]

---

25. Phil Palaveev, *The Ensemble Practice: A Team-Based Approach to Building a Superior Wealth Management Firm* (Hoboken, NJ: John Wiley & Sons, 2013), 5.

The 2011 Top Wealth Managers Survey conducted by Fusion Advisor Network shows that large practices such as ensemble practices have relationships that are seven to eight times larger than those of smaller firms.[26]

So, while it is not typically a good idea to have two advisors who are equal partners in a leadership role in one practice, it is a good idea to build a team composed of people who have different roles and responsibilities. Palaveev reports that clients prefer ensemble teams for two primary reasons: expertise and continuity.[27] A team of advisors can contribute a much broader realm of knowledge, expertise, and wisdom than a solo advisor can. And, if something happens to one advisor, there will be no interruption in service to clients because his or team members already understand their financial situations and goals. Following this client-centric model should be the goal of every professional advisor.

Even if you have only one assistant, you can put that person's picture on your website with yours. You can introduce him or her to your clients when they come in for a meeting. They will get to know your assistant and realize that you and that person make up a team. They will realize that if they can't reach you for some reason, they can call your assistant, and he or she will be able to help them. In their eyes, you and your team member(s) are the practice. They will recognize and appreciate that more than one person is watching out for them, taking care of their matters, and understanding their situation.

Some advisors joke, "My clients like my assistant better than they like me." Sometimes it is actually true. Even if you are managing a small practice, it is important to get your team members in front of your clients. Treating your team members well in front of the client sends a ton of desirable signals to the client.

Always think about what is going to create a superior client experience. Most likely, that involves pooling the talents of several professionals to create a Practice on Purpose that delivers a high level of value.

Envision the Future

Henry David Thoreau said, "Go confidently in the direction of your dreams. Live the life you have imagined." The key is to imagine your practice as it can look in the future.

---

26. Ibid., 12.
27. Ibid., 13.

Someone once asked Tom Watson, "What was your mindset when you started IBM?"

He replied, "I had a vision of what the company would look like in ten years, and I began behaving exactly like that."

He was able to envision the future—the bigger picture—as opposed to limiting his vision to what he had experienced so far. We have a similar story about Coley Bloomfield, who was the president of Minnesota Life. A reporter from the St. Paul newspaper asked him, "To what do you attribute your success?"

He said, "No matter what my job in the company, I always made decisions as if I were running the whole company, which clearly at the time I was not. So from whatever responsibilities I had, no matter how small they were, I would always try to have the perspective that if I was running the company, what would I do in that situation? I have done that in every job I have had, and sure enough, next thing you know, I was running the company."

That shows vision and perspective. You are totally defensible at that point. If someone asks, "Why did you do that?" you can say, "I tried to take in the scope of the whole enterprise when I made that decision the best I could." Think in terms of what your practice will become, not what it is today. The million-dollar practice for many advisors is the Holy Grail. We encourage our advisors to reach for that milestone.

Not every advisor is going to achieve a million-dollar practice or even reach the $500,000 level of revenue. They just can't handle it mentally or emotionally; they don't want the pressure. And that's OK, but they should probably be junior advisors for an advisor who is at the million-dollar level. This book is for those advisors who do have the skills and passion to take their practices to the next level.

* * * *

As you process the material in this chapter, be mindful that the goal is to create a business model that works even when you don't. By building your model with your team members, the processes you establish will proceed even in your absence because others will continue to propel the marketing systems you've established. When this goal is established, revenue streams in your practice will occur that enhance the value of your business and make it attractive to future potential buyers. If your practice produces revenue only when you are at work, then what you will have for sale will be a job, and nobody wants to buy a job!

> ### Todd's Story: How I Achieved Balance by Designing My Practice with a Purpose
>
> Todd D. Bramson, CFP®, ChFC®, CLU®, CFS®—Senior Partner, North Star Resource Group
>
> After attending a fine MDRT meeting in Boston and reading noted economist Paul Pilzner's book *Unlimited Wealth*, I was transformed. Up until then, I only understood the concept of working hard and the income and success would follow.
>
> I had a young family—two kids—and wanted to work less, not more. So one year, when writing out my goals, I wrote, "How I retired at age thirty-three, without retiring." The premise was that every year from that point forward, I had to accomplish three things each year: grow the business, work less, *and* have more fun. Those sound mutually exclusive, but they aren't if you apply the techniques as shared in this chapter and book.
>
> Basically, delegate lower-dollar-per-hour work, embrace training and mentoring, leverage your time with technology, and You Really Can Have It All. In fact, that was the topic of a speech I gave at a breakout session at MDRT in Anaheim. It was a thrill to give back to this great industry as those before me have done with me.
>
> I encourage all readers of this chapter/book to read, reread, and apply these concepts. If you take some time to map out a plan, you will be rewarded richly, beyond your dreams. I encourage you to start with the question, "What is the Fairy Tale?" Dream of your perfect life, and then use the ideas that Gary, Phil, and Ed present to go out and achieve that Fairy Tale.

Applying the Concepts to *Your* Practice on Purpose

1. Are you a solo practitioner? If so, how badly do you want to become the CEO of a thriving team-based Practice on Purpose? What steps will you take to make that transition?

_____
_____
_____
_____
_____

2. If you are a solo practitioner, whom could you hire to help take your practice to the next level? What would his or her title, role, and responsibilities be?

3. What level of revenue would you like your practice to reach? What steps do you need to take to reach that level, and when do you intend to reach it?

4. To what extent do you make every decision with the future in mind?

The Inner Game of Financial Advising

CHAPTER 6

> "The mind is everything. What you think, you become."
>
> **—Buddha**

The ultimate goal for the advisor who manages a Practice on Purpose is to achieve practice growth. When the advisor grows, the practice grows. Growth is the path that allows the advisor to help more people achieve financial dignity, build personal wealth, and eventually leave a legacy through a practice that outlasts him or her. Through coaching, we can lead advisors to achieve reasonable growth—typically 10 to 20 percent growth per year.

Achieving growth is 80 percent mental and 20 percent tactical. It is important to focus on both—your feet are in clay, and you are gazing up at the stars.

In his books, author Tim Gallwey discusses the vital role an optimum mental state plays in peak performance among athletes. He wrote *The Inner Game of Tennis* and *The Inner Game of Golf*. In the first book, he explains how the most accomplished tennis players do not think about the mechanics of each stroke of the tennis racquet. Their peak performance never happens when they are thinking about it. Instead, they play "unconsciously." About the accomplished athlete, Gallwey says, "He is conscious, but not thinking, *not overtrying*. A player in this state knows where he wants the ball to go, but he doesn't have to 'try hard' to send it there…. The player seems to be immersed in a flow of action that requires his energy, yet results in greater power and accuracy."[28] Gallwey says this is the ideal mental state—to have your mind so concentrated and focused that it is *still*. "When a player is in this state, there is little to interfere with the full expression of his potential to perform, learn, and enjoy."[29]

---

28. W. Timothy Gallwey, *The Inner Game of Tennis: The Classic Guide to the Mental Side of Peak Performance* (New York: Random House Trade Paperbacks), 7.

29. Ibid., 8.

Being a successful advisor with a thriving practice requires a similar mindset. The mechanical, tactical part of being an advisor is not that hard. The inner game is where 80 percent of the success comes from—mental preparation and awareness.

Goal Setting: A Mental and Tactical Process

In previous chapters, we discussed the importance of your overarching purpose, both as a person and as an advisor. That purpose likely revolves around helping people build financial dignity. Defining your purpose is a mental process. We also discussed the importance of deciding how to differentiate the services you are going to provide and of segmenting your clients. Those are tactical processes. Defining your goals is a hybrid step—a mental process that requires tactical steps to execute.

At North Star, when we work with advisors to take their practices to the next level, we use an assessment form that allows us to determine the current status of an advisor's practice. It is thirty pages long. We have never met an advisor who has completed it entirely. It is a diagnostic tool—a workbook, really—that reveals key details about an advisor's practice such as marketing efforts, staff, strategies for meeting new clients, and methods of serving clients. (If you have questions about this document, please contact the authors.)

We also have a "scope of engagement agreement" that contains six steps to working with advisors. What comes out of these assessment exercises is a list of specific goals for the advisor.

I met with an advisor recently who is doing well. We discussed the two most important things he learned in the year that had just ended. I asked him how he would integrate those lessons into the new year. I asked him, "When we meet in December, what do you want your practice to look like?" We decided to make those two areas—the biggest lessons he learned in the previous year—the goals he would work on to move his practice ahead. I mentioned that we can do anything; we just cannot do everything.

From there, we worked on some metrics and defined key outcomes he wanted to achieve. This process required the advisor to go through the mental exercise of deciding where he wanted to take his practice, and it required him to identify the tactical steps that would help him achieve the goal.

Pygmalion: The Power of Goal Setting

Pygmalion is the name of a talented sculptor in ancient Greek mythology. He created a statue of a woman from a piece of ivory. Upon finishing it, Pygmalion thought it was so beautiful that he clothed the figure, adorned it with jewels, and named it Galatea ("sleeping love"). Pygmalion went to the temple of Aphrodite (Venus), the goddess of love and beauty, to pray for a wife just like the statue. When Aphrodite heard him, she went to his home and was delighted when she saw Galatea. She thought the statue looked like herself, so she brought it to life. When Pygmalion returned home, he found Galatea alive. They married, and to thank Aphrodite for their good fortune, they took gifts to her altar as long as they lived. Aphrodite blessed them with happiness and love in return.

George Bernard Shaw created a play called *Pygmalion* that was first performed on stage in 1912. Decades later, it was made into the musical *My Fair Lady*, which was first performed on Broadway in 1956. In the play and musical, a professor/phoneticist works with a Cockney girl to refine her speech and manner so that she can pass as a well-born woman.

The idea is that when you believe in something so passionately and so clearly that it becomes your total devotion, you can make it become real. That is the power of goal setting; it creates a self-fulfilling prophecy.

When people refer to "the Pygmalion effect," they are referring to studies that researchers conducted with children. In the well-known Rosenthal–Jacobson study from 1968, researchers told elementary-school teachers that certain students had tested higher than their peers on an IQ test, even though they had not. However, those students ended up performing better academically throughout the year than the other students did, indicating that teacher expectations can influence student achievement.

Many years ago, I was a breakout speaker at a GAMA LAMP meeting. I was presenting on a successful coaching program that Terry Sullivan, Leslie Millikan, and I developed at Securian Financial Group called Breakthrough. At the end of the presentation, a participant approached me and asked, "How did you know if the increase in practice growth was attributable to the tactical prescriptions the advisor implemented or if it was because you demonstrated that you cared about them?"

My answer was, "Aren't they the same thing?" It's all because we believe in their ability to execute the actions necessary for practice growth, and we believe in them as people.

This concept of the self-fulfilling prophecy has intrigued me for many years. In 1995, when I was the Director of Field Development for Minnesota Mutual, I wrote a letter on this topic to our field leaders in the company. That letter appears in the appendix.

You Are What You Think About

When an advisor decides he wants to grow his practice by 20 percent, that specific goal creates positive energy that propels him to achieve the goal.

Maybe I am being a little mystical, but I think once you profess a goal, your mind works on that goal in ways we do not completely understand. Whatever you are looking for is looking for you. Your brain is sorting your behavior and filtering your environment to fit that goal. Once your intentions are clear, you will start noticing that things begin going in that direction.

Be careful what you wish for with all your mind and heart.

Back in 1956, Earl Nightingale (1921–1989) recorded a talk titled "The Strangest Secret." Its focus was along these lines—that you are what you think about. If you think financial advice will be successful in your practice, the odds of that happening are astronomically higher than if you think your clients will fight the financial-advice concept all the way. Again, it is a self-fulfilling prophecy.

When he was thirty-five, Nightingale launched an insurance agency. He conducted meetings for his salespeople on Saturdays. At one point, he decided to go on an extended vacation, and his sales manager encouraged him to record some thoughts for the sales force so they could hear them while Nightingale was out of the office. He prepared this twenty-five-minute talk for them and recorded it. It was one of those life accidents where if he had just said the same information during a meeting one day and walked out of the room, it would have been lost to time. But because he recorded the information on tape, it became permanent. It contains such a powerful message that thousands, then hundreds of thousands of people requested a copy. "The Strangest Secret" was the first nonmusic record to reach Gold Record status.[30]

I have a CD deck in my car that contains eight CDs, and number 8 is Earl Nightingale's "The Strangest Secret." Once in a great while, during one of the long commutes Ed and I both cherish, I will put on number 8 and listen to Earl Nightingale. It is always just what I need that day.

In 1960, Nightingale cofounded a highly successful motivational and professional development company, the Nightingale–Conant organization.

One of the examples he gives in the speech that resonates with me is that the human mind is like a field. It is like the soil itself. It knows no biases, and just like a field, the human mind will give back whatever is planted in it. If you plant corn in a field, the field will produce corn. If you plant nightshade, a poisonous plant, it will produce nightshade. The human mind is exactly the same. Whatever you plant into it, it will produce and yield. You become what you think about. Be careful, guarded, and deliberate in what you think about and the information you put into your mind because that is what it will return to you.

---

30. To hear a recording and read a transcript of the talk, visit http://www.18mind.com/mind/the_strangest_secret. To read more about Nightingale and the history of "The Strangest Secret," visit http://www.blacksgonegeek.org/Documents/The_Strangest_Secret.pdf.

At Ameriprise, when someone shared an important concept like that, we called it "thought leadership." You can provide thought leadership to yourself through self-talk. This is an important concept because once you decide on your purpose, then you can think about it and focus on it on a daily basis. In doing so, you are connecting your thoughts with your purpose on a daily basis. Then, as you interact with clients or with other advisors, your purpose will be clear to them. I have always liked the saying, "Your behavior may be the only Bible some people will know." Realizing that may encourage you to behave in a way that exemplifies integrity and leadership.

Growing through the People around You and the Books You Read

Tim Schmidt, CLF®, LUTCF®, FIC®, a Managing Partner with Thrivent Financial for Lutherans, spoke at one of our winter meetings recently. He cowrote an excellent book called *What Really Works*.[31] It is a great growth resource. He and his co-author, Paul Batz, use thousands of surveys and more than fifty personal interviews to explore how seven critical elements—faith, family, finances, fitness, friends, fun, and future—can help people achieve harmony and success in life. Tim says, "You grow by whom you choose to interact with and by the books you read."

I agree that both are vital. When I was graduating from the University of Minnesota with my undergraduate business degree, I felt I had missed a broad education—I had too much business and not enough liberal arts. I mentioned this to my academic advisor, and he connected me with a professor in the English Literature department. After several meetings with her, I walked away with a handwritten list of the fifty best books I needed to read in the next five years. The list included *Ulysses* by James Joyce, *A Passage to India* by E. M. Forster, *The Age of Innocence* by Edith Wharton, and *Faust* by Johann Wolfgang von Goethe. It took me five years, but I finished. I later bought the whole collection, and I still have the hard-copy edition of *The Oxford Companion to American Literature* and *The Oxford Companion to European Literature* among my books. Reading such a wide range of literature broadened my knowledge in a way that nothing else could.

At the back of this book is a list of books the authors recommend on practice management and other related topics. Reading the wisdom others have published can help you achieve exponential personal growth for a minuscule investment of time and money.

---

31. Paul Batz and Tim Schmidt, *What Really Works: Blending the Seven Fs for the Life You Imagine* (Edina, MN: Beaver's Pond Press), 2011.

Your Practice's Ultimate Value

When we work with advisors, we ask, "What does your practice need to be worth before work is an option for you and you can retire?" If the advisor replies, "I need my practice to be worth three million dollars, and it's worth maybe five hundred thousand today," that conversation is a lot of fun for us. We can help him get there. At that point, we ask the advisor, "How do you meet clients? Do you segment your clients? How do you get new clients? Are you entering into ongoing financial-advice relationships? Are you personally developing as a human being yourself?" That's when we begin leading the advisor to build a Practice on Purpose.

> Most advisors do poor financial planning for themselves, even when they do a great job for their clients.

To accomplish that ultimate goal—to have the practice be worth a certain amount when the advisor retires—requires a thorough financial plan. Most advisors do poor financial planning for themselves, even when they do a great job for their clients.

According to a 2013 *InvestmentNews* article, about 68 percent of advisors have no formal succession plan for their business. Of those who do have a plan, about 39 percent say they do not know to whom they will transition their business. In the article, John Anderson, head of practice management at SEI Advisor Network, says, "Unless [advisors] make a dedicated effort to making sure they have the right clients and the right infrastructure, they are not going to have anything to sell." To help ensure that their businesses have future worth, Anderson recommends that advisors harmonize processes and procedures, examine their client base, and employ a plan to attract younger clients. One way advisors can do that, he says, is have "the next generation of leaders" in their practices who can bring in younger clients. Because only 3 percent of advisors are under the age of thirty, that can be a challenge. Anderson suggests that, to attract the next generation, advisors embrace technology, offer training programs, and use a team environment when teaching young advisors.[32]

We encourage our advisors to team up with another financial advisor to create financial plans for one another. Often they are reluctant to do this because they don't want to share their personal financials with their peers. But it is a necessary exercise. Once they have a specific number in their head—the amount they need the practice to be worth before they can retire comfortably—the goals associated with that outcome become easier to reach. If we

---

32. Liz Skinner, "Advisors Neglect Own Retirement Planning," *InvestmentNews*, March 13, 2013.

structure the plan for growth in alignment with who the advisor is and what his purpose is, it typically works out well.

Too often, people—some advisors included—go from one year to the next, just plodding along. They get to their forties or fifties, and one day they look up and say, "How did I get here?" That's what happens when you do not have a sense of what you are trying to achieve—a specific goal.

Sometimes we come across an advisor who says, "You know, I'm OK with a hundred fifty thousand of net income. I don't know if I want new clients. They're a lot of work." When we hear that, we think, *OK. I'll wave at you down the hallway. Hope you have a good day.* That advisor will likely never progress past that point.

It might seem logical for an advisor to start out as a rookie in the insurance and financial planning career, then progress steadily toward the $1 million mark, hitting all of the other major revenue milestones along the way. But what often happens is that advisors back into a goal, and this is often a successful strategy. Once we know the number the advisor is aiming for, we work backward toward that goal by defining how much revenue the advisor will have to do each year, then each month and each day. Start with the end in mind.

We encourage our advisors is to lead their clients to feel like the advisors are running million-dollar practices before they actually are. This requires advisors to recognize the value they provide, as we discussed earlier, and to lead clients to derive optimum benefit from the practice. That, too, is a mental process. Remember, practice growth is 80 percent mental and 20 percent tactical. It's a door only you can go through.

Goals: The Bridge from Vision to Execution

Your purpose is the genesis of your practice's success. Once you define your purpose, then you create a vision for what you want from your practice. Your purpose and vision are big concepts. They need to be defined into goals, which are more tactical and specific. They are more short-term and immediate. Having goals allows you to put your purpose in gear and move you ahead to get the outcome you want. Goals make it possible for you to determine what you have to do in a specific time frame to achieve the level of success you want to achieve.

Tony Gordon is the author of *It Can Only Get Better: Tony Gordon's Route to Sales Success*, which has sold more than 100,000 copies. In the book, he sums up the critical relationship between purpose and execution in this observation about top achievers: "They seem to have a sense of purpose. Success is never an accident. It comes to those who can define it, break it down into its daily tasks, and then discipline themselves to do the job. They know success will come—they don't know when, but it is never in doubt."[33]

Sometimes we have to do things we don't want to do, but doing those things separates successful people from failures. In 1940, Albert Gray, vice president for the Prudential Life Insurance Company, gave a speech at the National Association of Life Underwriters convention. He said, "The common denominator of success—the secret of success of every man who has ever been successful—lies in the fact that he formed the habit of doing things that failures don't like to do."[34] Successful people don't like doing those unpleasant tasks any more than other people do, but they are focused on pleasurable results, not the methods. Those advisors who don't hit their goals are typically more focused on pleasurable methods, not pleasurable results. The successful person realizes that setting goals is one of those necessary tasks that is necessary but may not be pleasant. Again, it is a process that requires mental discipline.

> The successful person realizes that setting goals is one of those necessary tasks that is necessary but may not be pleasant.

North Star has a goal-setting template we use with each of our internally coached advisors. Most advisors are reluctant to complete this exercise on their own. It takes leadership from someone they trust and someone they know has an authentic interest in their growth. We want what they want. We as leaders just need to know what will light them up and make the year exciting for them. Once these goals are on paper and we can break them down into monthly and weekly mileposts, we can make progress.

We know that people who state their goals tend to reach them. People who don't set goals often don't go anywhere. And people who lose sight of the fundamentals often go out of business. That is the lesson in this story from *Be the First Believer* by Ed Deutschlander and Rich Campe:

> Here is a story that captures the reason people don't achieve their goals and objectives.
>
> A gentleman owns a fish market on the waterfront. It is a simple fish market that is reflected by the sign that hangs over the market. The sign reads, "Fresh Fish for Sale." Over time, some of the patrons approach the owner of the market.

---

33. Tony Gordon, *It Can Only Get Better: Tony Gordon's Route to Sales Success* (Bristol, UK: Redcliffe Associates, 2000), 152–153.

34. Tim Enochs, "Wisdom from 1940," Irrefutable Success blog, last modified October 22, 2012, http://www.irrefutablesuccess.com/2010/10/timeless-wisdom-from-1940/; Albert E. N. Gray, "The Common Denominator of Success, http://www.amnesta.net/mba/thecommondenominatorofsuccess-albertengray.pdf.

"You know," the patrons say to him, "we can tell that your market sells fresh fish. You're right on the waterfront, and you go out every morning for the daily catch. You really don't need to have the word 'fresh' on your sign."

The market owner considers this and decides his patrons are right. So he removes the word "fresh" from the sign. Now, the sign reads just "Fish for Sale." Time passes, and the same group of patrons approaches the owner again.

"We know that your business is for profit," they explain. "We know you sell fish for a profit. Do you really think you need the words 'for sale' on your sign?"

Again, the owner considers their insight and decides to remove the words "for sale" from his sign. Now the sign says just "Fish." More time passes, and the same group of patrons approaches the owner once again.

"Listen," they say, "it's obvious that you sell fish. We smell the aroma as we walk down the pier every day, and we can see the fish as we approach your market, so we really don't think you need to advertise that you have fish."

The owner ponders this, and he decides to remove the word "Fish." Therefore, he removes his sign altogether.

A year later, the market goes out of business.

The moral of the story is that people don't hit their goals because of the slow erosion of the fundamentals. This erosion does not happen overnight. It happens slowly over time. All of a sudden, a business owner realizes he is ignoring the foundation of his business. He has neglected the most important aspects of his business, and over time, they have become rusty. So the point is that we all have to pay attention to the little things.[35]

Only the Advisor Can Fuel Growth

Although our advisor development team serves as a catalyst to lead advisors to optimum results, practice growth is fueled by the advisor alone. Again, it's a door only the advisor can go through. There are some doors that only an individual can go through. It is a personal journey and, at times, a solitary one. It's that deep introspection to decide who you really are. The father of Taoism, Lao Tzu, who lived in the sixth century BC, said, "When I let go of what I am, I become what I might be."

---

35. Deutschlander and Campe, *Be the First Believer*, 93–94.

Here is an often perplexing question: Why do 20 percent of our advisors make the million-dollar gross-revenue level, yet so many others get to the $500,000 mark and cannot progress any further, even though they all have the same type of products, training, technology, office environment, and leadership? It's because those who make it to the top decide to go through a different door. They do the things failures don't want to do because they have a sense of purpose and specific goals. Plus, they are open to advice and coaching. Those advisors are at the top of the firm.

> With the right support, the group of advisors in the middle of a firm can make it to the million-dollar level, even though they may not get there on their own.

With the right support, the group of advisors in the middle of a firm can make it to the million-dollar level, even though they may not get there on their own. To show you an example of how we support advisors in reaching the next level through goal setting, I have included in the appendix several e-mails I have sent to advisors I have been coaching. In the e-mails, I recapped what we discussed during our meetings to discuss the growth of the advisors' practices. Also included is an e-mail an advisor sent to me following one of our coaching sessions.

As for the advisors at the bottom of the firm, unfortunately we just cannot propel them forward. We are not miracle workers, and again, the advisor drives growth—we don't. Other than quitting the business, the only option for those advisors is to team up with someone who is ahead of them and will always be ahead of them. And life goes on.

Three Types of Goals

To make goal setting really effective, try setting three levels of goals: Your BHAG, your primary goal, and your objective.

1. At the highest level is your BHAG—your "big, hairy, audacious goal." Jim Collins and Jerry Porras introduced this term in their 1994 book *Built to Last: Successful Habits of Visionary Companies*. This is a highly ambitious goal, and it will be a stretch for you to reach it. But it is possible if the stars align and you do everything in your power to make it happen. This is typically a longer-term goal, such as reaching the $500,000 mark with your practice. The danger with this type of goal is that if it's too much of a stretch, you might lose interest. If you set your goals too high, you may not make progress. If your practice is at $250,000 today, the $1 million mark might be too lofty a goal at this point.

2. Next, you have your primary goal. That might be to move from $300,000 to $400,000. It is a realistic goal.
3. At the third level, you set up the "failsafe." This is your *objective*, which might be to reach the $325,000 mark. This is a level of performance that should automatically happen, no matter what, if you stay on your current track. If you don't achieve your objective, you really have to question a lot of things you're doing.

A college student's BHAG might be to achieve a 4.0 grade point average. Her goal might be a 3.5, and her objective might be a 3.0. If she doesn't achieve a 3.0 GPA, she really needs to question her commitment to being in college at this point in her life.

Setting these three levels of goals will give you a comfort level and also keep you motivated. If you shoot for the BHAG, you are likely to reach your primary goal. This strategy has led a lot of our advisors to achieve great results.

Setting goals is effective in any endeavor, at any age. Recently my seventeen-year-old daughter, Maddie, worked as a nanny in Spain with her prior au pair's children. When she returned, she took my wife, Laura, and me out to lunch. During the meal, Maddie announced three changes she wanted to make in her life. One was to serve in a school leadership role—she wanted to run for student council. Several days later, a box with Chinese lettering printed on it showed up on our doorstep. In the box were five hundred fortune cookies that contained the message "Maddie Schwartz for Student Council." She handed them out to her high school classmates as part of her successful campaign. This showed a clear sense of purpose, a will to win, and execution. It has since opened many doors for her.

The Goal Trilogy: What, Why, and How

Many advisors focus only on *what* the goal is. That is a great start. It's more than many advisors have, and it is tangible and measurable. But that is only one part of the equation. There are three components to goal setting: What is your goal, why is it your goal, and how will you reach it?

Where advisors often get off course is in failing to identify *why* they have specified a certain goal. When we focus only on the what, we don't have clarity. We don't take the time to connect the head (what the goal is) with the heart (why that is the goal).

For example, an advisor might say her goal is to have a practice that produces $1 million in revenue and to take $600,000 income from the practice. Why $600,000? What is special about that number? Obviously, the advisor is not envisioning sitting at a big table with stacks of money that total $600,000. It is not the accumulation of the money or the earning of the money that drives her; it is what that money is going to do for her. That is the why. Maybe that $600,000 is going to allow her to pay for her daughter's wedding in two years. Maybe it will enable her to send her son to the college he wants to attend. Maybe it will give her and her husband the opportunity to donate to a particular cause that has been meaningful in their lives.

When we set goals, we are all going to encounter obstacles and roadblocks along the way. Knowing the why behind your goal will enable you to persevere when you are trying to move the dial on your practice from $300,000 in revenue to $400,000.

Once you know the what and the why, then you can focus on the how—the tactical steps you will take to reach your goal. Maybe you need to host three different client-appreciation events. Maybe you need to invest in a part-time marketing coordinator to free up ten hours a week of your time so you can get in front of your top clients more often and generate more recommendations. Or maybe you need to memorize that recommendation presentation you have neglected to implement for the past six months.

The what, the why, and the how all must be aligned. This is a huge part of North Star's culture and a key element in the success of those advisors whose practices achieve consistent growth. It is also a key component of the inner game—the mental process—of financial advising.

Jane's Story: Goals Turn Vision into Reality

Jane M. LaLonde, CFP®, Partner, North Star Resource Group

I have been in this wonderful business for more than thirty years and recognize the increasing importance of setting goals for my practice every year. These goals are important for me as well as my team. As the authors stated, "You become what you think." Going from deciding your purpose to setting goals and then thinking or focusing on these goals daily will make the type of practice you want to own become a reality. In addition, it will be rewarding because you and your team saw the vision and then turned the vision into a reality.

When I transition to an ongoing advice relationship with clients, I tell them I want to have an even more active role in their financial plan and that we have many more tools that make it easier for us to be financially organized. I tell them that, in addition to managing what I already do, I want to integrate their entire situation into the financial plan. And this takes time. I have only so much time (just like everyone else!). If I am not going to be paid appropriately, then I'd rather do something else with my limited time. If I

(continued)

> ### Jane's Story: Goals Turn Vision into Reality (continued)
>
> need to choose between (1) going to my son's baseball game or my daughter's lacrosse game or (2) working for free, it usually is an easy choice. Of course I don't get paid for everything I do, but I decided early on that I need to limit the amount of work I do for free. Plus, I have an outstanding team, and they get paid regardless of what I charge. The worst-case scenario: I work for free, then lose money because I always need to pay my staff.
>
> In an ongoing advice relationship, I feel committed, and I believe the clients do as well. In addition, I have the luxury of doing more complete work and a better job because I am being compensated to help them with their entire situation. I also feel that my advice is not based on a need to sell something to earn my keep. Of course I want to sell something if it is appropriate for a client, but there are times when people need help, not a product. I want to retain my clients for a long time on this path, do my best, give clients peace of mind that we are doing the best work...and then go to either the baseball or lacrosse game!

Applying the Concepts to *Your* Practice on Purpose

1. Practice growth is 80 percent mental and 20 percent tactical, and you are what you think about. What do you think about? To what extent are your thoughts and your self-talk positive? If they are not as positive as they could be, what positive message will you begin focusing on?

   _____
   _____
   _____
   _____
   _____
   _____

2. The most successful advisors always have three levels of goals identified: a BHAG (big, hairy, audacious goal) that is somewhat of a stretch, a primary goal that is realistic, and an objective that will definitely come to fruition if they stay on their current path. What is your BHAG for your practice for the coming year? What is your primary goal? What is your objective?

   My BHAG is to:

   _____

   _____

   My primary goal is to:

   _____

   _____

   My objective is to:

   _____

   _____

3. Now that you have defined what your primary goal is (in question number 2), why is that your goal?

   _____

   _____

   _____

   _____

   _____

4. What specific tactical steps will you take to reach that goal?

   _____

   _____

   _____

   _____

   _____

The Big Five: Five Traits Common Among the Most Successful Advisors

CHAPTER

7

"Strive not to be a success but rather to be of value."

—**Albert Einstein**

One of the recurring themes in this book is that when the advisor grows, the practice grows. As you strive to build a million-dollar Practice on Purpose, the self-awareness we discussed earlier is paramount to helping you achieve that goal. Self-awareness is an incredible journey. Knowing who you are, what your values are, and how others perceive you can be extremely liberating. The more you know about yourself—your strengths and weaknesses, what motivates you, what you believe in—the more control and command you will have over your future. Knowing what you do well and what you could improve on can help you build the infrastructure of your practice. It will give you illuminating clarity about the gifts and talents you have to offer and the areas you need to work on. It will help you surround yourself with people who are gifted in the specific areas you need help with so you can leverage their strengths and catapult your practice to the next level.

In this chapter, we review assessment instruments that have been proven effective at assessing personality characteristics. Then we present the five characteristics we believe differentiate superior advisors from average advisors and offer our recommendations for using that insight to propel your practice forward.

As you work to emulate the characteristics that are common among the most successful advisors, do so in a way that honors and reinforces the values that define you as a person and as an advisor.

Personality Assessments Have Been Used for Centuries

Many psychiatrists, psychologists, behavioral experts, philosophers, and researchers have conducted extensive research for centuries in an effort to categorize personality traits and to determine the characteristics that are common among the most successful people. There is a great deal of intricate science behind this research. Here are some highlights from the extensive history of personality assessment:

1. As early as 2200 BC, the Chinese used oral examinations to hire and retain civil servants.

2. In ancient Greece, the physician Hippocrates (460–377 BC) described the four temperaments of people as "humors," or moods. They were based on the four elements of fire, air, water, and earth, and each was believed to be responsible for a different type of behavior. Hippocrates recorded the first known personality model, theorizing that a person's personality is based on these four moods.

3. Around 340 BC, Plato described the four temperaments as Philosopher, Guardian, Artisan, and Scientist.

4. From 200 to about 800 AD, various people dabbled with the idea that bodily fluids determined personality—for example, an excess of blood made a person sanguine, and an excess of phlegm made one phlegmatic, or slow and stolid.

5. The concept of psychological testing as we know it today really got its start in 1869, when Sir Francis Galton of England reported measurable differences among individuals' minds. He was evidently the first person to apply statistical methods to the study of human differences and to the inheritance of intelligence. He introduced the use of questionnaires and surveys for collecting data on human communities.

6. In 1917, the American Psychological Association asked American psychologist Robert Woodworth to devise a test to assess emotional stability. He came up with the Woodworth Personal Data Sheet, which was the first modern personality test. First used in 1919, it was designed to help the US Army screen out recruits who might be susceptible to shell shock.

7. One of the most popular assessment tools, the Myers–Briggs Type Indicator, was introduced in 1923 after forty years of development. Isabel Briggs Myers and her mother, Katharine Cook Briggs, developed the tool based on ideas of Carl Jung's four psychological

types: Sensing, Intuitive, Feeling, and Thinking. The questionnaire is intended to identify the personality type that will help a person succeed most in life.[36]

The "Big Five" Personality Traits

Based on all of that history and science, researchers have, to some extent, agreed that five dimensions (not types) of human personality can be categorized as follows:

- Extraversion (your level of sociability and enthusiasm)
- Agreeableness (your level of friendliness and kindness)
- Conscientiousness (your level of organization and work ethic)
- Emotional stability (your level of calmness and tranquility)
- Intellect (your level of creativity and curiosity)

Acronyms commonly used to refer to the five traits collectively are OCEAN, NEOAC, and CANOE. Related to each of the five factors is a cluster of correlated specific traits. For example, extraversion includes related qualities such as gregariousness, assertiveness, a tendency to seek excitement, warmth, activity, and positive emotions.

Now let's talk about some modern assessments we have actually seen being used with positive results.

The Craft Personality Questionnaire (CPQ)

Dr. Larry Craft is a behavioral scientist who had extensive experience as a manager in the financial services industry prior to becoming a leader in the employment assessment industry. Dr. Craft's research on drive and motivation is widely quoted.[37]

He developed the Craft Personality Questionnaire (CPQ®), a seventy-five-item assessment of eight job-related personality traits that have been proven to predict job performance and employee retention. Thousands of managers use this tool in employee selection and development. Dr. Craft refined the CPQ through thirty years of exhaustive applied research.

---

36. Ellen Borowka, "Cracking the Personality Code" blog, last modified August 6, 2008, http://crackingthepersonalitycode.com/blog/2008/08/condensed-history-of-personality-tests.html. This blog posting presents a detailed history of the development of personality assessments.

37. You can read more about Dr. Larry Craft on his website, http://www.craftmetrics.com/.

The CPQ assesses eight work-related personality traits, which he refers to as the "Basic Eight" traits. There are four "ego-drive traits" (goal orientation, need for control, social confidence, and social drive) and four "empathy traits" (detail orientation, good impression, need to nurture, and skepticism).[38]

The Craft*Metrics* Personality Inventory (CMPI)

Dr. Craft's newest assessment tool is the Craft*Metrics* Personality Inventory (CMPI). This unique assessment measures the primary and secondary personality traits that have been found to predict performance in numerous industries and job descriptions. It asks a candidate to select the statements that best describe an introductory paragraph. Candidates are told how important it is to avoid the temptation to "sell themselves" to leave an unrealistically favorable impression. Then candidates take a brief vocabulary test that can be customized to any industry's terminology. This part of the assessment determines how familiar a candidate is with an industry. Applicants are then asked to describe the "ideal or perfect candidate" before describing themselves. Throughout the twenty-minute questionnaire, interactive technologies analyze each response to determine its accuracy and then intervene with a warning if indicators are "triggered."

The California Psychological Inventory (CPI™)

The California Psychological Inventory (CPI™) model helps individuals discover their orientations toward people and interpersonal experiences, rules, values, and inner feelings. Results of this assessment indicate which of four different ways of living, or lifestyles (Implementer, Supporter, Innovator, Visualizer) best describes them and provide insights about how they see themselves and how others see them. The CPI instruments help people gain a clearer picture of their personal and work-related characteristics, motivations, and thinking styles—as well as how they manage themselves and deal with others. These tools also provide a view into candidates' strengths and developmental opportunities.[39]

OPQ or OPQ32 Assessments

The Occupational Personality Questionnaires, commonly referred to as "OPQ" or "OPQ32," are widely used occupational personality questionnaires

---

38. "Craft Personality Questionnaire Development," Pearson Education, Inc., 2008, http://us.talentlens.com/wp-content/uploads/pdf/CPQ_Development_of_the_CPQ.pdf.

39. The CPI assessment was created by Harrison Gough and currently published by Consulting Psychologists Press (CPP). The CPI is made up of 434 true–false questions and is scored on eighteen scales. It takes about forty-five to sixty minutes to complete. You can read more about this tool at https://www.cpp.com/products/cpi/index.aspx.

launched by Saville and Holdsworth Ltd. in 1984. This tool indicates an individual's preferred behavioral style at work. It helps employers gauge how candidates will fit into certain work environments, work with other people, and cope with various job requirements. It can be completed in about thirty minutes.[40]

The OPQ instrument recognizes the following traits:

- **Controlling:** Likes to be in charge, takes the lead
- **Caring:** Sympathetic and considerate toward others
- **Evaluative:** Employs critical thinking
- **Innovative:** Generates new ideas, thinks of original solutions
- **Nontrusting:** Is not fooled easily

Our List of Five Differentiating Traits

In 2011 and 2012, North Star participated in a study with Dr. Craft. We administered the CMPI to sixty-eight actively practicing financial advisors. Because we had information about these advisors' production histories, we were able to demonstrate statistically significant traits that were correlated with production. Two traits that stood out were intensity (drive/dominance) and independence. We have built our list of common traits that tend to characterize top-performing advisors on that study, other research, and our collective experience working closely with advisors (more than 110 years for the three authors combined).

We believe the following five traits differentiate superior advisors from average advisors:

- **Dominance:** Intensity, drive, "the mind of a capitalist," the relentless pursuit of a goal, a will to win, a sense of urgency and purpose, compulsion (a refusal) not to lose
- **Independence:** The ability to be a self-advocate, self-assuredness, and poise
- **Responsibility:** Conscientiousness, reliability, the ability to own your work ("If it's going to be, it's up to me") and to learn from your environment and experience (an "I own it" attitude)
- **Well-being:** A positive, optimistic outlook; an authentic concern for others; and "the heart of a social worker"
- **Ruggedness:** Tough-mindedness, persistence, perseverance, the ability to overcome obstacles, a "marathon" energy, the ability to shrug off discouragement

---

40. More information about the OPQ is available at http://www.shl.com/assets/resources/opq-uk.pdf.

Other traits are certainly important, but we think these stand out as the most critical. We use them to assess an advisor's current readiness to move his or her practice to the next level and to focus on specific areas for advisor growth. If you have all five of these traits, chances are, you are a leader among your peers—or at least you have the potential to be. If you determine, using the self-assessments provided here, that you are not as strong in one of these traits as you would like to be, it would benefit you to work on developing that trait. Remember, when the advisor grows, the practice grows.

Let's examine each one of these traits more closely and look at some examples of advisors who exhibit them.

Dominance

Ed describes our top-performing advisors as "goal-driven machines." There is an intensity about them—in the way they act, move, and even speak—and they seem to be propelled forward by a driving force to get things done. That driving force is usually a specific goal. In their relentless pursuit of that goal, they have the attitude, "Get out of my way; I'm going to reach that goal. If it is not today, it will be tomorrow or the day after, but I am going to hit it." We see the dominance characteristic in advisors and other people who really know how to manage an enterprise effectively.

A great example of this characteristic is the story of Sonia Sotomayor. Since 2009, she has served as an Associate Justice of the Supreme Court of the United States. She is the Supreme Court's first Hispanic Justice. In her autobiography, *My Beloved World*, she writes that she was born to struggling Puerto Rican parents. Her father was an alcoholic, and her mother's way of coping was to avoid being at home with him. She had to give herself painful insulin shots for diabetes starting around age eight. She says she was "blessed" with a "stubborn perseverance." She wasn't originally a top student, so she did "something very unusual" in fifth grade—she approached one of the smartest girls in the class to "ask her how to study." Soon she was getting top grades.[41] Justice Sotomayor graduated *summa cum laude* from Princeton University in 1976 and earned her JD from Yale Law School in 1979, where she was an editor at the *Yale Law Journal*.

An article in *The New York Times* says, "The point of this example is not, 'See, it's easy to climb out of poverty in America.' On the contrary, Justice Sotomayor's story illustrates just how extraordinary a person has to be to overcome the odds stacked against her." The article goes on to say that, according to research, perseverance and motivation can be taught, especially to young children.[42]

---

41. Sonia Sotomayor, *My Beloved World* (New York: Random House LLC), 91.

42. Amy Chua and Jed Rubenfeld, "What Drives Success?" *The New York Times*, January 25, 2014, http://www.nytimes.com/2014/01/26/opinion/sunday/what-drives-success.html?_r=0.

Ed also notes that, in addition to being driven to win, advisors who exhibit dominance hate to lose. They are highly competitive and refuse to be in second or third place. Sometimes, not wanting to lose is an even greater motivator than wanting to win.

> Advisors who exhibit dominance hate to lose.

In Chapter 1, we talked about "locus of control," which is the extent to which individuals believe they can control events that affect them. Advisors with dominance exhibit the attitude, "I am happening to the world" versus "The world is happening to me." They are outer-directed. They are influencing their environment. They are a force to be dealt with, a life in action, a life force. We hear this about people sometimes: "He is just a life force." Advisors with dominance say, "I can't help people I don't meet, so I need to go meet people. I need to be with my clients. I need to exercise influence and persuasion over my universe." They go and make things happen.

On the flip side are people who think the world is happening to them. They're powerless. They tend to get discouraged, and they can't throw off discouragement. People who are outer-directed can deal with discouragement. They can shrug it off and keep going. They heed the wise advice from Henry Ford: "When everything seems to be going against you, remember that the airplane takes off against the wind, not with it."

Advisors who have the dominance trait also have a strong and positive self-image. They recognize the value they provide to clients. One day, one of our advisors was at a cocktail reception with some thirty-year-old millionaires who worked at start-up firms. The advisor told me about the reception later and said he had been bashful about approaching these great prospects about working with them. He said, "I don't know why they'd want to work with me. They probably have their own advisors."

I said, "We've got to stop the conversation for a minute. I want to talk to you about that. I think they'd be really lucky to work with you. You have every right to play big and in this case, you played little." He did not exhibit dominance. He missed a huge opportunity that time to be more influential in his environment. There will be a next time.

Independence

An advisor who has the trait of independence wants to be his own person, define his own success, and be outside the influence of a boss. Independent advisors think in terms of solutions and see their work from different angles. They are self-governing and self-reliant. The saying "Eagles don't flock" applies here. Independent advisors do not flock together. They have fierce spirits and get things done without relying heavily on others. They are their own people, and they do things their way.

Responsibility

Winston Churchill said, "The price of greatness is responsibility." Proverbs 10:5 says, "A wise youth makes hay while the sun shines, but what a shame to see a lad who sleeps away his hour of opportunity." Jodi Johnson, a regional VP for Ameriprise, used to say, "If it's going to be, it's up to me." Those quotes all exemplify the trait of responsibility.

Strong advisors have a sense of responsibility to a number of constituents—first of all, a responsibility to themselves to use their skills well. Remember the Venn diagram from Chapter 1, where skills, financial reward, and passion intersect? As an advisor, your first obligation is to be in that zone where those three components come together. Advisors also have a responsibility to their family, to be good providers, spouses, and parents. Next, they have a responsibility to their clients, to make a positive change in their clients' lives, leave them better off than they found them, and help them achieve the financial dignity and choices they should have because they worked with an advisor. People who have a keen sense of responsibility say, "If it's going to be, it's up to me." They own it. It's theirs.

Failure with excuses is not as much fun as success. Responsible people own their success, and they take responsibility for getting better and for growing.

In Chapter 1, we mentioned the Demontreville silent retreat that Ed and Phil attend every year. A few years ago, one of the statements Ed heard at the retreat that resonated with him was, "People demonstrate their gratefulness by being responsible for whatever it is they're grateful for." To put that in the context of a top advisor, that advisor is going to be extremely responsible with his career or profession, but chances are, he is pretty grateful for it. He is thankful for the chance to do what he does every single day. He is grateful for the various people who brought him into the business and developed him. A lot of times, when people get to the top of the hill, they believe they climbed the mountain on their own. They tend to forget the Sherpa guide who was there to help them in so many ways on the climb.

Sherpa guides, by the way, are an excellent example of servant leadership. As advisors, we are the Sherpa guides of financial advice. Here is a brief story to show you the impact a Sherpa guide can have on someone's life. On May 29, 1953, Sir Edmund Hillary, a mountaineer, explorer, and philanthropist from New Zealand, climbed to the peak of Mt. Everest. He was guided by a Nepalese Sherpa named Tenzing Norgay. They were the first climbers to be confirmed as having reached the summit of Mt. Everest. In appreciation for Tenzing's contribution to this achievement, Hillary started a trust to benefit the people of Nepal. *Time* magazine named Hillary as one of the one hundred most influential people of the twentieth century.

Whatever a responsible person is grateful for, he or she will be responsible for it—career, family, volunteer work—whatever it is. When Ed speaks with college students, he uses the example of grandparents. He says, "Maybe your grandparents gifted you and your family some money so that you can go to college. How do you demonstrate to Grandma and Grandpa that you really are thankful for that gift of an education? You do it by being responsible for it, and you get great grades, and you take pride in that. You graduate with honors instead of having the mindset of a minimalist and doing the least amount of work possible to get through."

> Whatever a responsible person is grateful for, he or she will be responsible for it—career, family, volunteer work—whatever it is.

A form of responsibility is captured in my theory of attribution: We attribute our success only to ourselves, and we attribute our failures to everyone else. Or as the other saying goes, "Success has many parents, and failure is an orphan. And to fail is to learn, to be educated. Education, after all, is the sacrament of transformation."

Well-Being

One aspect of well-being is to have an authentic concern for others. We've used that phrase "the mind of a capitalist, the heart of a social worker." This is the "heart of a social worker" side of it. Advisors who exhibit this trait are compassionate. The top advisors really care about their clients and their clients' families. They tend to have a community view about what they do; they want to make their communities better by helping people achieve financial security.

Few people have as much impact on a community as advisors do. In 2013, North Star advisors paid out 249 death claims for a total of $30.4 million. And that is just the life insurance side of our business. That is huge.

Ed gives a presentation in which he demonstrates the financial impact of what advisors do. He notes that when New York City hosted the 2014 Super Bowl game, the city took in about $700 million in revenue. In comparison, North Star Resource Group advisors have $46 billion worth of protection (life, disability, long-term care, etc.) in place with clients. That is more than sixty-six times the financial impact of the Super Bowl.

At North Star, we have at least a dozen advisors whose financial impact eclipses a Super Bowl—by themselves—when you factor in life insurance, annuities, and other protection products.

If you are having a difficult time acknowledging the significant impact you have on people's lives and on your community, take an hour or two out of your life to calculate the financial impact and contribution you are making as an advisor. That is your sense of well-being. A simple way to assess your impact on clients is to calculate how much protection your clients have in place:

Disability income: _____

Life insurance: _____

Term life: _____

Whole life: _____

Long-term care: _____

Assets under management: _____

Total: _____

Another aspect of well-being is having a blended life—you know who you are, and you demonstrate your values whether you are at work, at home, or in the community. You are always who you are, no matter where you are. You are content wherever you are. Phil has the following quote framed outside his office door at North Star: "A master in the art of living draws no sharp distinction between his work and his play, his labour and his leisure, his mind and his body, his education and his recreation. He hardly knows which is which. He simply pursues his vision of excellence through whatever he is doing and leaves others to determine whether he is working or playing. To himself he always seems to be doing both. Enough for him that he does it well." English educator, philosopher, and Unitarian minister Lawrence Pearsall Jacks (1860–1955) wrote that often-repeated passage in 1932.

Advisors who have a strong sense of well-being tend to be humble. We like C. S. Lewis's definition of humility: "Humility is not thinking less of yourself but thinking of yourself less."

Ruggedness

Ruggedness is a trait we associate with resilience, toughness, and perseverance. Hebrews 12:1 says, "Let us run with perseverance the race that is marked out for us."

This trait indicates a person's ability to withstand rejection and overcome obstacles. In Harold Cummings's book *Prescription for Tomorrow*, he says, "Never doubt it. You can gauge your size by the size of the things that life throws you."[43] What is throwing you? Is some little thing causing you to falter, and you just can't shrug it off? Well, if that small thing is throwing you, then that is how big of a person you are. If you encounter a small obstacle, move on. Tell yourself, "I'm bigger than that, and I am going to succeed in spite of it."

---

43. Harold J. Cummings, *Prescription for Tomorrow: The Way to Live Today to Bring Peace to the World Tomorrow* (Farnsworth Publishing Company, 1980).

Some of us just need to toughen up and develop a thicker skin. One time I was agonizing over something that happened to me. Ed looked at me and said, "Gary, we're Germans. Buck up." I had to laugh because he was imposing ruggedness on me. He was basically telling me, "Gary, be more rugged." That is actually really good advice.

A high energy level is also associated with ruggedness. Ed uses the term "marathon energy" to refer to advisors who are always on the go, making things happen. Their energy doesn't come in spurts; there is a consistency, a rhythm, about their energy, both when they are working and in their lives in general. If you have ever run a marathon, you know that the energy required to finish a 26.2-mile run has to be consistent and steady. You develop a pace and maintain it for the duration of the race.

Phil often comments on practices that are "energy-filled places." He appreciates people who have a high kick to their step and walk with purpose, quickly. In his book *The Sky Is Not the Limit*, Phil notes that one of the questions he likes to ask candidates is, "When was the last time you got a speeding ticket?" In his book, he says, "I actually like people who get speeding tickets because I like people around me who are in a hurry even when they don't have a particular reason to be. The energy they bring to a firm, a team, or a meeting is infectious."[44]

How would you rate yourself in terms of these five valuable characteristics? Use the following chart for your self-assessment.

Are You Leading the Life You Imagine?

Choose the number between 1 and 10 that honestly describes how well you think you exemplify the following characteristics of top-performing advisors.

	Low			Medium			High		
Dominance / Intensity / Drive — Intensity, drive, "the mind of a capitalist," the relentless pursuit of a goal, a will to win, a sense of urgency and purpose, compulsion (a refusal) not to lose									
1	2	3	4	5	6	7	8	9	10
Independence — The ability to be a self-advocate, self-assured, and poised									
1	2	3	4	5	6	7	8	9	10
Responsibility — Conscientiousness, reliability, the ability to own your work ("If it's going to be, it's up to me") and to learn from your environment and experience (an "I own it" attitude)									
1	2	3	4	5	6	7	8	9	10
Well-being — A positive, optimistic; an authentic concern for others; and "the heart of a social worker"									
1	2	3	4	5	6	7	8	9	10
Ruggedness — Tough-mindedness, persistence, perseverance, the ability to overcome obstacles, a "marathon" energy, the ability to throw off/shrug off discouragement									
1	2	3	4	5	6	7	8	9	10

---

44. Richards, *The Sky Is Not the Limit*, 32.

Now that you know these are differentiating factors in a million-dollar practice, the critical question is, what will you do about it? Here are our recommendations:

1. First, be self-aware about the extent to which you exemplify those characteristics.
2. Then do what you can to integrate them into your practice. Try to apply them in an active way in your daily decision making and the way you interact with clients.
3. If you do not feel you have a good sense about how well those traits describe you, ask someone who knows you well. Or take one of the assessments we describe in this chapter. Maybe you're not empathetic enough toward clients; you are too business-focused and concerned more about how much money you can make than on helping clients achieve dignified retirements. Or maybe you need to leverage the talents of the people around you.

    Recently, I met with an advisor who is very self-sufficient, but his practice has not reached its potential, and we knew it would not grow any bigger until he began to leverage other people. We brought in his team member to sit with us, and she had four really good ideas she could implement right away to help him grow his practice. He said, "I don't know why I didn't think of that before." Now they are going to meet every Monday and go through their calendar. She is going to call clients and schedule meetings for him. And after he meets with a client, she will visit with him about what does she need to do. Now he will be able to grow—just by leveraging the people around him.

4. Determine how your pursuit of these characteristics of top-performing advisors will align with your personal and professional values. In his book *Financial Intelligence*, Doug Lennick says our values help us determine how we individually express certain principles. "For example, responsibility is a key principle, but our values help us choose how we individually express the principle of responsibility.... We can align our life choices with those values and with the principle of responsibility."[45]

Self-examination takes courage and a passionate desire to grow. Knowing to what extent you exemplify these five characteristics can help you grow your practice to a level you might have thought was out of reach.

One of the best examples of an advisor who possesses these five traits is Shaun McDuffee. Shaun serves as a Senior Vice President at North Star Re-

---

45. Doug Lennick, CFP®, with Kathleen Jordan, PhD, *Financial Intelligence: How to Make Smart, Values-Based Decisions with Your Money and Your Life* (Denver, CO: FPA Press, 2010).

source Group. In addition to his management and leadership responsibilities, Shaun is also our firm's top advisor. His success includes being a perennial MDRT Top of the Table qualifier and being recognized, numerous times, as Securian's Advisor of the Year, selected from among more than one thousand advisors. *Medical Economics* has featured Shaun as one of the top advisors in the country for specialty physicians. Many regional and national publications have awarded Shaun distinctive advisor honors.

Shaun's consistent performance over the past quarter century has allowed him to serve thousands of clients, write several books, and speak at top industry meetings. Yet Shaun's greatest joy stems from developing the future of our industry as he personally mentors new advisors; many of them have gone on to be top performers as well.

We have asked Shaun to share stories about the advisors he leads and the way they exemplify these five critical traits.

Shaun's Story: Six Top Producers Who Exemplify the "Big Five"

P. Shaun McDuffee, AEP®, CLU®, ChFC®, CEPA®, Senior Vice President; Senior Partner; and Founder, North Star Medical Division, North Star Resource Group

When I was asked to review the chapter on the "Big Five Traits" top producers possess, I couldn't help but immediately identify those traits with leaders in my Division. My top producers/mentors possess all five of those traits. Interestingly enough, they all possess all five, yet each of them has an "extra helping" of a few traits that makes them uniquely successful.

When I look at Craig Molldrem and Michael Paulus, "dominance" is front of mind. They have a relentless attitude when it comes to this career and winning. If there is a list out there, they *will* be at the top of it. Both were Securian's National New Advisor of the Year (2010 and 2012). They are driven, focused, and refuse to accept defeat. Not coincidentally, they were both scholarship athletes at the University of Minnesota— Craig was a dominant fastball pitcher who carried that mindset into this career. Michael was a standout gymnast who was/is relentless in his pursuit of excellence.

Well-being and ruggedness come to mind when I think of my other very successful leaders/producers: Laura Vaughn, Marcus Stone, James Jaderborg, and Mark Miller. All of them are extremely focused on always doing the right thing and keeping others' needs ahead of their own. Even though Laura was also a National New Advisor of the Year (2011), you wouldn't

(continued)

> ### Shaun's Story: Six Top Producers Who Exemplify the "Big Five" (continued)
>
> know she was new because she got there with a dogged sense of serving others. These top advisors also shrug off rejection because they focus on what the end goal is: helping others, even if others don't realize they need help. Mark runs marathons, and he takes the exact same approach to this career—he realizes that by staying the course, he will win. These four leaders inspire greatness in others, and they don't accept obstacles when they appear—they simply view them as something to overcome.
>
> All of my leadership team members have one overriding trait that is tied into responsibility: They *all* have an amazing "attitude of gratitude." They truly are grateful for any and all opportunities afforded to them, and they truly appreciate the gifts they have been given. As a result, they feel a sense of responsibility to give back and to be successful so as to not squander the opportunities they have been given. That sense of responsibility and gratitude are what make them a true blessing to be around, and that is why this organization will stand the test of time.)

Applying the Concepts to *Your* Practice on Purpose

1. On a scale of 1–5, with 1 being lowest and 5 being highest, to what extent do you think you exemplify the characteristic of *dominance* (intensity, drive, and a force in getting things done—the mind of a capitalist)? What are some examples of ways in which this characteristic describes you? What specific steps can you take to have a more dominant personality?

   _____
   _____
   _____
   _____
   _____
   _____

2. On a scale of 1–5, with 1 being lowest and 5 being highest, to what extent do you think you exemplify the characteristic of *independence* (being a self-advocate, self-assured, and poised)? What are some examples of ways in which this characteristic describes you? What specific steps can you take to have a more independent personality?

_____

_____

_____

_____

3. On a scale of 1–5, with 1 being lowest and 5 being highest, to what extent do you think you exemplify the characteristic of *responsibility* (an attitude characterized by owning your work ["If it's going to be, it's up to me"] and learning from your environment and experience)? What are some examples of ways in which this characteristic describes you? What specific steps can you take to have a more responsible personality?

_____

_____

_____

_____

4. On a scale of 1–5, with 1 being lowest and 5 being highest, to what extent do you think you exemplify the characteristic of *well-being* (positive, optimistic, authentic concern for others—the heart of a social worker)? What are some examples of ways in which this characteristic describes you? What specific steps can you take to focus more on others' well-being?

_____

_____

_____

_____

5. On a scale of 1–5, with 1 being lowest and 5 being highest, to what extent do you think you exemplify the characteristic of *ruggedness* (tough-mindedness, persistence, perseverance, the ability to overcome obstacles)? What are some examples of ways in which this characteristic describes you? What specific steps can you take to have a more rugged personality?

_____
_____
_____
_____
_____

6. How will your pursuit of these five personality characteristics of top-performing advisors align with your personal and professional values?

_____
_____
_____
_____
_____

Valuing Your Life's Work

CHAPTER 8

Everything you do is built on your personal purpose in life, which defines the purpose of your practice. You are contributing to people attaining financial integrity and build stress-free retirements. Because of your expertise, your passion, and your values, you are making your community a better place.

And, as a by-product of helping people, you are building personal wealth for yourself and your family. Your practice is a financial resource for your own retirement. The personal wealth you build translates into cars, weddings, homes, vacations, and a college education for your children—some of the things you value most in life. For many advisors, their practice is the most significant asset they will have in retirement. Therefore, it is important to view your practice as a lifetime investment you eventually can sell for a profit. This important mindset allows you to approach your practice as a business rather than as a job.

Some advisors balk at the thought that someday, another advisor might manage the practice they worked so hard to build from the ground up. We like to remind them that, in the spirit of the quote presented above, the new advisor will succeed, not replace, the original advisor.

As we mentioned in the Preface, the Holy Grail in our industry is to build a million-dollar practice—ideally, a million-dollar practice in which 60 to 80 percent of the revenue recurs, or repeats. A practice like that will probably be worth $1.5 to $2 million eventually if the advisor has the right business-continuation strategy in place.

You are already employing your values to help people and make an impact in your community, so why wouldn't you want to provide these valuable and needed financial services to more people? An advisor's practice is highly scalable. So once you have a physical plan or blueprint in place that defines your prac-

> When Thomas Jefferson presented his credentials as US minister to France, the French premier remarked, "I see that you have come to replace Benjamin Franklin."
>
> "I have merely come to succeed him," corrected Jefferson politely. "No one can replace him."

tice's path, growth becomes quite manageable and achievable. I challenge advisors that I could drop $25 million of assets into their practice and they would hardly break a sweat because they know where to invest it, they have the staff to handle it, and they can service new clients. Most $300,000 to $500,000 practices already have the infrastructure in place for $1 million of revenue. It's like throwing a couple of extra bales into the truck—you already have everything you need, so why not just do more of it?

> Most $300,000 to $500,000 practices already have the infrastructure in place for $1 million of revenue.

Sometimes advisors cannot take their practices to the next level because they see themselves as being at a certain level and cannot picture what they could become. This is a limiting mindset that must be conquered.

Jeff Jarnes is an advisor at North Star with one of our wealth practices, which is called Fortune Financial. When Jeff spoke at one of our winter meetings recently, someone asked him, "Jeff, are you more talented than everybody else? Why are you so successful?"

He replied, "I am not more talented than anyone else. Virtually everyone in this room is more talented than I am. I just always did twenty percent more. If I had a certain number of appointments one week, I would try to add twenty percent more. Or I would try to add twenty percent more assets. Sometimes I would even challenge myself to reach, by the end of the third quarter, where I was at the end of the previous year."

Jeff added that you don't need a massive lift in activity in your practice to make a real difference. A solid, incremental lift like 20 percent will compound every four years (3.4 years using the Rule of 72). He has a mindset that is focused on growth, activity, goal setting, and doing more than everyone else. That is why he is so successful.

Once your practice does reach $1 million in gross revenue, it is wise to consult with an outside firm such as Moss Adams to value your practice. Also keep in mind that if you are considering selling your practice or buying another advisor's practice, you will need to consult with a CPA to determine the tax implications of the sale or purchase.

The mechanics of practice valuation are beyond the scope of this book. A phenomenal book on the topic is *How to Value, Buy, or Sell a Financial Advisory Practice* by Mark Tibergien and Owen Dahl. It is by far the best resource on this topic. What we do want to accomplish in this chapter is to impart the importance of knowing what you want your practice to be worth ultimately, conducting your business in a way that moves you closer toward that goal, and being prepared for emergencies that could interrupt your achievement of that goal.

Begin with the End in Mind

As Stephen Covey, author of *The 7 Habits of Highly Effective People*, says, "Begin with the end in mind." Decide what you want your practice to be worth at the end of your career, and then structure your Practice on Purpose so that it meets those objectives and goals. Even brand-new advisors who are just starting out in the industry and building a client base should begin with the end in mind. Always be looking ahead to the future, and make sure that everything you do on a daily business contributes to your ultimate goal.

We have asked this question before, and it's a critical one: How much does your practice need to be worth for work to be an option for you? If you know that number, then everything you do will be driving your practice to reach it. A few advisors know that number, but most don't. Most advisors do not do financial plans for themselves, so they don't have a solid grasp of that critical number. It's like the old saying, "The cobbler's kids have no shoes." The cobbler is so busy making shoes for other people, to make a living, that he doesn't have time to make shoes for his own children. That concept applies in our business, too. Most advisors are extremely private about their personal finances and feel uncomfortable having their peers know details about their financial situation. We encourage them to team up with one advisor they trust and complete financial plans for one another.

Industry Changes That Affect Succession Planning

Our business has changed drastically over the past few decades. Viewing a practice as an entity that holds value, has a market, and can be sold is a relatively new phenomenon. Historically, most advisors have not viewed their practices this way. In the past, advisors would rely on life insurance policies as a future source of funds. Now our practices are much broader in terms of product array, and they have more significant and recurring revenue. Life insurance renewals have declined significantly, to the point where the new life insurance policies tend to be front-end compensation with very low trails going out into the future. Insurance companies have not individually chosen to reduce the advisor competition but have responded to the marketplace, which, in the final analysis, ultimately determines compensation. The positive news is that this has been good for the consumer because it has made life insurance products far more cost-effective. It is not unusual for a company's premium to have been reduced significantly over the past fifty years from 3.8 percent annually as a percentage of the death benefit to less than 1 percent per annum on a whole life product.

We see a lot of reports that the number of advisors in the workforce is shrinking. According to Cerulli Associates, a research firm specializing in the financial services industry, our industry will lose more than 25,000 advisors by

2017, mostly because of retirement.[46] The National Association of Insurance and Financial Advisors has seen its membership drop from a high of 142,000 to approximately 41,000 today.

Because of our shrinking advisor pool, there are now fewer incoming advisors for senior advisors to sell their practices to once they retire. At North Star, however, we do not see droves of older advisors running for the door. Our experience has been, instead, that many senior advisors prefer to stay in the business and work part-time rather than retire. Where else can you work two days a week and make $100,000 a year? It's a great career, and they have earned it. Other advisors stay in the business because they have trouble letting go of their clients. They have made promises to their clients over the years, and they feel obligated to follow those obligations through. And frankly, some advisors just don't know how to quit. They have not found someone to take over their clients and be their business continuation partner. When you put an effective business continuation plan in place, you are honoring your clients.

> When you put an effective business continuation plan in place, you are honoring your clients.

Don McLaughlin, while a VP at Principal Financial Group, enginecrod hundreds of succession plans, overcoming the three challenges advisors have when considering a successor: loss of control, perceived loss of income, and divorce (which is what happens if the newer advisor doesn't work out). North Star has employed his methods with excellent early results.

Another change that our industry is experiencing is that our advisor pool is aging. According to a 2013 *Time* magazine article, the average financial advisor age in the United States is fifty. Wealth managers are growing old in a line of work with a slow replacement rate, and financial advisors past the age of sixty control $2.3 trillion of client assets. "Most alarming: These trillions of dollars will be up for grabs over the next decade as fewer than one in three advisers has a formal plan for handing off their client list," the article says.[47] In this environment of a shrinking and aging advisor pool, succession planning for practices is a must.

Also, millions of Baby Boomers are retiring at the same time as their aging financial advisors. This can lead to costly gaps and disruptions in planning

---

46. Dan Jamieson and Jeff Benjamin, "Retiring Boomer Advisors Leaving Talent Vacuum," *InvestmentNews*, last modified September 22, 2013, http://www.investmentnews.com/article/20130922/REG/309229995.

47. Dan Cadlec, "Close to Retiring? Uh-Oh, So Is Your Financial Adviser," *Time* website, last modified July 18, 2013, http://business.time.com/2013/07/18/close-to-retiring-uh-oh-so-is-your-financial-adviser/.

for consumers, but it presents a huge opportunity for advisors to serve this burgeoning segment of the population.

North Star does not fit the aging-advisor profile, however; it is a youthful organization in comparison to the norm. In fact, 43 percent of our advisors are thirty-five or younger, 24 percent are thirty-six to fifty years of age, and 33 percent are fifty-one or older. In our organization, there are ample choices for successful, younger advisors to carry on the legacy of an older advisor who wants to scale down his business or retire. One of our tactics is to replace the word "retire" with the word "rewire." The intended implication is that the desirable transition should be one that accommodates the senior advisor's needs and feelings.

One of the reasons we have a younger advisor workforce is that we recruit from college campuses. That drives that demographic to a great extent. Also, we have experienced extensive growth through our recruiting efforts, which Ed has led successfully. We have focused on building the bottom of the pyramid with people who are just starting out in the career. This strategy allows us to maintain our culture of faith, integrity, growth, gratitude, and service because young college graduates are like a liquid that takes the form of whatever vessel it's poured into.

Succession planning in advisor practices can be a challenge. When addressing large groups of our advisors, we used to joke that half of the advisors in the room should sell their practices to the other half. That would be an easy solution.

Are You Growing or Dying?

Advisors often don't know when their practices are at their peak value. If you are not getting new clients coming in, if you have not worked with your client's children, or if you haven't grown professionally or personally, you could be at the top of your career and not know it.

Think of a big mall or a big office building. You see one escalator going up and another escalator going down. They meet about halfway. That's what advisors are like—some of their practices are on their way up to the peak, and some are actually declining in value. Usually, the advisors who are on the way up know it, but the ones who are on the way down often don't realize it. They do not have the self-awareness we talked about earlier. Knowing where you are in your practice is critical as you strive to have your practice be worth what you would like when you retire.

Ed often asks advisors, "Are you growing, or are you dying?" You are doing one or the other. Someone he used to work with referred to the status quo as "a managed decline." If you are not growing, in essence you are experiencing a managed decline because you are just managing the inevitable. No one ever thinks they are at the peak; they think their success will keep coming. But if they really look in the mirror—if they really try to be self-aware—they might see that they are in that state of managed decline or that they are flat-out dying and not growing.

Here are some questions Ed uses with advisors to help determine if they are growing or "dying":

Am I Growing or Dying?

1. Did I bring aboard more new clients over the previous year?
2. Did I generate more cases?
3. Did I earn more money (15 percent)?
4. Did I earn a designation this year?
5. Did I obtain another license?
6. Did I attend LSMF/MDRT/NAIFA/FPA?
7. Did I formally mentor someone?
8. Did I add staff/invest in my practice/business? If so, what percent?

In *Good to Great*, Jim Collins talks about how we need to "confront the brutal facts." At some point, we need to have the courage to do that. Ed has a list of questions he calls "the X-ray questions." He and Phil use them often. They are questions we ask advisors to determine the status of their practices. It takes only a few minutes to answer these questions, but the answers are quite revealing; they basically allow you to take an X-ray of your practice. They encourage you to be honest about where you stand. If you have more "no" than "yes" answers to these questions, it is a wake-up call. It is an awareness issue.

Ed compares this scenario to smoking. If you smoke cigarettes over a period of many years, the detrimental health effects might not be readily apparent, so you keep smoking. But if you look at your own damaged lungs via an MRI one day or see a cadaver's smoke-damaged lungs, you realize that the damage is cumulative, corrosive, and detrimental. It's the same way with an advisor's practice—you have to get a clear picture of the long-term effects of your daily activities to know your true status.

The X-Ray Questions

1. What am I great at?
2. What am I lousy at?
3. What is going well/right?
4. What is not going well/right?

5. What do I need to start doing?
6. What do I need to stop doing?
7. What are my billable hours?
8. If I were to write a book about financial planning, what would the executive summary say? One message!
9. How much money is entrusted to me?
10. What is the fairy tale?
11. What are three words I want my clients to associate with me/use to describe me?

Often, especially when we are experiencing a great tailwind from an "up" market, an advisor might say, "My revenue was up, and I had a great year." On the surface, the advisor may have had a great year. The market went up 25 percent, and his assets went up 25 percent. But if we look at that practice more closely in terms of long-term growth, how many new clients or households did he bring into the mix?

Growth is by far one of the most overlooked metrics in an advisor's practice and one of the most important. As long as you are in a building mode, and as long as you are bringing in new clients at a healthy, productive rate, your practice is going to be valued at a higher level and is going to be more robust.

Often, advisors look at just total revenue, which can be deceiving. If you are not bringing in new clients, especially as your clientele ages, your clients begin to move into the distribution mode of your planning phase—they begin using their assets to sustain them during their retirement, and they may begin distributing their assets to relatives and charities. Those assets can flee your practice at an incredible rate, resulting in a radical drop in your managed assets.

Being aware of the true status of your practice is a must for reaching the next level.

A Mindful Approach to Practice Growth

In this book, we talk a lot about the importance of self-awareness for advisors who want to reach that Holy Grail—the million-dollar practice. In some circles, self-awareness is called "mindfulness." According to a 2013 Mayo Clinic special report, mindfulness is, in general, "a conscious effort to be completely present, setting aside worries, expectations, and other thoughts to be fully aware of the current moment." The report says mindfulness training can help people reduce pain, increase quality of life, and even cope with cancer.[48]

---

48. Ginger Plumbo, "Calmer Minds, Better Health with Mindfulness," Mayo Clinic News Network, last modified October 29, 2013, http://newsnetwork.mayoclinic.org/discussion/calmer-minds-better-health-with-mindfulness.

One of the most prominent researchers in the area of mindfulness is Ellen Langer, PhD. A social psychologist, Dr. Langer is the first female professor to gain tenure in the Psychology Department at Harvard University. She is hailed as "the mother of mindfulness," and she is the author of eleven books and more than two hundred research articles on mindfulness. She believes that by paying attention to what's going on around us, we can reduce stress, unlock creativity, and boost performance. She says, "Life consists only of moments, nothing more than that. So if you make the moment matter, it all matters. When you're doing anything, be mindful, notice new things, make it meaningful to you, and you'll prosper."[49]

Being mindful may sound easy, but it can be a challenge for a busy, stressed person. I did my first episode of yoga recently. It's called "yoga flow." It involves relaxing more than exercise. You lie down on your mat in a quiet room, and a person reads to you and plays pleasant music. You do some stretching and lifting, and you change your body posture to inflate your lungs with air. By the end of the hour, I was a marshmallow. I realized how tense and preoccupied I had been. The purpose of the class is to get you to unplug and be mindful of your breathing, the room, the people around you, and what's important to happen in your life today. It was an interesting exercise for realizing how we are so busy plowing ahead that we are not aware of ourselves, our health, and the choices we are making.

> By paying attention to what's going on around us, we can reduce stress, unlock creativity, and boost performance.

Simply put, try to be where you are. Be in the moment. Many times, we will be at work but thinking about what's going on at home. Or we will be at home worrying about something at work. Be focused. When you are in front of a client, focus on her; try not to think about the errands you need to run. When you are at home, be fully engaged with your family. Too many of us are looking over the fence at the other thing, and we rob ourselves of being fully in the moment and giving those around us the full extent of our personality and being.

Phil says, "When you're in the office, be there. Monday-morning quarterbacking of the Vikings or the Cardinals is robbing somebody—either your clients who need you and your advice or your family who wants and deserves more of your time. Don't vacation at the office!"

Phil and I knew the remarkable Coley Bloomfield, who was chairman and CEO of Minnesota Life. He had a spectacular gift of being so focused on the person he was speaking with that you were absolutely convinced you were the

---

49. Alison Beard, "Mindfulness in the Age of Complexity," An Interview with Ellen Langer by Alison Beard, *Harvard Business Review*, March 2014, http://hbr.org/2014/03/mindfulness-in-the-age-of-complexity/ar/pr.

only person in his life and the only thought that was important to him. Clearly it was not true, but he made you feel that way. That is a gift. Being mindful and self-aware can help you become a better listener, build trust among clients, and compartmentalize your life and work issues in a way that optimizes the time and energy you devote to all of them.

What Has Value for Another Advisor?

Early in my career, I worked in corporate relocation. I noticed an interesting phenomenon among people who were preparing to sell their homes to move to another part of the country for their careers. They perceived their homes to be worth more than the market proved them to be worth. Because they raised their family in that home and had many fond memories of it, owners would exaggerate their perception of how much their home was really worth. The reality is that a home is worth only what a willing buyer will pay for it. Technically, a home is primarily dirt, lumber, location, and fixtures. When it gets down to it, that's how appraisers value houses; they look at how much it would cost to construct it again in that location. But there is an emotional or goodwill factor inherent in that process, and it is hard to quantify.

An advisor's practice is the same way: It is worth only the amount another advisor will pay for it. When an advisor considers buying an existing practice, he will look at factors like his ability to obtain and secure additional client relationships in the practice, the quality of relationships the current owner has with his clients, the assets and products the practice represents, the potential for obtaining recommendations, and the manner in which clients will transition to the new practice. That is where the economic value lies.

Sometimes it's difficult for advisors to see the economic value in their practices. They can see the value in other practices, but not their own. One day, one of my advisors called me and said he had had enough and wanted to sell his practice. I was impressed with him and knew he had considerable potential. So I removed the names from his client data and printed it all out. I sat down with him and said I had a sample practice that would show him how practices are valued. I walked through all of the practice data and summary reports with him. I did a rough calculation to show what it might be worth to a motivated buyer. He studied the data and said to me, "If I could buy this practice, I would do so in a minute because I can see all the opportunities in the practice." He started pointing out individual clients and what he would present to them to move them to their potential goals.

I said, "Really? Well, I have news for you. You already own this practice. It's your practice. I took the names off." Once he got over the fact that I had gamed him a bit, he laughed and said he should probably keep his practice and view it differently.

That advisor stayed in the business. Today, he has a partner, a talented advisor I referred to him. They manage one of the top practices at Ameriprise and will soon cross the million-dollar-revenue practice level. This advisor was recognized recently in *The Wall Street Journal*.

An inspiring book on the subject of discovering wealth in your own backyard is *Acres of Diamonds: Life-Changing Classics* by Russell Conwell and John Wanamaker. Conwell, the founder of Temple University, was referred to as the penniless millionaire. He left a legacy that is still changing countless lives today. His famous "Acres of Diamonds" message challenges readers to seek opportunities to find true wealth right in their own realm without getting sidetracked by greed.

Try to see your practice as others see it.

One Man's Ceiling Is Another Man's Floor

The way clients are moved from one practice to another affects the value of the practice that is being sold.

A group of clients might not hold value for one advisor anymore, but another advisor might see great value in those clients. It reminds me of the old Paul Simon song, "One Man's Ceiling Is Another Man's Floor." Here are several different types of sales transactions that can take place for advisor practices.

Partial Sales

A partial sale is when an advisor looks at his practice and realizes that he has a group of clients who just don't fit where he is going. They are unresponsive, they are not savers, they don't act on advice, differences in values have become more pronounced, or they don't fit the demographic profile he has decided on as a specialty or focus in his practice. So the advisor will sell those client files to another advisor. Sometimes the transaction happens because an advisor is in the same building with another advisor, or maybe we introduce them to each other. What I think is not working for my practice anymore might be a pretty good arrangement for another advisor. We are in favor of partial sales. We owe it to all of our clients to have an advisor engage with them actively. If no advisor is doing that, then we should do those clients a favor and transition them to somebody who will take an interest in them.

Whole Sales

The whole sale is just what it sounds like—an advisor sells his entire business. He might be retiring or leaving the industry. Sometimes an advisor will sell his business to someone who has been a competitor through the years. Or he might sell to an advisor he has worked with in the past.

Fire Sales

A fire sale takes place because a time-sensitive event has taken place. It happens when an advisor is being terminated because of a compliance violation, and he has to sell his practice in thirty days. It also happens when an advisor gets divorced and has to sell all of his practice or a huge portion of it to meet the terms of the divorce settlement. At Ameriprise, I worked with a woman who was a fantastic advisor and had a large practice. Her husband was not a nice person, and eventually she had enough. She had to sell a pretty good chunk of her practice to settle the bad separation and subsequent divorce. It was a considerable asset.

Some advisors have a fire sale because they file for bankruptcy. They need the money from the sale of their practice or else they will no longer be able to be affiliated with their company. Other fire sales are initiated because of death or disability of the advisor.

In a fire sale, the value of the practice is depressed, and the selling advisor is usually in a tough spot.

Living Transition Sales

A living transition with known successors has the maximum practice value. In earlier chapters, we talked about the value of having a team in place that is composed of people who know the clients, and the clients know them. The selling advisor is leaving a legacy of value and, because he has a competent team in place, they will deliver on the promises they made to clients through the team they built.

> A living transition with known successors has the maximum practice value.

Many times, what happens is that once an advisor decides to retire in five years, he will begin selling parts of his practice to other associates who are already in the practice. This is the model that has the most value.

Who Owns the Client?

Transitioning clients from one practice to another can involve some tension because there is often disagreement regarding who "owns" a client. Sometimes home offices or companies think they "own" the client, and often the advisor thinks he or she owns the client. But the fundamental reality is that the client owns the client. The client gets to pick his or her advisor.

When financial-planning companies recruit experienced advisors, what happens is that an advisor brings his client base over to his new company. He is often surprised when clients don't move with him, and he gets his feelings hurt. On the other hand, sometimes clients make the move with an advisor, and the advisor thought for sure they wouldn't. So advisors are not always the best judges of whether they have influence or control over a client. Advisors tend to overestimate their level of control and their ability to influence clients. This is not necessarily a bad thing; it just is.

> A successful practice transition should plan how to keep the clients' interests in mind and how clients will work with the new advisor.

When I first joined Ameriprise, I talked with the 250 advisors I worked with initially. I asked them, "Did you buy a partial practice or a full practice from another advisor?" About half of them did. The amazing thing was that all of them were happy with their sale price, whether they had sold a practice or bought one from another advisor. That tells me that the selling advisors probably weren't doing much with that group of clients and were therefore happy to have them gone. The advisors who bought practices were happy with what they got because they were acquiring new relationships, which revitalized their practices, and the clients liked being part of a vibrant new practice. Often, that is not the case when you are buying or selling for value. Usually one party benefits and the other one does not.

A successful practice transition should plan how to keep the clients' interests in mind and how clients will work with the new advisor.

When I was with Ameriprise, we would have two or three partial practice sales a month. One day, I got a phone call from a client. He said, "Gary, are you the leader? I just received a letter saying I have been reassigned to a new advisor. I got traded like a baseball card."

That was his comment. I could tell he was feeling bad, so I said, "Well, when was the last time you heard from your current advisor?"

"Oh, it's been about three years."

I told him, "Someone new has purchased the right to meet with you. He paid money to meet with you, and it didn't come out of your pocket; it came out of his pocket. He bought the right to give you a phone call, and he wants to work with you. If you don't get better service, I will be really surprised." I asked him if he wanted to interview other advisors, and he said no.

I gave him my cell phone number and said, "Please call me in three months and let me know if that situation worked out."

Of course I never heard from him. Right after the client called me, I called the receiving advisor and said, "Look, this individual called me. I want you to call him right away and then tell me how it went." So he called the client right away, called me back, and explained that they had an appointment set up, and it worked out fine.

Building Value as You Go

"Building value as you go" is the process of managing your personal finances in a way that results in your turning the corner on meeting your household budget. If you can control yourself from not buying every darn thing on the planet and start putting some of your earnings away for your personal retirement, you will eventually have a net margin of 20 percent profitability, of retained earnings, that you can set aside. You can use that money to increase your personal wealth, or you can invest it back into your practice. We strongly recommend that you invest in your practice.

Many advisors take all of their earnings home, all the time, every day, for their entire careers. They do not invest in their practices. As a result, they are not as financially well-off as they could be. They are like a consumer who has no advisor—they spent everything they make.

To think more like business owners, it is wise for advisors to know the appropriate margin or income for them to take home versus taking home everything they net. They need to decide what percentage of their top-line revenue should be spent on staff, rent, overhead, and retained earnings. That is the amount they need to maintain their personal lifestyle, the amount they have already set aside to fund their retirement, and what is left over, or retained.

We believe retained earnings should go into building your personal wealth, which is nonqualified wealth. Putting money into a retirement plan is "qualified" money, by IRS definition. This approach changes the way you think about your business. If you take home everything that is left over, you are not really thinking through what is the appropriate reward for you as a business owner, the CEO of your practice.

When we ask advisors what their goals are for the next year, often they just tack on 10 or 15 percent onto their current revenue. It is an interesting exercise to stop them for a minute and ask them to think about the talent, credentials, and business-management experience they have. We ask them to think about the opportunity costs of running their practice: "What else could you be doing in the world that you are giving up to be in this career? Do you know what your relative worth is, how much should you be paid for the risk you are taking, for the capital you have invested in your education, physical space, staff, and liability from clients?" That requires a lot more thought and planning than just tacking on 10 percent to what you did last year. Are you a $300,000-a-year advisor or a $500,000-a-year advisor? Your business ought to be driving that value.

And if you are at $250,000 right now, what is going to get you to $500,000? Are you really worth $500,000? We look at advisors and wonder what is standing between them and a doubled income. This conversation gets them thinking bigger and encourages them to reset their perspective. If they can't get paid fairly for what they are doing, they should either change their practice or sell it and go do something else.

The best investment you can make is in your practice. There is no better investment than in yourself. If you adopt this mindset, you will feel an urge to invest back in your practice whenever you feel there would be a return greater than whatever that investment is, especially on an annual basis rather than on a one-time basis. This is how you "build as you go." Start with the amount of money you want to take home, then use any excess funds for investment and to hire a support person or a CFA into your practice. At North Star, we provide marketing support as a resource to our advisors so they don't have to hire their own full-time marketing directors. If you do not work for a firm like North Star that provides marketing support, you might want to consider hiring a marketing director. Before you take that step, be reasonably certain you have the capacity to serve the additional clientele that might be generated from that effort. Advisors who have anywhere from 150 to 250 clients are maxed out; they don't have time to serve additional clients. If you hire a marketing director, you will generate new clientele, so you also will have to hire a junior partner to do some of that additional work.

When advisors add more capacity to their practices, they grow. Sometimes you have to take a temporary reduction in your margin to get that next burst of growth, but eventually it will pay off. All you have to do is realize that, eventually, the return on those dollars will be greater than the value of the dollars themselves. One of the admonitions in Phil's first two books is that if you do $10-an-hour work, you'll make $10 an hour. If you want to earn $250 an hour, you must do $250-per-hour work. Hiring others to do the $10-an-hour work frees you to make use of your skills, experience, wisdom, and relationships.

It is ideal to think about adding a new team member when you think the margin of revenue will be able to support the new person within twelve months. If you are going to hire a second full-time staff person, the revenue you are going to generate initially is not going to be sufficient for you to break even on that person. You will need to pay for training, and the interaction among all of the people within your practice can slow your processes down at first. But by the end of the first year, you should be fairly confident that you have a margin of revenue that exceeds your annual costs associated with hiring that person.

Most practices are one-, two-, or three-person operations. A good rule of thumb is that every $250,000 of gross revenue equates to one full-time staff member. Maybe 20 percent or more of your net take-home pay should be devoted to hiring a new team member. When you get to the $250,000 point, maybe that is the time to take $50,000 or $75,000 out of your earnings and hire a new person.

At North Star, when an advisor hires his or her first full-time person, that team member typically does administrative work. The second person an advisor hires is often the person who handles the tasks the advisor does not like to do. (This aligns with the exercise in Phil's book *The Sky Is Not the Limit*, which we discussed in Chapter 5, that requires you to determine what you like to do most and what you like to do least and delegate those tasks you do not enjoy doing). Every new person who joins your practice should be doing something different. It is part of the design of a Practice on Purpose.

How to Value a Practice

When we value a practice, there are two types of revenue: recurring revenue and nonrecurring revenue. We will also discuss multiple earnings.

Recurring Revenue

Generally speaking, a risk-based management advisor's income, assuming he has been in the business five years or longer, is the median income of his clientele. This rule of thumb should encourage advisors to work upmarket to obtain recommendations and to grow with clients. The average income of your clients becomes your average income. This guideline applies in financial planning as well as in life insurance. The longer you are an advisor, the more your income should shift from being a commission or other one-time kind of revenue to being recurring fee revenue.

> The average income of your clients becomes your average income.

Recurring revenue is a bit unique to our industry. Dental and medical practices, real estate offices, and car dealerships do not have the predictable recurring revenue we do. If you go to a dentist, there is no assurance that if your dentist retires, you are going to keep going there. A client has no real tie to that dentist other than maybe habit or location. But in financial services, an advisor has possession of a client's money and protection products, so the tie is a lot stronger, and that is fortunate for us.

Recurring, or bookable, revenue has a higher value than nonrecurring revenue. One type of recurring revenue is 12b-1 fees, also known as distribution fees. They allow mutual funds to use their assets to pay for marketing and distribution expenses, such as compensation of financial advisors. Like life insurance and annuity trails, investment IA management and ongoing advice fees have a history of repeating. Typically, about 80 percent of advice fees will recur.

When you work on a partial sale of a practice, recurring revenue is about the only thing you look at. Typically, the multiple for recurring revenue is 1.5 to 2.5 times. In other words, your practice could be worth 1.5 to 2.5 times your recurring revenue. That is based on studies conducted by the Financial Planning Association and Moss Adams. Recurring revenue is really important. In a healthy practice, about 50 to 60 percent of its revenue is recurring. That revenue is going to be of great value in a practice you are selling.

> When you work on a partial sale of a practice, recurring revenue is about the only thing you look at.

For example, let's say an advisor has $100,000 in contractual product renewals from life insurance, annuities, disability income; $150,000 in wrap/money management fees; $50,000 in C shares; and $75,000 in 12b-1 fees. In a perfect transition, the new advisor would realize $375,000 of recurring revenue. So if the multiples on this are from 1.5 to 2.5 times, the estimated value from recurring revenue would be $562,500 to $937,500, with a mean of $750,000.

This is a substantial number and not one most purchasing advisors could cover in a single check. These transactions are complex and are best done when there is time to prepare. North Star has been successful in structuring these transactions. Each of them has its own characteristics and outcome.

Nonrecurring Revenue

Nonrecurring business is just what it sounds like: It is the business that occurs because you meet with a client to solve a specific, just-in-time issue. It would be like an A share or First Year Commission (FYC). You could also look at it like a store people walk into to make a purchase. Sometimes we call this "goodwill business" or "ongoing business." Often, one client or customer makes just one purchase from that particular store. This is not predictable and therefore is valued less than recurring revenue. Typically 0.8 to 1.2 is the multiple for historic annual nonrecurring revenue.

Blended Multiple of Earnings

The value of your practice is a combination of recurring and nonrecurring avenue. The calculation needs to be done separately for those two types of revenue and then added together. The blended multiple of earnings represents the value of your practice. From this thinking, then, an advisor would be well served to increase the amount of recurring revenue in his or her practice. It's not uncommon for a highly functioning practice to have 60 to 70 percent of its total revenue as recurring revenue. That is a healthy balance between having new business coming in along with recurring revenue that essentially shows up every year. It's a balance between hunting for new revenue and harvesting existing revenue.

Why a Buy/Sell Agreement Is a Must: Two Stories

We have two stories that demonstrate why it is critical for every advisor to have a buy/sell agreement in place for his or her practice. The first story is about an advisor who was not prepared, and the second one is about an advisor who was prepared.

Matthew's Story

I worked with an advisor named Matthew and knew him well. He ran a practice on the east side of the Twin Cities, and his wife worked in the practice. Matthew was a pretty good advisor. He was active in his community and did well. He had been born with a heart condition. He was public about it and always had to be a little careful because of his heart condition.

One night, Matthew and his wife went out to dinner. He went to the restroom and didn't come out. He passed away. He was only in his late thirties. Later in the day, another advisor called me and told me that Matthew had passed away. I have a lot of phone numbers in my smartphone, and Matthew's number was one of them. As I was sitting in a parking lot, my phone rang, and the digital readout said it was Matthew who was calling. I thought, *This could be a heck of a phone call.*

I answered it, and it was Matthew's widow. She was distressed. She said, "Gary, what am I going to do? We do not have a buy/sell arrangement. The children and I need the money that is in the practice. It is serious." So I put together some statistics about Matthew's practice. Word got out, and before the funeral took place, advisors were calling me, asking, "What's going to happen to Matthew's practice?" With the permission of Matthew's widow, we communicated some details regarding the practice.

We ended up with twelve serious bidders. We screened them, narrowed the pool down to the best potential buyers, and finally selected one. Because many advisors were competing for the practice, the bidding process increased the final price. The price got to be almost a three-times multiple, and it was a cash deal, which is unusual. A gentleman bought the practice, Matthew's widow got paid in cash, and it was a great outcome.

One day, the advisor who bought it said, "Gary, I think I may have paid too much for the practice."

I replied, "I don't know, but I do know that time will fix that. You didn't necessarily pay too much, but you might have to wait a little longer before you recoup your investment."

Because the buyer paid three times the value of the practice, in essence, he had to wait three years before he would turn the corner, unless additional business came from that practice. The purchasing advisor was an excellent advisor and had a strong practice team, so it was likely that not too many clients would leave the practice. I anticipated that he would eventually reap financial rewards from buying the practice.

Matthew's widow and I hosted a reception for the clients who were a part of the practice. We introduced them to the new advisor, and most of that practice stayed with the new advisor. The outcome was extremely positive.

I tell that rather long story to make two points. First, many times, an advisor does not have a buy/sell agreement in place when he dies, but that doesn't mean it is the end of the world. When you work with a firm like North Star, we will make an appropriate valuation of the advisor's life work and make sure that other advisors see the value of the practice. Unfortunately, an advisor who is with an independent broker–dealer and is in a solo practice, or is the only advisor in a small town, is at risk if he or she dies without an agreement in place. This is a preventable tragedy.

> Have a buy/sell agreement in place, and seek legal advice to specify what will happen to your practice if something happens to you.

It serves advisors well to be prepared. Have a buy/sell agreement in place, and seek legal advice to specify what will happen to your practice if something happens to you. A buy/sell is critical for the unplanned or surprise situation. An advisor who does not have a firm like North Star behind him does not always get to pick a successor and will lose control of the process in the event of an emergency. If that happens, his staff won't know if they are going to stay employed, and the clients will lose confidence about their financial situation. It is imperative to have a buy/sell agreement for your practice. North Star has templates for buy/sells, and we help advisors establish these agreements.

Keith's Story

The second story is about Matthew's training manager, whose name was Keith. He had a large practice, which he shared with two other people. They all had buy/sell agreements. Keith was on a weekend fishing trip with a group of fellow advisors. They were taking an afternoon break, and Keith did not come back. He was later found by the others; he had drowned. A number of people took many difficult actions that day to inform the family and to honor Keith. We witnessed some tremendous acts of kindness, courage, and respect that day and in the weeks that followed.

If there is anything good about this situation, it is the success of a transition plan working to its maximum benefit. Keith's practice and clients transferred within twenty-four hours. By Monday, all of the clients were in the names of the other two advisors. Those advisors had asked their team members to go to the office on the weekend. They set up a schedule to go out and meet with all of Keith's clients. They did not lose a single client. They had marketed themselves as a practice, and the clients had met the other partners over the years, although Keith had been the primary advisor.

The buy/sell funded the practice to continue Keith's legacy. The money in the buy/sell did not go to the family; it went to the practice. The practice members, in turn, made a settlement with Keith's estate. Keith believed in life insurance for his clients and for himself. The life insurance settlement is where the family found the greatest financial security. The value of the practice was also realized through the well-designed and well-executed buy/sells the advisors had in place.

During our time working with Keith, we developed a strong relationship with his widow. We would often have her come and talk to advisor groups about the importance of succession planning, buy/sells, and being prepared for the unexpected. She is a wonderful person. They have since formed a charitable golf tournament named after Keith. He remains part of the whole culture of the firm.

So, as you can see, with a little bit of planning, even in a difficult situation, you can recognize the value of your practice, and you or your family can reap that benefit in the event of an emergency.

Types of Financing

There are different ways to structure the handoff of a practice. When an advisor buys a practice, he can make lump-sum payments, a buyout, or an earn-out. Sometimes an advisor will pay for a practice using the profit he makes from that practice. So they are paying the multiple but they have taken over all the service and work in the practice.

Sometimes an advisor will structure the deal so that if he grows the practice after he acquires it, the seller will get some of the profit, too. Often, there is seller financing. If the seller is still in the picture, he offers financing. The buyer might put down 20 percent of the value up front, and the seller finances the rest. That type of arrangement motivates the seller to stay involved in the practice. It's a win for the purchasing advisor to have the original advisor remain active in the practice, and it's a win for the selling advisor, who will raise the security of getting future payments if he or she stays involved.

At North Star, we help advisors purchase practices. We ensure that both sides of the deal are respected and that there is a maximum transfer of value. Financing from banks is very rare because banks don't really understand our business. Also, client relationships are not good collateral; they do not hold the type of tangible value that equipment or a building does. There are some small business administration loans for advisors, but they tend to be pretty low amounts of financing, and the regulation is significant.

★ ★ ★ ★

Your practice is probably the most significant asset you will have in retirement. Even if retirement is a long way off for you, it is important to view your practice as a lifetime investment you eventually can sell for a profit. As you work every day to create comfortable, dignified retirements for your clients, strive also to achieve optimum value in your practice so that you and your own family have a comfortable, dignified retirement as well.

Paul's Story—From the Seller's Vantage Point: The Financial and Psychological Value of an Advisor's Legacy

Paul J. Coufal, Financial Representative, Registered Representative, North Star Resource Group

Many years ago, a research psychologist was a main speaker at a conference I attended. In his attempt to find the "pervasive truths of our lives," he visited several senior living facilities. He asked the occupants about the importance of their lives, what they wished they had done that they hadn't. He condensed their answers into these three activities: They wished they had risked more, reflected more, and left something behind.

In this chapter, the authors have outlined various formulas for building value in our practices. When I began my career forty-plus years ago, this formula was not discussed. It was expected that we would be examples of what we espoused—i.e., we would be financially successful. Therefore, we prepared for a successful retirement. Was I recently surprised to find that there was also financial value in my practice? Absolutely! Bonus time!

So, while I'm mindful and grateful that I did take various forms of calculated risks and that I reflect daily on this quandary of life, I now find that the greatest compensation from my work is psychological. I am convinced that my life's work will positively affect my insureds'/investors' lives in many ways for several years. There is even a possibility that this good will be intergenerational. I have left something behind. I am prosperous.

> ### Rick's Story—From the Buyer's Vantage Point: The Financial and Psychological Value of an Advisor's Legacy
>
> Richard D. Schultenover, CFP®, Senior Financial Advisor and Partner, The Vitality Group, North Star Resource Group
>
> Working with Paul on a transition strategy for his practice has been an exciting experience. We hit it off almost instantly, and after nearly two years of communicating (both with Paul and his clients), I feel a great sense of accomplishment—not only in seeing my practice grow and strengthen, but also in seeing Paul's legacy continue on through me.
>
> In Paul's forty-plus-year career, he has built significant relationships and a massive amount of trust with the families he has served. I have some very big shoes to fill as Paul closes this chapter in his life, and I am humbled and honored that he is trusting me with his life's work. It has also been very humbling to see how open his clients have been to be "handed off" to me with little resistance. This speaks volumes about Paul, as his final recommendation to clients is to put their trust in someone they've only just met...especially after building such a close friendship with Paul.

Applying the Concepts to *Your* Practice on Purpose

1. What do you want your practice to be worth when you retire (or rewire)? Write down a specific number.

   _____
   _____
   _____
   _____
   _____
   _____

2. Do you have a buy/sell agreement in place? If not, when will you commit to getting one prepared?

3. If your practice has at least $1 million in gross revenue, have you ever had a valuation conducted by an independent firm? If you are at that level, when will you commit to having a valuation done?

4. Are you at a point with your practice that you should consider investing in another team member to hand off some of those tasks you don't enjoy? Should that investment be for a part-time or full-time addition? If premature now, when should you consider this action?

5. To what extent do you think you see your practice as others see it and recognize its true value? If you do not think you can assess its value objectively, whom can you ask to help you assess it?

___

___

___

___

___

___

Where the World Is Going

CHAPTER 9

We have discussed the many ways in which you and your clients benefit when they are engaged in a financial advice relationship. We know this is a better way to run a practice, and we know it is the type of practice your top clients deserve. But what you may not realize is that someday, *this may be the only way you can be an advisor in this country.*

We think that in the future, advice will become the standard, and product compensation will become obsolete.

Larry Barton, PhD, CAP®, Chancellor of The American College, believes the consequence of regulations or legislation preventing commissions on financial products will merely result in middle-class Americans being left without advice or needed products. This presents a significant opportunity for advisors to provide value to millions of Americans.

We only need to look beyond our shores to see this coming. In several countries, legislation has been enacted that essentially outlaws product compensation. The UK, Netherlands, and Australia have enacted outright or partial bans on commission payments to financial advisors, while regulators in Canada, Hong Kong, and Singapore have decided to increase disclosures about fees paid by investors.[50] Here are some examples of recent regulatory changes worldwide:

1. In Australia, a ban was enacted on product commissions, volume-based benefits, asset-based fees on borrowed funds, and volume-related shelf-space fees as of July 1, 2013.[51]

> "Progress is impossible without change, and those who cannot change their minds cannot change anything."
>
> —**George Bernard Shaw**
> Irish Playwright

---

50. Chris Flood, "Fighting Financial Product Mis-Selling," FT.com (Financial Times, UK), last modified February 21, 2014, http://www.ft.com/intl/cms/s/0/af1ab8e0-9a4f-11e3-8e06-00144feab7de.html.

51. "Future of Financial Advice, PWC (Australia) website, http://www.pwc.com.au/industry/financial-services-regulation/fofa.htm.

2. In the Netherlands, the Dutch parliament agreed to a complete ban on inducements under an amendment to the country's Market Conduct Supervision Decree. The ban went into effect on January 1, 2014. The new rules, which affect portfolio management, investment advice, and execution-only services, apply only to retail investors. A ban on inducements for mortgages and life insurance policies sold by banks was already in force in the Netherlands.[52]

3. In Finland, the Finnish Insurance Mediation Act prohibits payment of insurers' commissions to brokers. The broker is able to receive fees from the client. The provision covers both life and nonlife activities and business with retail and corporate clients.[53]

4. In the UK, the UK Retail Distribution Review has imposed an educational mandate. Before beginning to practice, advisors must obtain a qualification that can involve extensive study and multiple exams. They also must complete thirty-five hours of continuing education each year.[54]

5. Two proposals being discussed in the United States would impose a "fiduciary standard" on advisors, requiring them to always put client interests ahead of their own. Currently, many advisors working for brokerages are required only to make recommendations that are "suitable," but not necessarily best, for their clients.[55]

6. In Singapore, where Phil and Ed recently spoke at GAMA Asia, this is *the* topic. In September 2013, the Monetary Authority of Singapore (MAS) issued its response to the public consultation on the recommendations of the Financial Advisory Industry Review (FAIR). The purpose of the review, which began in April 2012 with the appointment of the FAIR Panel, was to raise the standards and professionalism of the financial advisory (FA) industry and enhance the market efficiency for the distribution of life insurance and investment products in Singapore. The FAIR Panel's recommendations were published in January 2013 and were open for public consultation from March to June 2013. The majority of the responses received from the

---

52. Attracta Mooney, "Netherlands Enacts Ban on Inducements," FT.com, last modified December 26, 2013, http://www.ft.com/intl/cms/s/0/4f8bc83a-6e33-11e3-8dff-00144feabdc0.html#axzz2uqNMjfBu.

53. "Finnish Act on Intermediation and the Remuneration Model for Brokers," last modified March 20, 2013, http://www.sven-giegold.de/wp-content/uploads/2013/03/EP-Breakfast-Finish-contribution.pdf.

54. Robert C. Pozen, "Regulators Ban Financial Advice Fees and Conflicts," Brookings.edu, last modified September 9, 2013, http://www.brookings.edu/research/opinions/2013/09/09-financial-regulator-ban-advising-fees-pozen.

55. Ibid.

public consultation were in support of the recommendations made by the FAIR Panel. Of the FAIR Panel's twenty-eight recommendations, MAS has fully accepted nineteen, modified eight, and dropped one.[56]

The new requirements will apply only to FA firms and representatives serving retail clients, except where it is otherwise stated. However, FA representatives who work only with accredited and institutional investors are strongly encouraged to adopt similar standards. This legislation to ban product compensation was tabled for two years due to a push back from the financial services industry. That is fully expected to be a temporary status, however, and it is widely anticipated that the ban will be back in the next few years.

In an October 2013 news release, the Life Insurance Association of Singapore (LIA) said the industry welcomed the MAS's Response to Public Consultation on Recommendations of the Financial Advisory Industry Review, stating that it is another milestone in the evolution of the life insurance industry in driving best outcomes for consumers as well as the industry. The press release included this statement that highlights the value of ongoing financial advice: "Customised life insurance solutions require highly qualified advice at the time of purchase and personalised service long after the purchase on an ongoing basis."[57]

> Major regulatory changes will be implemented in Singapore in 2015.

One of the authors of this book, Phil Richards, is close friends with Mr. Mohd Amin, who is the CEO of MAA Financial Planning in Singapore. Mr. Amin has been in the life insurance industry in Singapore for more than fifty years. He spent many years with Prudential Assurance and Great Eastern Life. He is a Fellow of the Life Underwriters Association of Singapore, and he was the first Singaporean to receive the designation of Chartered Insurance Agency Manager (CIAM). He has spoken at many seminars and conventions, both in Singapore and abroad, and he has won many prestigious industry awards. He was the first Asian to serve as a board member of GAMA International.

---

56. "MAS Issues Response to Consultation on Recommendations of Financial Advisory Industry Review," Monetary Authority of Singapore, last modified September 30, 2013, http://www.mas.gov.sg/News-and-Publications/Press-Releases/2013/MAS-Issues-Response-to-Consultation-on-Recommendations-of-Financial-Advisory-Industry-Review.aspx.

57. "Life Insurance Association Backs MAS Proposals to Raise Financial Adviser Competency," *Singapore Business Review*, last modified October 1, 2013, http://sbr.com.sg/financial-services/more-news/life-insurance-association-*backs-mas-proposals-raise-financial-adviser-.

Mr. Amin is witnessing the radical shift in the financial-planning industry in Singapore. Here are his observations: "Major regulatory changes will be implemented in Singapore in 2015. It is very timely and appropriate that your new book on fees instead of commission could be introduced to our advisers. Earlier, the Monetary Authority of Singapore, the regulators, had wanted to abolish commission payment but due to unfavourable feedback, they decided to postpone the idea."

It is for this reason that the AFA of Singapore invited the three authors of this book to be the keynote speakers of its annual conference in Singapore in July 2014, where this book will be introduced for the first time.

Driven by Consumers More than the Government

In some countries, this trend toward a ban on product compensation is driven by the regulators and the legislatures. In the United States, the regulators and legislatures have struggled with implementing the Dodd–Frank legislation five years after its introduction. We expect the movement to a fee environment in the United States to be driven more by consumer interests and industry pressure than by government regulation.

> We expect the movement to a fee environment in the United States to be driven more by consumer interests and industry pressure than by government regulation.

A 2014 *InvestmentNews* article says a number of forces are pushing the advice sector toward customer loyalty and care. An executive of a fiduciary care firm said, "I think it's a combination not only of the regulatory pressure but also the competitive pressures and client demand."[58]

The Registered Investment Advisor (RIA)-only platform is the most rapidly growing way for advisors to work with affluent clients. They are particularly forward in representing the fiduciary standard as they compete for the mass affluent and the simply affluent. The transparency inherent in having the advisor represent only the best interests of the client has a strong appeal to both advisors and consumers.

Our industry has a history characterized by commission products being king. But now, instead of "buyer beware," it's "seller beware." It is the age of the consumer. Consumers today have unprecedented information, power,

---

58. Mark Schoeff, Jr., "Facing Down the Inevitable Fiduciary Standard," *InvestmentNews*, last modified April 6, 2014.

and choices. Some of us will remember 8 percent mutual fund compensation and when life insurance had relevant trail compensation. Today it's essentially an A share. We know there is significant downward pressure on wrap fees. There has been considerable discussion on imposing breakpoints in the wrap business, and some companies have wisely introduced their own breakpoint formulas. We are all aware of the discussion around 12b-1's and questions about their relevance. They were originally introduced to help the mutual fund industry get off the ground. Financial products are truly open-market commodities. This is good for the consumer. Our concern here, however, is that this trend may not be good for the middle class, who may be more resistant to the payment of fees. It is essential that we all work to strategize ways that include advice to this hard-working majority of our citizens.

People value transparency in service providers, especially among those who handle their money. The fee-only model provides transparency, which means that advisors will provide full disclosure to clients about their financial recommendations and services. It also means you will not withhold pertinent information related to an investor's options.

As we discussed in Chapter 3, a fee-only model optimizes the experience for your clients because it allows them to take full advantage of the knowledge, wisdom, discipline, encouragement, emotional competence, and peace of mind you provide them.

The Hybrid Advisor

A 2011 report from Charles Schwab & Co., Inc.,[59] discussed the pros and cons of a "hybrid" advisor model—one that allows an advisor to conduct both broker and advisory business. The hybrid business model is one of the fastest-growing segments of the financial advisory business. It involves both a dual revenue structure and dual registration with the US Securities and Exchange Commission or the applicable state securities regulatory authorities, as well as the Financial Industry Regulatory Authority (FINRA).

According to the report, RIA firms with dually registered advisors experienced almost three times the growth of RIA-only firms from 2004 to 2009—14.7 percent growth versus 5 percent growth. This growth, measured by the number of firms, advisor head count, and assets, is expected to continue for the next several years.

One of the drivers of this growth is the increasing competitive pressure independent broker dealers (IBDs) are experiencing to increase their assets under

---

59. Charles Schwab & Co., Inc., "Understanding the Hybrid Practice: Considerations for Advisors in Transition."

management and to respond to their advisors' desire for advisory fee solutions. As a result, many IBDs have encouraged the growth of advisory business.

The two primary practice models within the hybrid channel are as follows:

1. The semi-captive hybrid model, in which the advisor joins a corporate RIA of an independent broker–dealer (IBD)
2. The dually registered hybrid model in which the advisor starts or joins an independent registered investment advisor (RIA) firm

The report notes that a dually registered model may be a better choice than a semi-captive model for advisors who want to own their own firms or conduct an advisory-only practice. It allows advisors to own a legal entity that can be monetized and sold.

The Value of Being a Fiduciary Advisor

You are not a commodity. Your experience and wisdom, how much you care, and the discipline you bring to a family's financial resources are priceless. Without our influence and sometimes intervention, the consumer is unlikely to ever engage in one of these wonderful commodities. They need us more than ever, for reasons repeatedly presented in this book. Because we are not commodities and each advisor is unique, we present an opportunity for open-minded clients to select an advisor who fits their long-term needs and interests. Our advice takes them where they want to go.

An unfortunate fact in this business is that investments work, but investors don't. When investors involve their emotions in financial decisions, they underperform the market. Our research shows that in the twenty-year period ending in 2013, the S & P averaged an 11½ percent return, while the average investor averaged only 4½ percent. Advisors' discipline and advice were probably a factor in keeping panicked investors in the market rather than selling low.

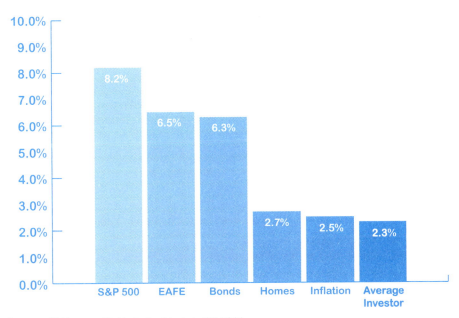

Source: JP Morgan, Guide to the Markets Q1-2014

Indexes: Bonds, Barclays Capital U.S. Aggregate Index; EAFE, MSCI EAFE; Homes, median sale price of existing single-family homes; Inflation, CPI. Average asset allocation investor return is based on an analysis by Dalbar, Inc., which utilizes the net of aggregate mutual fund sales, redemptions, and exchanges each month as a measure of investor behavior.

As an advisor, you can help your clients close that gap. You can help them avoid falling victim to doing what everyone else does, which is to panic, then buy high, sell low, and fail to insure themselves properly. So, although there is considerable downward pressure on financial product compensation, the value of your knowledge and advice is increasing in value. People are drowning in information but starved for wisdom and advice.

We just mentioned that more advisors are becoming "hybrid" advisors. They are on both a broker–dealer platform and an RIA platform and are compensated for both parts and labor, to use a car-repair analogy. Unfortunately, it also requires that they straddle the suitability world with the fiduciary world. In the suitability world, a more expensive product could still be more suitable than a less expensive one, while in the fiduciary world, it would be the most cost-effective product. We know, for example, that a more expensive/higher-fee wrap account does not necessarily perform better. For these reasons, more and more investors want to be clients of a fiduciary advisor.

A 2014 *InvestmentNews* article reported that brokers are morphing themselves into advisors. The article says, "The transition gives advisors a steadier stream of income, based on the fee charged on assets, and more closely synchronizes their welfare with that of clients: They will get paid more as their clients' accounts grow."[60]

What this means in regard to providing advice for a fee is this appears to be where the world is going. Diversifying your revenue sources to include offering service for a fee strengthens your practice, gives your clients alternatives, and, in the end, may be the only way we can or should work with affluent clients. That is why we are such strong advocates for this way of working with clients and why we are so determined to provide the leadership needed to move advisors to adopt this model.

A favorite German proverb of ours says, "A good part of the journey is already behind you once you leave your front door." Once you decide to capture the value of your advice in an ongoing advice relationship, your world and your clients' world changes for the better. It is a door that only you, the advisor, can go through, and when you do, you will not come back. You will remove the stake from the ground.

That is where the world is going. Achieving a Practice on Purpose aligns with that path. It also provides your clients with the service and advice they deserve and helps you build the personal wealth you desire.

Brad's Story: How to Grow as a Fiduciary Advisor

Brad K. North, CFP®, Financial Planner, North Star Resource Group

Advisors committed to a proactive, goals-focused, and planning-driven process will be rewarded! Plan first, strategize second! The business of an advisor is about three things: the protection of a standard of living, proactive ongoing advice, and proper execution. The right advice at the right time is the reason for our existence. A financial plan and the advice it drives will be recognized for its value in the free-market enterprise system. If you're not busy growing as a fiduciary, you're busy dying. Working as an advice-based advisor is where the entire industry is headed. As Confucius said, "Choose a job you love, and you will never have to work a day in your life."

---

60. Mark Schoeff, Jr., "Facing Down the Inevitable Fiduciary Standard," *InvestmentNews*, last modified April 6, 2014.

Applying the Concepts to *Your* Practice on Purpose

1. To what extent are you aware of the changing regulatory climate that is likely to favor advice over product compensation? What will you do to learn more about how this imminent shift in the industry may affect you and the way you manage your practice?

2. What fundamental changes will you need to make in your practice if the United States joins the ranks of those countries that have outlawed product compensation and enacted outright or partial bans on commission payments to financial advisors? Early preparation and anticipation of this shift will be critical to the survival and success of your practice in the future.

3. To what extent are you familiar with the pros and cons of a "hybrid" advisor model—one that allows an advisor to conduct both broker and advisory business? Does this model have implications for your practice?

A Time to Review and Execute

CHAPTER 10

Losing sight of the shore—venturing outside of your comfort zone to try to achieve a higher level of success—is typically scary but usually rewarding. It is thrilling for us when we work with an advisor who has a $250,000 practice and are able to lead him or her to build a practice worth two to four times that much. It is actually a quite logical process. There is no mystery to it—except for the mystery surrounding why some advisors have stayed at the same performance plateau for years without progressing, even though they have all of the tools they need to serve more clients.

Let's review the key concepts we have discussed so far.

> "You can never cross the ocean until you have the courage to lose sight of the shore."
>
> **—Christopher Columbus**

What Is Your Purpose?

We started our discussion by challenging you to know your purpose. Why are you here? What is your purpose? Where do your passions combine with your skills and then create financial rewards and eventual wealth? How are you using that combination to help people improve their financial situations?

What Are Your Values?

We then moved on to consider the values that underpin that purpose. Values matter; you can feel it when you are aware of your values and when your practice aligns with them. We are all driven by our values. This is true whether you articulate them and know them or they are under the surface and in your subconscious. We mentioned how a deck of values cards can help you select your five most important values from the deck of fifty. Once you know your values, you can articulate your vision for the future.

What Is an Exceptional Client Experience?

How can you bring those values to the good for the people who have chosen to work with you and have let you into their lives? What is an exceptional client experience? What would we want if we were in their position?

What Is the Value of Your Financial Advice?

Advice is the product of formal learning and the lessons of life experiences. Advice is knowledge in action, applied to a real situation that improves an outcome. Your clients who are receptive benefit magnificently from your advice. You guide them so they can make better decisions about their money and with their money. This advice has its own value to your clients and in the marketplace. The impact of this advice dwarfs the value of product solutions. Without your expertise, clients do not know which products are in their best interests, they will not have the sustained discipline to take action, and they will not know if they are getting further away or closer to their goals. The true meaning of your work is captured in your advice.

> Advice is knowledge in action.

How Do You Acquire People You Can Help the Most?

We cannot help people we do not meet. The key to a Practice on Purpose is to work with the people you can help the most. Not everyone should be in your practice. One of the reasons this is a great profession is that only those people with the "big five" traits can find enough of the right people. The ladder of success is not crowded at the top. We discussed some of the timeless ways to identify and attract the right people to your work, and we discussed some of the new ways social media and crafted events can lead you to these people.

What Is the Best Design for Your Practice?

Your Practice on Purpose is a business. Not only do you have to be a great financial advisor; you have to be an effective business owner as well. We discussed the evolution from being a solo practitioner to being a CEO. We discussed the value of building a team of people whose skills complement yours. We discussed the value of clients being clients of the practice so that they can realize a greater value proposition. And we shared our thoughts regarding the growth of a practice that produces increasing amounts of recurring revenue, even during your absence. This is the superior method of building value in your practice instead of creating a labor-intensive model that is little more than a job that no one wants to buy.

What Causes the Practice to Grow?

The practice grows when the advisor grows. This is a fundamental premise of the Practice on Purpose. The advisor is the engine that moves the practice. (You cannot outperform your self-image.) The advisor has the vision, the expectations, the talent, and the passion to grow. The growth can be sustainable, predictable, and serve the best interests of the client as well as the advisor.

You are what you think about, and what you think about is rooted in your values. Your character, applied, becomes the destiny of your practice. Greek philosopher Heraclitus said, "A man's character is his fate."

What Are the Traits of the Most Successful Advisors?

To be a successful financial advisor is to live large. We know it takes drive, it takes someone who is responsible, it takes someone who is independent and confident, it takes someone who authentically cares about the well-being of others, and it takes someone who is rugged and durable.

What Is Your Life's Work Worth?

We discussed the monetary value that can be derived from your practice. This is in contrast to the good that advisors do for their clients and their community. Here we looked at how value is created by a strong client service experience, the development of multiple streams of revenue from a variety of services, building a significant recurring revenue stream that is worth multiples of annual revenue, and then value from ongoing business operations. We discussed the structure of business continuation arrangements, including buy/sells, purchase agreements, financial arrangements, and successors.

Although most advisors have an idea that their practice has value, few do practice valuations routinely or know what drives practice value, and even fewer have a value number tied to a retirement or net-worth goal. Deriving value from your practice while doing good for others is to have a Practice on Purpose that honors your professional accumulated value.

Where Do We Go from Here?

When I first graduated from the University of Minnesota, I joined what was then the Minnesota Mutual Life Insurance Company. I relocated to Seattle, Washington. As part of my responsibilities, I called on mortgage bankers. On a cold, rainy day, I found myself in the office of a banker in Bellingham, Washington. On his wall was an attractively framed quote from William Thompson: "At the edge of history, the future is blowing wildly in our faces…sometimes brightening the air and sometimes blinding us."

That was many years ago, and it started my habit of collecting quotes on recipe cards. That collection today contains more than 250 pearls of wisdom that became part of me and the words I use. A few are included throughout this book.

The future is bright for financial advisors and our profession. We are needed more than ever, and there are fewer of us than there were ten years ago. People need our comprehensive financial advice and our guidance in implementing product solutions that meet a fiduciary standard. This important point bears repeating: Most people will earn a fortune in their lifetimes, but without a financial advisor, few people will have anything to show for it. Our advice is timeless. Short of a surgeon or a religious leader, few people will have as great an impact on an individual or a family as we will.

What may be blinding us is the way we do this work. Product compensation continues to thin and compress. As we have discussed, in some countries, product compensation is no longer an option. Regulators and legislators, in the interest of pursuing what is transparent, compensation-agnostic, and consumer-centric, have brought us to the doorstep of the financial advisor model.

Hopefully this book has provided a working template of this model. We have built it on the chassis of creating a practice that serves your purpose in this life and is run on purpose so that you lead the practice and it does not lead you. In the end, we hope you achieve the practice you desire and your clients deserve. And remember, building a Practice on Purpose is a door that only you can go through.

Clarisa's Story: When You Know the "Why," You Can Handle Any "How"

Clarisa M. Hernandez, Partner, North Star Resource Group

I am the daughter of Mexican immigrants, and that has shaped my worldview. When my brother, sister, and I were growing up in Arizona, we didn't have a lot of money. As immigrants with limited resources, my parents believed the number one gateway to success is a good education. They made it their top priority to get us into the best schools—Xavier, an all-girls' Catholic high school, for my sister and me, and Brophy, an all-boys' Catholic high school, for my brother. We couldn't afford the tuition, so we were on financial aid. Because of my parents' efforts, we were exposed to a high caliber of success and academic excellence, and our peers were aiming for a higher degree of academic excellence than students in other schools. My parents put us in that environment and exposed us to that life, and I did well as a result.

(continued)

Clarisa's Story: When You Know the "Why," You Can Handle Any "How" (continued)

I am grateful, so I want to give back, to pay it forward. Philanthropic causes are an essential part of who I am. But when I first got out of college, I was not in a position to give money to my former school. When you first come into this business, you're broke. All you've got is your drive!

Then, while working with the Xavier and Brophy alumni associations, doing financial planning presentations, I found out that instead of paying the premium (sales) tax to the state, insurance companies in some states have the option to redirect those dollars as a charitable contribution to qualifying educational institutions. I had just started my career and did not feel comfortable about going to the various insurance companies we work with to ask them to donate funds to the high schools. Phil [Richards] rallied for the cause and put me in front of people in key roles at several insurance companies. I asked them if they would consider Xavier and Brophy as the recipients of some of these charitable donations. A handful of them agreed to do so. As a result, we have raised more than $120,000 for my family's former high schools. All of that money goes toward students' tuition—no buildings or faculty salaries, just tuition.

Through this arrangement, I was able to give a lot more money to the schools, a lot sooner, than I would have been able to do on my own.

When I was a kid, my dad found out he had stage 4 melanoma. He was diagnosed as terminally ill for a long time. We were living off of private disability insurance. He had no benefits through his job; he was a business owner. For two years, our family of five lived on $1,500 a month. Forget having vacations—putting food on the table was our concern for a long time. My father was a miracle case—he was one of the 10 percent of people who survive that type of cancer. He got us back on track, and our family stayed together.

My parents, as immigrants, were learning the system from the ground up. Somewhere along the line, someone told them, "You should get disability insurance." I am so grateful for that because while that period of our lives was stressful, at least the mortgage was paid. They struggled for many years, so I want to help them catch up. I also want to make sure I am not in that situation. There is a fear for me that other families, just out of ignorance, will miss the opportunity to make good financial decisions. It is important for me to help as many families as I can.

If you don't have a long-term vision of what you're looking to accomplish, the day-to-day can be mundane and almost demotivating. The thing that keeps you going, and the reason you strive to progress onward and upward is having a vision of what you're looking to accomplish. For me, the only way to get there is to continue to strive to make things better—taking care of my parents and reaching a level of success that allows me to not only have a comfortable lifestyle but also to continue pay forward the opportunities that were presented to me.

Leading and Coaching Advisors: An Encore Chapter

CHAPTER 11

> "Before you are a leader, success is all about growing yourself. When you become a leader, success is all about growing others."
>
> **—Jack Welch**
> CEO of General Electric, 1981–2001

An advisor's practice contributes to his or her life's purpose. This is equally true of leaders. Just as advisors run their practices to serve *their* clients—people who need leadership regarding their finances—we, as leaders, run our Practices on Purpose to serve *our* clients—advisors who need or want guidance in leading their practices.

And just as the advisor's personal sense of purpose drives the purpose of his or practice, yours should as well.

What Does *Your* Practice on Purpose Look Like?

Articulating your specific purpose and communicating it consistently and often allows everyone around you to understand your motives and help you achieve them. Leaders repeat, repeat, and repeat.

I carry around two purposes in my head when I lead advisors:

1. **To leave advisors better than I found them**—We are all passing through each other's lives. As Shakespeare said, "All the world is a stage, and each of us has our entrances and exits. In our time, we will play many roles." No matter how long we work with our advisors and the various roles we play to support them, we should challenge ourselves to leave them collectively and individually better than we found them.

2. **To allow myself to grow and be better as an individual because of my relationship with these advisors and their leaders**—How much you grow is a product of how much you want to grow, how open you are to not being perfect, and how passionate you are about being a "learning animal."

We are running practices, too. Our clients are our advisors, and we can run our businesses on purpose and with a purpose. As a field leader, you have a choice to decide what your own Practice on Purpose will look like and how you will execute your leadership skills. It's about being intentional and engaged.

North Star's Coaching Approach

Field leaders take financial advisors to a place they probably would not go on their own—a place where they might not even know they need to be or realize they can be. Advisors who have at least five years in the business and at least $250,000 of gross revenue are succeeding in a difficult, highly competitive, and ever-changing industry. The next question—one you can help them answer—is how and why they will continue to be in the business.

Coaching advisors to create Practices on Purpose is what the three of us do on a daily basis, and it is what makes North Star what it is today and what it will be tomorrow.

When we enter into a coaching relationship with an advisor, we have found that it is helpful to be specific about defining what the advisor can expect. We are deliberate in our expectation that both parties—the advisor and the coach—have ownership of the outcome. If the advisor is not working on this as hard as we are, the relationship will not work.

When advisors at North Star learn that we are here to contribute to taking their practices to the next level, they are not sure what our coaching approach involves. We have been asked about this so often that we created the following summary of the key actions we take when working with advisors.

Advisor Coaching Approach

North Star Resource Group

1. Listening, observing, and exploring

We work together to think broadly and creatively to define what you want from your practice. Why are you an advisor? What does it mean to your clients? We will discuss your readiness for change and your responsiveness to coaching. Are you running a Practice on Purpose, or is the practice running you?

(continued)

Advisor Coaching Approach (continued)

2. Defining values and vision

We will identify what we are trying to accomplish. What is the picture of success for you? Is there a point of arrival? What are your personal values, and how does your practice align with those values? What are your five core values?

3. Conducting a preliminary analysis

Where is your practice today? How many clients do you serve? What is your product mix? What does your client-service model look like? What do your client segmentation, gross revenue, marketing, and new-client-acquisition strategy look like? What is your tenure as an advisor? What is the history of your results?

4. Defining priorities and specific goals

What are the key strengths you can leverage? Where are the weaknesses you need to address? Where are your greatest opportunities? What threats need to be mitigated? Where do you want to be in one, two, and three years on key metrics?

5. Identifying, evaluating, and implementing action steps

What are three key actions that will move the practice ahead? What are you authentically committed to doing that will change the future and increase the value of your practice? What does your Practice on Purpose look like?

6. Tracking progress, taking corrective action, and celebrating success

We are focused on taking a keen interest in your practice. It's not about accountability; it's about you getting what you want. If you are working as hard as we are on your practice, you will bend your growth curve.

7. Posing a challenge for your personal growth

When the advisor grows, the practice will grow as well. We review the energy around growing, deepening, and honoring your five core values.

8. Conducting an annual review and assessment

Once a year, we will conduct a deep dive to look at the big picture again. We will review your values, goals, and progress on key metrics; establish next year's goals; adjust action steps; and repeat these eight steps.

Thought Leadership

A good way to supplement your coaching is to infuse your firm with thought leadership from industry speakers. At North Star, we regularly invite well-known, highly respected industry speakers to share their wisdom and knowledge with our advisors and management team. The following list includes some of the industry experts who have spoken at our Summer Summit meetings over the past eight years. Please get in touch with us if you would like their contact information.

- David Alarid
- Nate Bennett
- Jack Bobo
- Conk Buckley
- Rich Campe
- Dr. Richard Caselli
- Lou Cassera
- Mike Conley
- Nate Crowther
- Joey Davenport
- Steve Earhart
- Mark Feldman
- Mike Gabrielian
- Michael Goldberg
- Tony Gordon
- Steve Hammer
- Phil Harriman
- Harry Hoopis
- John Huggard
- Joe Jordan
- Garry Kinder
- Bob Krumroy
- Doug Lennick
- Norm Levine
- Jim Mars
- Jim McCormick
- Van Mueller
- Chris Noonan
- Mark Rooney
- Bob Savage
- Tim Schmidt
- Bob Senkler
- Jim Shoemaker
- Charlie Smith
- Maury Stewart
- Gene Storms
- Bob Veninga
- Athan Vorilas
- Norb Winter
- David Woods

Splitting Their Atom and Worshipping the Deity within Them

In a nuclear reaction, unstable atoms are split apart, and when the bonds that held the atom together come apart, tremendous energy is released. What causes the atom to split is a strong outside influence. What makes them vulnerable is the fact that they are ready to be split, and what creates the energy is the freeing of old bonds. This is how we think about coaching advisors. If we can find that "atom" in an advisor that can be and needs to be split, it's our calling to extract that energy and help them release it.

In some Far Eastern cultures, a common greeting is for a person to place his palms together in front of his chest and then lower his head toward you.

In doing so, he is worshipping the deity that is in you, acknowledging the God that is in you. When we lead advisors, we are recognizing the potential that is inside of them.

Ten Touches

In Chapter 7, we referenced ruggedness as one of the top five traits of successful advisors. Ameriprise had a Senior Vice President named Brian Heath. He has since retired and runs a winery in Texas. Brian was the personification of ruggedness, and I learned many things from him. The most important was the Ten Touches Rule. Its premise is that until you have made ten touches (interactions with an advisor) or ten "deposits" into an advisor's development, you are not going to influence him, nor do you have a right to influence him. Leadership with an advisor is earned.

The touches can be many kinds of interactions, big and small. You can refer a prospect to advisors, go to their children's soccer games, fix a problem with a product company, bring them a sales idea, give them a book on a topic that interests them, give them a heads-up that their wedding anniversary is approaching (particularly good for guys), match them to a practice for sale, or find them junior advisors. We tend to stay away from activities like golf, sporting events, and dinners and focus more on practice- and family-related touches.

When I was a new advisor, I received a memorable personal touch from one of the best new-advisor leaders I have ever known, John McConneloug. He flew out to see me shortly after I moved to Seattle right out of college and rode with me for several days while I visited clients and prospects. Then he returned to Minnesota, where my parents also lived. Over the weekend, without my knowledge, John called my parents to tell them how well I was doing and that they should be proud of me. He also asked if there was anything he could do for them to help them adjust to my move away from home. That was a big touch. You don't leave companies like that, and you never forget people like that.

Think about touches you can make that will make a significant positive impact in your advisors' lives.

Advisors Know when It's Not about Them

In Chapter 7, we noted C. S. Lewis's definition of humility: "Humility is not thinking less of yourself but thinking of yourself less." To be an effective leader requires humility.

There is an old story that demonstrates a colossal lack of humility. A sales manager takes a new advisor recruit out for a drive. He drives by the top country club in town and says to the recruit, "I want you to look at that and really take it in." Then he drives past the most prestigious neighborhood in town, points to a house high on the hill, and says, "I want you to look at that mansion and really take it in." Finally, he drives to the marina on the lake, points to a large cabin cruiser, and says, "See that? Think about that. What I want you to know is that if you work really hard and do what I ask, someday that country club membership, that home, and that boat will all be mine."

Advisors have sharp sensors for detecting when it is not about them, when they are not your top priority. Being authentic and real is the only way to build sustainable trust and relationships. Advisors don't expect leaders to be perfect. They do, and should, expect that we have their best interests at heart.

Someone interviewed Celine Dion, the singer, once, and asked her, "What's your favorite song?"

Her answer was, "Whatever song I'm singing at the time."

That is a great example of being intentional and self-aware—being in the moment.

Who is your favorite advisor? The one you are speaking with at the moment. To feel and act any other way is a disservice to that advisor.

Joel Barker, the futurist mentioned in Chapter 1, tells the story of a runner on a beach who stoops down to toss starfish back into the ocean one at a time while he runs. A stranger stops him and says, "You cannot possibly make a difference with all those starfish washed up on the shore."

The runner tossed another starfish into the ocean and replied, "Tell it to that one."

Every advisor matters.

Buy a Ticket

An elderly man is plagued with myriad family and financial worries. Every week, he goes to the chapel and pleads with his god that he has to win the lottery. He pleads passionately every time, and this goes on for years. One day when he goes into the chapel, drops to his knees, and is about to start his plea, a booming voice comes out of the ceiling and says, "This is God. You have to meet me halfway. Buy a ticket!"

We have all had advisors in our lives who just wouldn't put in enough effort for us to help them. When you conduct advisor meetings, you have probably looked out at the audience and seen what I call the "arm crosses." In just about every group of advisors, there will be a few sitting in their chairs with their arms crossed, skepticism written all over their faces, waiting for you to deliver. They will keep you at a distance until you can prove to them you ware worth their time.

In Phil's first book, *Twenty-Five Secrets to Sustainable Success*, is a chapter titled "Coach, Don't Coax." He notes that, as leaders trying to grow advisors and their practices, we must ask ourselves if we care more than they do about this mission. If we care more, we are coaxing, not coaching.

As leaders, it is incumbent on us to ask for and invite active engagement from our advisors. When we have the buy-in of both parties, we can arrive at a better solution. We each have to buy a ticket.

At North Star, we use a document called the Five Levels of Leadership and Problem Solving, shown below. At the lowest level of leadership, Level 1, is the person who is quick to point out the problem and attribute blame to someone else. At the most advanced level of leadership, Level 5, is the person who is fully engaged in the solution. That is the level to strive for.

Five Levels of Leadership and Problem Solving

Level of Leadership	Identifying Characteristics of the Leadership Style
Level 5	• Has a compelling vision of the future. • Anticipates challenges and opportunities. • Articulates the situation clearly. • Solicits input on decision making. • Identifies resources. • Empowers others to act. • Guides execution. • Follows up through completion.
Level 4	• Identifies the problem. • Identifies possible solutions. • Evaluates solutions. • Selects a course of action. • Gathers resources and support. • Communicates actions and the expected outcome. • Owns the outcome. • Assures execution. • Learns from the experience.
Level 3	• Identifies the problem. • Identifies possible solutions. • Evaluates solutions. • Makes a recommendation to the decision-making authority. • Supports efforts to address. • Learns from the experience.
Level 2	• Identifies the problem. • Considers some alternatives and solutions. • Shares his or her opinion with others.
Level 1	• Identifies the problem. • Attributes cause and responsibility to others.

When we coach advisors, it is all about having them be engaged in the solution and own their part of the solution. Recall the 1960s phrase, "If you are not part of the solution, you are part of the problem."

Develop an Advisor Service Model

In Chapter 2, we discussed how important it is for advisors to develop a client-service model as a tool for creating an exceptional client experience. We can apply the same model to field leaders and their advisors. That means segmenting advisors, conducting meetings with a purpose, establishing and honoring meetings at specific intervals, taking meeting notes, sending a summary of the notes to the advisors, identifying action steps before the next meeting, tracking progress against key metrics, and recognizing advisors' success.

I coach about thirty advisors every two weeks or once a month. I will disappoint them and myself if I do not take notes that include key actions for the next meeting. Last year, the advisors I coach directly had a 20 percent lift in their gross revenue. We cannot achieve these results if I do not drive the practices with documentation. Taking the meeting notes, sharing them with advisors, and following up on the action items allow me to make "touches" and to show advisors that I respect them.

Would your advisors know they are top advisors by your behavior toward them? One of our authors, Phil Richards, does this better than any field leader I know. When I coach advisors who have worked with Phil, they tell me stories of the "Phil touches" and the way he makes them feel. Every month, Phil sends every advisor his copy of their production report, along with his coaching comments. The advisors not only keep these reports; they show them to me and ask that I work with them on Phil's ideas. One of them, Tom Haunty, has every one of these notes for the past thirty years in a file in his desk. All three authors use an Advisor Engagement Model or Service Model when working with advisors.

As Ed says, you cannot manage time. Time just keeps on running along. But you can manage priorities. You can always be guided by doing the important, rather than the urgent, things. If I saw your calendar, would I know your advisors are a priority? Could I tell which ones are your top advisors?

Are You Worth Their Time?

A few years ago, I was assigned to work with a $2.3 million gross-revenue advisor. He had a reputation of being difficult and having a strong distain for field leaders. So I called him up for an appointment. He was hard to reach but eventually called me back. With attitude, he stated, "My standard fee is one thousand dollars an hour. You will have to pay me that amount because I am giving up a client meeting to see you." He ended the call by saying, "Bring your checkbook."

I walked into his office a few days later and set my checkbook on the conference table between us. We proceeded to go through his practice reports. What I knew and he did not know was that he was $20,000 away from a production bonus of 1 percent. I had a practice report that showed more than $1.2 million of cash in client accounts older than six months that could be put to use for the clients' benefit. I found where at least $20,000 of increased revenue could come from and then the $23,000 pay increase (1 percent on $2.3 million). Then I said to him, "I will need you to get out your checkbook. My hourly fee is twenty-three thousand dollars."

We never had that $1,000-dollar-an-hour discussion again. It was, however, a good lesson in perspective. That advisor was right—when leaders meet with advisors, it, in effect, costs the advisors revenue. If we challenge ourselves to discover multiples of $1,000 of increased revenue in their practice as the result of our meeting, we have won the day.

By habit, I end our coaching meetings—just as my allergist ended my appointment all those years ago—with the questions "Has this been a good meeting? Did you find value?" Or I might ask, "What were two of the best things you got from this meeting?" If I ask advisors to say it, it becomes more real to them.

You know it's working when advisors who are not working with you call and ask to meet with you because they heard something good from another of your advisors. Recently, an advisor who was reluctant to be coached asked for my help after he talked with an advisor who was experiencing success as a result of receiving coaching. I agreed to work with him and asked him, given the number of years he had been in business and the infrastructure he had in place, "Why aren't you bigger?" Then I asked him why he wanted to grow his practice. He explained that his wife had to work but did not want to. His compelling "why" was to be able to go home and tell his wife she no longer had to work. Remember, if you know the *why*, you can live any *how*.

Be a Curve Bender

Most advisors have a propensity to grow. It's in their nature. They are entrepreneurial, they want to build wealth, and they want to provide for their families. Their growth curve is usually upward and to the right. The challenge for us as leaders is to be curve benders. Can we bend their growth curve upward? Can we get them to where they want to go more quickly? Can we do it in a way that honors their values and contributes to their purpose?

It's not unusual for some advisors to have significant life challenges as they are growing their practices. They might have issues with children, aging parents, chemical dependency, divorce, personal health issues, and even financial issues. In these cases, bending the growth curve is not as important as simply keeping the curve moving to the right. Having a coach can make all the difference in encouraging them to stay in the business and continue helping people by living out their purpose.

The good news is that, in most cases, advisors can quickly navigate obstacles, get in the clear, and accelerate. It is our role as leaders and coaches to be pushing down on the accelerator right along with them.

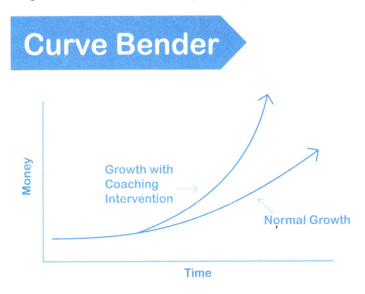

Try to Get Yourself Fired

At least once a year, I try to get myself fired by each of the advisors I coach. It's my way of testing to see if we are both still "buying tickets." As I mentioned, I try to end each meeting with a value check: "Has this been a good meeting? Can you share with me the most important thing you got from the meeting?" It is my way of verifying if I'm delivering value. Having them profess out loud that it was valuable solidifies their belief that it was indeed of value to them.

Now, here is the key. Once a year I share with the advisors I coach a full year's assessment of their progress. I will say, "We have made real progress this year. I want to ask you if you think you want to proceed on your own from here. I have enjoyed our relationship, but I don't want to overstay my welcome. What do you think we should do?"

What almost always happens is they want to keep going. Sometimes we change the frequency of the meetings or change the day, location, or other logistical details. But I have not been fired yet. I have discontinued a coaching relationship when I thought I was more engaged than the advisor was, but I have not been fired. (Yet!)

This big value check cements the relationship and assures that we are both spending our time well.

Recruit Your Own Advisors

Our first responsibility as field leaders is to recruit our own advisors—in other words, to create a supportive and dynamic environment that facilitates advisors' personal and professional growth.

Advisors who are candid with me tell me when they get recruiting calls. We should not deceive ourselves; they get calls several times a week and are heavily wooed. This is our reality. This is their reality. We cannot and should not try to control those calls. Instead of worrying about which advisors we might lose to another company, we can choose to focus on what we can control and on our strengths—our value proposition and our ability to grow advisors with that value proposition.

Other companies may have more money to offer an advisor in the short term, but they should not care more about our advisors than we do.

Build Relationships with Wholesalers

Product wholesalers are a valuable and often overlooked resource to us as field leaders. They have the same audience we do—our advisors. They can be an extension of us and can be our eyes and ears on the ground. They often give us a heads up if an advisor needs some attention or if they see things we could be doing better. They can also be a third-party advocate for us in front of our own advisors.

We reach out early in the year to our primary wholesalers to share the North Star strategic plan and our business plan for that particular year. When they know our values and goals as an organization, they can align with us and contribute to a better result. Most of these wholesalers are well trained, well educated, and frankly, extremely talented. We want them to bring practice-management tips and sales ideas to our advisors.

Wholesalers also have access to some of the leading authors, speakers, and practitioners in the country. We welcome these resources and find that it improves North Star's value proposition in front of our advisors when we secure these high-level resources they cannot get on their own. Also, wholesalers have financial resources for our advisors and for North Star; however, we are always respectful of their situation and do not "shake them down" for financial support. These are key relationships, and there is a strong wholesaler community in each of the communities we serve. We strive to earn their respect and the right to their business.

Don't Take Their "Monkey"

Field leaders often refer to advisors' problems as "monkeys"—as in "they have a monkey on their back." One of our important roles as leaders is to support advisors as they find their own solutions to problems. If we solve problems for them, we are not helping them grow. This quote admonishes us, as leaders, to encourage advisors to deal with their own monkeys: "Everyone has a monkey on their back. Don't take their monkey—don't let the monkey jump to your back. If it does, it never ends. Help them solve their monkey. If you take their monkey, they don't grow. You have all the time for them, but not their monkey."

Fix the Broken Windows

The broken-windows theory is a concept that social scientists James Q. Wilson and George L. Kelling first described in their 1982 article in *The Atlantic*.[61] They theorized that there is a significant link between disorder and crime. They used a broken window to symbolize unaccountability. They argued that if one window in a building is broken and no one replaces it, it is likely that the rest of the windows will be broken soon, too. William J. Bratton, who was New York City Mayor Rudy Giuliani's first police commissioner in 1994—and before that, the head of the New York City Transit Police—used this theory as his guiding principle in fighting crime. He had a zero-tolerance policy for petty crimes.

So if you don't care about your neighborhood, garbage is lying around, and buildings are broken down, then crime in that neighborhood is likely to increase because people figure no one really cares. But if you fix the windows, mow the lawns, and pick up the garbage, it looks like someone cares about the community. And that makes people treat it with respect.

In the world of advisor leadership, we sometimes encounter advisors who are metaphorically broken windows. They are unhappy, they are complaining, they are oppositional in meetings—that's a broken window. Or someone leaves your organization unhappy, and that can have a ripple effect. A good field leader fixes the broken windows. When people come into your environment and get the sense that people care about the organization, they will respect the environment and take care of it. If you let a broken window go unfixed for too long, your culture starts eroding. In a positive culture, broken windows are fixed.

---

61. James Q. Wilson and George L. Kelling, "Broken Windows," The Atlantic Online, March 1982, http://www.lantm.lth.se/fileadmin/fastighetsvetenskap/utbildning/Fastighetsvaerderingssystem/BrokenWindowTheory.pdf.

Encourage Advisors to Get Up Off the Nail

A traveler was walking through a town in rural America. He walked along a street lined with beautiful old homes with porches out front. As he walked by one home, he saw a big dog lying on the porch. The dog was moaning and groaning. A gentleman was rocking in a chair on the porch. The traveler asked, "Sir, is there something wrong with your dog?"

The man replied, "Yep, he is lying on a nail, and it bothers him."

"Well, why doesn't he get up and move?" the traveler asked.

"It doesn't bother him that much."

Recently, I coached an advisor who has a team-member issue. A person on his team who has worked for him for many years is preventing the advisor from taking his practice to the next level. But he will not address the issue with her because he does not want to upset her. I told him, "I will not meet with you again unless you address this issue. You just cannot lie on the nail and not do something about it. I want it to bother you a little more. Get rid of the nail."

Sometimes, our job as leaders is to recognize when advisors are lying on the proverbial nail and then nudge them to get up off of it.

Be More than a Boat Bumper

When I first started as a field leader at Ameriprise, one of our franchise consultants called me and asked me to go see him. When I walked into his office, he said to me, "I've heard good things about you, and I want to know why you would take this job. You are just a boat bumper."

I asked him to say more.

"Well, it's like this," he explained. "The home office is the dock on the shore, the advisors are the boats, and you are the white squishy thing between the boats and dock to make sure nobody gets hurt."

It was good for a laugh. But I stressed to him that I was not interested in being only a boat bumper—instead, I wanted to lead the advisors to make the boat bumper unnecessary. I wanted to reframe the relationship. He eventually became a good friend and a guy I could count on to give me real perspective.

In reality, there is an element of that in any field leadership position. Just don't let advisors make you into a full-time boat bumper.

Crabs, Eagles, and Kittens

Building a culture in which advisors feel supported starts at the top. It's our job to set that standard and to reinforce an abundance mentality—the concept that when an advisor succeeds, we all win. Unfortunately, however, some people feel threatened when others succeed.

The term "crab mentality" is used to refer to the mindset of "If I cannot have it, neither can you." We know, as leaders of advisors, that the top advisors are like eagles—they don't come in flocks. They are their own people doing it their own way. Only the best of the best pull and encourage each other to fly higher. This is in stark contrast to the "crabby" advisors who pull each other down with comments like, "That won't work. I've tried that before" or "If I had better technology, I could get more clients" or "If I had a higher payout, I'd be more successful." As leaders, we need to make sure we are not running or allowing crab barrels to fester in our organizations. We want to soar with the eagles!

In his book *The Sky Is Not the Limit*, Phil tells a story that illustrates this story well:

> As a youngster, I'd pass a Polish delicatessen on 11th Street between Avenue A and Avenue B in Manhattan, inhaling the garlic odors emanating from the pickle barrel in the store. Beside the pickle barrel was a second barrel containing live crabs. However, only one of the barrels had a lid on it, and it wasn't the crab barrel. The pickle barrel had a lid on it to keep the garlic odors inside to flavor the pickles. The crab barrel didn't need a lid because as crabs neared the lip of the barrel to try to escape, the other crabs would pull them back in. It didn't escape me that some people are a lot like those crabs, and they're the ones to avoid.[62]

After one of Phil's many speaking engagements during which he shared the crab story, a participant came up to him with an observation. He said that if you place a number of kittens in a box, they will actually help each other out of the box.

★ ★ ★ ★

You know your purpose when you get notes like the one I will tell you about now.

In the process of writing this book, I reconnected with an individual I was lucky enough to hire and work with a few years ago, Larik Hall. I enjoyed watching Larik develop during our time together. We lost contact for a few years, and then he turned up as Chief Distribution Officer for AIG in Japan. Larik wrote this note to me recently: "Your wisdom, coaching, and demonstrated leadership continue to influence my actions and decisions on an al-

---

62. Richards, *The Sky Is Not the Limit*, 217.

most daily basis." To me, this is what it's all about. I'm fortunate to have met Larik and many others who have written and spoken grateful words to me over the years.

Closing Thought

All three of us have grown as much as, if not more than, the people who have let us into their lives. And that is the ultimate reward for doing what we do. Remember the Jack Welch quote at the beginning of this chapter: "Before you are a leader, success is all about growing yourself. When you become a leader, success is all about growing others."

We wish you great rewards as you lead advisors to conquering plateaus, achieving $1 million Practices on Purpose, and leaving client legacies that make our communities and world a better place.

Applying the Concepts to *Your* Practice on Purpose

1. What is your fundamental purpose as a leader who coaches and develops advisors?

   _____
   _____
   _____
   _____
   _____
   _____

2. In what ways do you "touch" your advisors to build trust and rapport with them? List some interactions you could initiate that you have never used before. Think of interactions that will make a significant impact on your advisors—personalized touches they will remember for a lifetime.

   _____
   _____
   _____
   _____
   _____
   _____

3. Will you commit to developing an Advisor Service Model? If so, when do you commit to completing and implementing it? Your model can include guidelines for segmenting advisors, conducting meetings with a purpose, establishing and honoring meetings at specific intervals, taking meeting notes, sending a summary of the notes to the advisors, identifying action steps before the next meeting, tracking progress against key metrics, and recognizing advisors' success.

_____
_____
_____
_____
_____
_____

4. How do you build value in your organization in a way that makes advisors want to stay on board and resist offers from other firms?

_____
_____
_____
_____
_____
_____

5. How strong are your relationships with product wholesalers? To what extent do you partner with them and rely on them to be advocates for you in front of your advisors? What specific steps can you take to build closer working relationships with wholesalers?

_____
_____
_____
_____
_____
_____

Appendix
Supporting Documents

Chapter 1

No supporting documents.

Chapter 2
North Star Resource Group Sample Service Menu

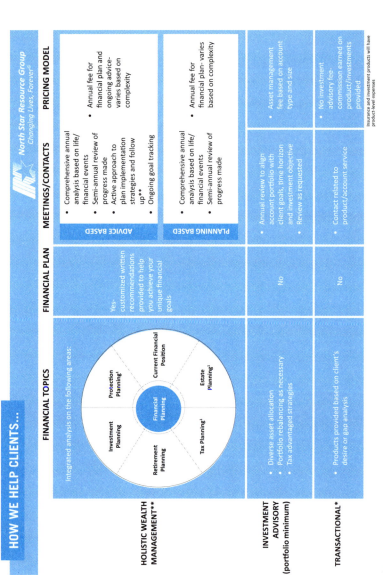

PERSONAL SERVICE RELATIONSHIPS

ACCOUNT TYPE	DESCRIPTION OF SERVICES	FEE RANGE
	FINANCIAL PLANNING SERVICES**	

COMPLEX	This level of service is appropriate for household incomes greater than $500,000 or a net worth in excess of $4,000,000. Services at this level include:
	• Semi-annual Review
	  – 2 to 3 meetings per calendar year
	  – Extensive meeting preparation work
	  – 2 Net Worth statements per year (mid-year & year-end)
	• Elite Reporting Package: (not less than once per year)
	  – Review of planning goals
	  – Analysis of existing financial plan
	  – Updated retirement analysis as needed
	  – Comparative Net Worth Statement
	  – Detailed Balance Sheet (E-Money)
	  – Investment Report (E-Money, Asset Allocation)
	• E-money access
	• Written Financial Plan and Recommendations
		$3,600 to $5,000 annually

INTERMEDIATE	This level of service is appropriate for household incomes greater than $250,000 or a net worth in excess of $2,000,000. Services at this level include:
	• Annual Review
	  – 1 meeting per calendar year
	  – 1 conference call per calendar year
	  – Extensive meeting preparation work
	  – 1 Net Worth statement per year (year-end)
	• Premium Reporting Package (choose up to 3 from Elite Reporting Package)
	• E-money access
	• Written Financial Plan and Recommendations
		$2,100 to $3,000 annually

BASIC	This level of service is appropriate for individuals or families seeking basic financial planning services such as Retirement Planning, Protection Planning, Investment Planning, Current Financial Position, etc. Services at this level include:
	• Annual Review
	  – 1 meeting per calendar year
	  – Meeting preparation work
	• Written Recommendation
		$1,500 annually

Choosing How to Work With Your Advisor

Every client prefers to work with his or her financial advisor differently. Use the chart below to evaluate your options, and determine what type of relationship will allow your financial advisor to best serve you.

RELATIONSHIP TYPE	TRANSACTIONAL	INVESTMENT ADVISORY	FINANCIAL PLANNING
SERVICES	Provide investment and insurance recommendations on accounts and assets	Provide proactive investment advice utilizing one of several investment advisory accounts and investment approaches	Provide detailed, integrated analysis of your personal financial goals and present recommendation designed to help you achieve them
FINANCIAL TOPICS	Advice on specific brokerage investments and insurance products based on your time frame, risk tolerance and investment objective	Ongoing investment advice and recommendations for assets held within the selected accounts based on your time frame, risk tolerance, and investment objective	Advice on key financial planning areas: • Cash and liabilities • Protection • Investments • Education • Accumulation Distribution • Tax strategies • Retirement • Estate planning • Business planning
MEETINGS / CONTACTS	Generally one meeting per year	Generally two meetings per year; minimum of 1	Generally two to four meetings per year; more in the first year
FINANCIAL PLAN?	No	No; however, you receive written investment advice on assets held within selected accounts	Yes – written recommendations on agreed upon areas of focus, along with goal tracking over time[1]
FEES	Sales loads, trading commissions, or compensation based on purchase of insurance product(s)	Asset-based fee; amount varies based on services selected, account size and your needs	Fixed or flat fee based on case complexity and your circumstances

[1] Goal tracking over time only available if ongoing financial planning is chosen.
Separate from the financial plan and our role as financial planner, we may recommend the purchase of specific investment or insurance products or accounts. These product recommendations are not part of the financial plan and you are under no obligation to follow them.

Fifty Meetings with a Purpose

In January 2014, I wrote an article for North Star's *Navigator* newsletter titled "Fifty Meetings with a Purpose." It discusses the benefits of conducting purposeful meetings with your top fifty clients.

What would happen if you had Fifty Meetings with a Purpose with the top fifty clients in your practice in the next ninety days? Most of the advisors I am fortunate to coach know the answer and are well on their way to making this real. The call to action is to engage with clients in the top quartile of your practice in the first quarter of the New Year. Here is why this could get you off to a fast start and well on your way to having your next year be your best year yet for you and your clients.

First, do you know which clients are in the top quarter? It's not unusual for advisors to not have a complete picture of who is in this group and why they are in this group. We have access to practice-management reports we can use to discover clients' revenue generated, assets under management, protection in place, cash on the sidelines, and other useful information. You get to pick the criteria, even down to who are the best referring clients. It's your practice, and it's your choice.

Next, once we know who these clients are, we can begin to develop a contact strategy. Who needs a face-to-face meeting? Should you call, or can your team call? Do they prefer conference calls or Fuze calls? Do they meet in your office or at their office or home? Have a specific contact method identified for each of the fifty households.

Then reach out and get them on your calendar for the next ninety days. If you need a script, it could be as simple as "It's the start of a New Year, and we would like to review your goals, look at progress we have made in the past year, and identify work that needs to be done to get you closer to those goals. What day works best for us to meet?"

Prepare a Discussion Agenda

When the client comes in, have a typed agenda that could look like this:

- Name of client and date of meeting at top of the page
- What is new since we last met? (Job changes, children updates, retirement, changes in employer benefits, tax returns, health, vacations, graduations, homes, a second home, etc.)
- Goal restatements and updates: "Is it still important to be able to make work an option by the time you are fifty-five?" "Is it still important to fund 75 percent of your children's education?" "Do you want to create a scholarship in your name at your college?" "Do you want a warm-climate vacation place?"

- Financial progress in investments since last year
- Protection review and any updates
- Review of financial plan implementation steps
- Simple retirement projection: "If we want to replace 80 percent of your family income in retirement in twenty years, what do you need to put aside each month?"
- Next meeting date and topics

Theme Your Meetings

Consider having a theme for your meetings from this point forward. While you can have a standard template of topics to be covered, I recommend that you have a specific theme during parts of the year. Let's start with retirement because this is virtually a universal desire and a place where you can make a huge impact. The Report on Retirement Statistics from the US Census Bureau indicates that average retirement savings of a fifty-year-old is $43,797. We know at least two things from this number: First, it is not enough money for retirement, and second, people with this amount of savings did not have an advisor providing them with retirement planning advice.

Run a basic retirement projection for each of the fifty meetings, regardless of your clients' ages. You have access to simple calculators. Make this a topic. It will lead to increased investment assets, protection sales, and financial advice fees. The theme for the second half of the year could be a protection review. Make an inventory of all protection in place and ask your client, "How do you know this is still the right amount and type of coverage? Would you like me to look into that?"

Reasons to Have Fifty Meetings with a Purpose

Here are eight good reasons to consider conducting fifty meetings with a purpose:

1. Your clients want you to be engaged and provide leadership to their situation.
2. They want meetings that are all about them and their goals.
3. They want meetings in which you come to understand their situation and what is important to them.
4. You will shield your clients and your practice from the competition. If your clients are not hearing from you in a proactive manner, they are susceptible to the next prospecting call. Your competitor, whether it is another advisor, their bank, their credit union, their professional association, or AARP, should not be more interested in your client than you are.

5. Great service gets referred. Over the holidays, another soccer parent asked me for a referral to a good dentist and oral surgeon. I couldn't wait to refer them to mine because they are both proactive; they pre-book our meetings; they are knowledgeable, recognized leaders in their profession; and they call after an appointment to check on my family to ask if they solved the problem and if it was a good experience. When you have fifty quality Meetings with Purpose, you are much more likely to keep those clients and get their recommendations.

6. Meetings are where accidents happen. My first sales trainer would get us in his car and go out and see people. He said that's where accidents happen. People took action and bought things because we were there and we asked. You do miss 100 percent of the shots you don't take.

    - We know the Pareto Principle (80/20 Rule) all too well. I wish it were not so true, but it is. The top quartile of your client base usually contributes about 80 percent of your revenue. Why would you not be engaged with and in front of this most important group? You are lucky to have them, and they are lucky to have you. The by-product of more face time with this more affluent group will no doubt result in better recommendations from them.

7. Finally, the gods of sales favor activity!

Chapter 3

The Power of Financial Advice

Gary H Schwartz, CLU ChFC CRPC
Senior Vice President-Advisor Growth and Development

This has been an exciting year for the Advisors at North Star who have embraced ongoing Financial Advice as part of the services offered by their practices. We are on track to pass one million dollars of gross revenue in Advice fees. More importantly, hundreds of individuals and families are engaged with their advisor in a shared purpose to reach their financial goals.

"The right advice at the right time can make a huge difference in a client's financial future."

What we know about individuals and families who engage in an ongoing advice relationship rather than a transaction relationship:

- They give their advisor higher client satisfaction scores.
- They have two times the level of assets with their advisor.
- They are more likely to refer them to a similar prospect.
- They purchase more product solutions with their advisor.
- They have higher retention with their advisor
- They have higher reported confidence about achieving their financial goals and financial independence.

Offering ongoing financial advice seems to be a natural evolution for some advisors. They started their career by addressing important risk exposures through protection products, then invested excess assets in mutual funds, added professional money management services (SEI etc) and then broadened their services by offering comprehensive financial advice in an ongoing advice relationship.

Ongoing financial advice is not appropriate nor suitable for every client. Many of you have developed a menu of services visual aid that can be used to explain to clients the various levels of service your practice can provide. It's helpful for your clients to know their options in how to work with you and what is the benefit to them at each level of the menu. A typical response is that some clients will wonder why you haven't offered this before and are interested in engaging at the advice level and others will only want service on products that are already in place.

Offering advice services starts with a mindset that the discipline and knowledge you bring to a client situation has its own value independent from a product. Most clients will literally earn a fortune in their lifetime. Without an advisor providing a certain level of discipline, few people will have anything to show for it. The articles tell us the average American has about $25,000 saved for retirement. That tells us they did not have the discipline that comes from having an Advisor. Discipline doesn't mean we are going to take all their fun. It means that an honest portion will be put aside for them to have more fun later.

Knowledge is the other key value that comes from the advice relationship. You are the sum total of your formal education, Industry reading/seminars, credentials and hours of client meetings. We don't go to the surgeon for their knowledge for our surgery only. We go to the surgeon for the 100 other surgeries they have experienced similar to ours. Your client gets the benefit of your experience of seeing really good financial decision making and some not so good decisions. They get it all and that has value.

Transitioning your practice to capture your advice for financial value starts with mindset and a bit of courage to have the conversation. This is often easier with new clients than existing clients. Yet with the right language and conviction both are possible. There is an appropriate proverb "A good part of the journey is already behind you once you leave your front door" Once you decide that your knowledge and discipline have value then talking about your top level of service becomes much easier.

There are some common comments I hear when working with Advisors on this transition. "I make enough from my IA business that I offer the advice for free" We need to be sensitive to value and revenue. I would suggest that you may want to reduce your IA fees to be very competitive and add ongoing Financial Advice in its place. We do know there is downward pressure on IA compensation and a more expensive IA does not necessarily perform better. On the other hand the value of advice is increasing as your client's financial lives become more complex. IA on its own also lacks context. How much is enough? What will you use it for? Why are you working so hard? How much do you need to not work another day? Comprehensive advice gives you and the clients context.

If your car is making a noise and you take it to the dealer. The mechanic lifts the hood, hooks up the diagnostic equipment and determines that your alternator bearings are bad. They offer to replace the alternator and then to assure it is working in concert with the battery, regulator, and computer to function properly as an integrated system. There was a margin to be made on the alternator (part) and then the knowledge to know it was the problem and then to get all the system to work together (labor). This is a simple story to explain that comprehensive advice is about parts and labor.

The related story I've heard from a North Star Advisor is that a surgeon would not say I make enough off of medicine and bandages that you don't need to pay me for my consultation and procedure...its mindset and language.

You will note that I have not used the words Financial Planning or selling a onetime plan or even a plan. While E-money is an important resource it is the machine behind the curtain. The Advisor with their knowledge and discipline is the leading value proposition. The plan is more for the advisor than the client. Language is everything in providing advice. Wisdom and knowledge trumps data and information.

A recent article in Financial Planning magazine by Mitch Anthony talks about Advisors providing a Return on Life for their clients through their Advice.

There were five key benefits for the client:

1. **Organization** — bringing order to a client's life
2. **Objectivity** — Provide untainted perspectives that lead to suitable and rational money decisions
3. **Proactivity** — Help clients anticipate life transitions and prepare financially
4. **Accountability** — Help clients follow through on their commitments
5. **Partnership** — Help clients make decisions that move them toward the best life possible with the money they have

It is in the partnership stage where ongoing advice between you and the client comes to life. As an advisor you get a more engaged client, who is shoulder to shoulder with you working on improving their financial situation. You get off the product transaction train and get on the advice train. You may buy a product to take advantage of an opportunity or to transfer a risk to an insurance company. With ongoing advice this will be a shared decision and you will find you and your client in the goal achievement business.

Money is a wonderful servant and a terrible master. Your ability to make money a servant for your clients is the outcome of providing the right advice at the right time. It will change the lives of your clients for the better and for those advisors who know this value and can capture it; their lives and their practice will be made better as well.

If you are interested in learning more about how to transition to offering ongoing advice please contact me. We have an excellent Financial Planning Resource Center that can work with you on deliverables production and Advice consultation. Carrie Hancock, John Nagel, Danelle Fiman and myself are all available to contribute to your efforts in this area. This is an important resource that is provided to you as part of the North Star value proposition.

Our congratulations and appreciation goes out to those North Star Advisors who are leading the way in this important evolution and service for our clients.

Chapter 4
Tips for Hosting a Party with Purpose

1. **Why do events?**
   - Staying face to face with your best clients is the most valuable thing you can do to insulate them from the competition and get introductions to their most qualified family, friends, business associates, and professional advisors.
   - Events deliver connections.
   - Even in today's hyperconnected world, face-to-face connections still power business.
   - Your prospective clients drive the buying process. They are smart, resourceful, and socially connected. They do their own research and can be up to 90 percent of the way through the buying process before even meeting you.
   - Events can get you closer to prospective clients faster and propel them through the buying process.
   - Events turn new and existing clients into brand enthusiasts. In the olden days, successful events caused attendees to tell their friends at work and call their friends and families to tell them about the event. Today, attendees send pictures to friends, post them to Facebook, and endorse the advisor on LinkedIn *during* the event.
   - Events give the people important to you and the growth of your business a real-time, genuine way to experience your brand and share it with the world.
   - No matter the technology, events done right leave memories that last a lifetime— a brand that is priceless and expensive to earn any other way.
   - Traditionally people think of doing events to appreciate clients or attract prospects. Just as important is to have events for your team, centers of influence, and peers in the industry.
   - One-third of your marketing budget should be spent on events.

2. **The one event every advisor must do every year that is also the easiest way to implement event strategies in your business**
   - This critical event is a client-appreciation event.
   - You do not need to invite your entire client base. Invite the A's and the B's who are going to be A's and anyone who has given you an A recommendation (whether they became a client or not).

- Clients in your desired profile are being invited to other financial advisor events several times a year through direct mail, friends, family, and their other professional advisors.
- Don't let them say, "My advisor isn't doing this."
- It gives you another opportunity to be face to face with people and show off your brand.
- It carries low risk for your brand.
- It gives you and them practice.
- It gives them comfort to bring someone to the next event.

3. **The secret sauce to a small, private dining event**
   - You want to start small.
   - Client retention: Invite two couples—a couple who was referred by the other couple.
   - Client acquisition: Invite two couples—a couple who referred the other couple—and ask them to each invite another couple.
   - Ask the two original couples where they'd like to go or what they'd like to celebrate.
   - This makes it easy to request a follow-up meeting.
   - You'll create a memory of a lifetime that the guests will talk about for just as long.

4. **The number one key to a successful event: Turn it inside out**
   - The event needs to be about what your clients want and need.
   - Doing that will make the whole process easier, from getting people there to getting people to meet with you after the event.
   - Because you have a Practice with a Purpose, their wants and needs will be in alignment with your values.
   - The number one reason people attend events is networking; a close second is education.
   - Make sure you invite the right people—create "event families," and make certain they have something in common.
   - What's their *why*? What do they want from you? What will make them feel better about having you for their advisor? What will make them want to show you off to their friends and family?
   - If you don't know it, ask them—informally or via a survey.

5. **4 P's to perfect prospecting parties**
   - Here are some tips to ensure that your next event won't waste your money or risk your brand.
     - Process—Plan the event starting with the ROI, and plan the follow-up before you pick the venue.
     - People—It's all about the people. Make sure you have guests who can do the party without you. If you invite the right people, getting them there and having them bring their friends is a snap.
     - Plant—The "plant" is composed of the venue, the invitations, the entertainment—every last detail that goes into making each and every guest feel special.
     - Pipeline—This isn't just a party. It's a huge investment of time, people, and money. Make sure you have a follow-up plan and process and track it for at least a year.

6. **Event whys**
   - The obvious: Appreciation, seminars
   - Generational event: Monies at risk (huge)
   - Market crash or market acceleration
   - Transition or succession
   - Helping clients grow their businesses
   - Celebrating a firm anniversary, your relationships with clients
   - Celebrating birthdays, anniversaries, etc.

7. **Three categories of event ideas**
   - Education
   - Health and wellness
   - Fun and lifestyle

8. **The biggest mistakes you can make**
   - Having unrealistic expectations
   - Doing one event, then quitting

Following these tips can enhance your brand and set the stage for meeting new clients.

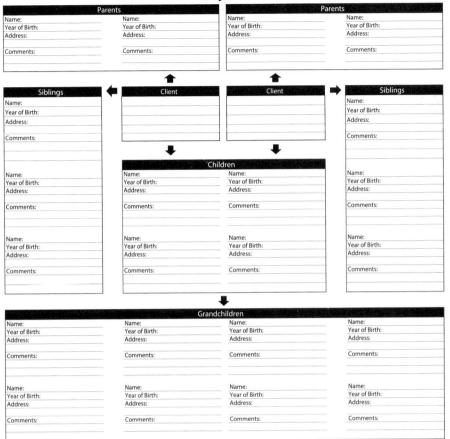

Chapter 5

No supporting documents.

Chapter 6

A Memo Written in 1995 on the Power of Goal Setting

To:	General Agents
From:	Gary Schwartz Director of Field Development, Minnesota Mutual
Date:	April 10, 1995
Subject:	The Power of Goal Setting

For the past several years, I have been making a concerted effort to study the characteristics of successful people. What has driven my curiosity is that I would often interview or meet people who had essentially the same background and native abilities who would, however, have very different levels of success. As a result of this curiosity, I changed my interview to include two questions:

1. What is the single most important reason for your success?
2. What role does goal setting play in your life?

While there are many factors that determine why some people have success in life and in work, I am convinced that there are at least two principal factors:

1. First, somewhere in their careers, someone really believed in them. This individual took a strong interest in them, built their self-esteem, and made them believe they were capable of great things. I can't tell you how many candidates and successful people I've worked with and interviewed who have attributed their success to someone believing in them.

    These mentors not only believed in them; they expected great things from them. Most people want to be successful and achieve great things. What they need is someone to instill in them a new framework of what is possible.

    When Roger Bannister ran the first four-minute mile, it looked like an insurmountable obstacle. However, since then, dozens of people have run a four-minute mile. Roger Bannister instilled in others a new framework of what was possible.

2. Second, these successful people set goals for themselves and stayed focused on them. Sometimes these goals were unwritten, broad, and visionary; other times, they were formal, frequently reviewed goals.

In any case, the common denominator was that they had goals. A recent article mentioned that only 5 percent of Americans have articulated their personal goals, but 95 percent of those people achieve their goals.

In my study of the characteristics of successful people, I read various textbooks, popular books, and assorted articles on the subject. The following two articles really stand out:

- **"Pygmalion in Management" by J. Sterling Livingston**—This is a classic in management literature. It captures what happens when we expect greatness in others. Most people want to achieve great things. What they need is someone to unlock the best in them and give them the permission and vision to be bigger than themselves, to play over their heads.

    While the author spoke to people early in their careers, the concept of playing Pygmalion is equally applicable at any stage of a person's career. We should also forgive the author for referring to developing "young men." This 1969 article was written before the enormous influx of women into the labor market in general and into business careers specifically.

- **"Goal Setting: A Motivational Technique That Works" by Gary P. Latham and Edwin A. Locke**—This short somewhat academic article illustrates the power of goal setting, which is a simple, straightforward, and highly effective technique for motivating individuals. Most management development fads for the past twenty years are based on some variation of goal setting.

What does this mean, day-to-day, for you and your agency?

1. Set high expectations for yourself, and share them with someone who will hold you accountable. At North Star, our advisors are encouraged to write their goals down, place them in a sealed envelope, and give the envelope to a mentor or member of the leadership team with a note on the envelope that says, "Open January 1, 2015 (the next year)." It is a highly effective way of setting goals and of building an inspirational way of asking a respected person to monitor that tactic.

2. A good example of setting high expectations is in the area of recruiting. We are much more likely to achieve our recruiting goals if we set high expectations for ourselves and have the activity that contributes to those expectations. All of us need a new framework of what is possible, so we can be the best in agent recruiting and development. We need to break our own four-minute mile.

3. Set high expectations for your agents and secure their agreement to hold them accountable for these expectations. This is particularly important for new agents early in their careers. They don't know what a four-minute mile is in telephone calls, appointments, and cases.
4. Demonstrate to those around you that you believe in them. Never underestimate the power of a word of encouragement, recognition, or empathy. Sometimes a person whom you think needs it the least really needs it the most.
5. Work jointly with agents to set goals each quarter and each year.
6. Monitor performance regularly and provide feedback. Let your agents know where they stand, remind them where they set their goals, and demonstrate your faith in their ability to get there. Managing the results at the end of the year will not cause someone to change behavior in the next year. If we don't change behavior, there is no growth.
7. Good leaders are good teachers. The definition of learning is a change in behavior. Good leaders, then, change behaviors in themselves and in others.

I hope you enjoy these two articles and draw some inspiration from their content. Having faith in the greatness of others and unlocking this potential through participative goal setting is the most powerful thing we can do as leaders.

Chapter 7

No supporting documents.

Chapter 8

No supporting documents.

Chapter 9

No supporting documents.

Chapter 10

Five E-Mails That Recap Goals Discussions with Advisors

Sending follow-up e-mails to advisors after you meet with them results in several benefits to both you and the advisor. It reiterates the action items, it allows you to invest in the advisor, and it shows the advisor that you respect him or her.

In this e-mail I wrote to an early-career advisor whom I coach for a partner company, I recapped six action steps we had discussed during a recent meeting with him to help him grow his Practice on Purpose from $240,000 to $350,000 in the next two years. This is the actual e-mail I sent to him.

November 26, 2013

Hello, Mike—

Great to see you today. I wanted to capture key points from our meeting today so we can remember them and set specific action steps.

We discussed the progress you have made in the past several years. Your production in 2011 was $137,000, in 2012 it was $173,000, and by the end of 2013 it is projected to be about $240,000. That means you gained nearly $100,000 of production in 24 months. This is an important improvement and a trend we can continue. I view our relationship as a curve bender. You will grow anyway, and if we can engage together, we can grow faster and better.

We have set a goal of $250,000 of production in 2014. I would suggest a goal of $275,000 in 2014 and $350,000 in 2015. We will need to see the 2015 grid to make sure you are maintaining or increasing your payout.

We discussed the opportunity to add a full-time team member. There are several keys to this strategy: This person should have different skills than you and/or like to do things that you either don't like to do or are below your pay grade. He or she should be doing revenue-generating activities and/or revenue-enhancing activities.

Your homework assignment is to write out a list of these two types of activities. I would include keeping your calendar full, setting appointments, developing a client-service model for each client group, learning the planning software so you can do retirement projections, develop and execute a premier client-service model, market events, develop meeting prep and meeting agendas, and hold yourself accountable to ask for referrals.

We discussed the menu of services. This is the type of treatment each client or segment of clients experiences in your practice. I will mail you some samples of menus of service. This is part of having a Practice on Purpose. You and your team need to have this down cold. I would suggest that you standardize your service, then customize. If you customize everything, you do not develop economies of scale, and you are less profitable. Clients want a predictable, repeatable experience. Let's get this produced for you early in the year.

We discussed conducting a retirement projection for each of your top 50 clients. This achieves a number of purposes. It is a strong deliverable. It will point out gaps in current status and goal status. It will cause clients to invest more with you. It may lead to insurance sales. It will be a significant service to your clients. Virtually all clients have retirement as a common goal. If we can contribute to your clients having a confident retirement, we will move into that top category of value to the client.

I will send you a document from the US government on retirement statistics. It is sobering. This is in the "why" category of being an advisor. We can be great money managers, but the money is usually out of context. How much is enough? Will it be enough? We can answer these questions.

We discussed how to ask for referrals in a client-service meeting. I would suggest that you make retirement your specialty. This is all about language. Here's an example of a conversation a potential client might begin with you:

"What do you do, Mike?"

"I work with busy, successful people so they can retire. I was working with a couple recently who wanted to make work an option as quickly as they can. We were able to do the math for them, and now they are well on their way to getting there. Would you be interested in seeing those numbers for you?"

You are an expert on uncertainty. The certainty of uncertainty. We don't know the future yet, but we can prepare for it. This on the lifeline/moneyline napkin talk.

We also discussed being more of a business owner and less of a social worker. You will never lose your concern for people. "Just because you can doesn't mean you should." Tighten up your conversations to shorten them and stay on topic. You can talk for two hours with a client, but I'm not sure you should.

Finally, we discussed the notion of leadership. Leadership is taking someone to a place they would not have gone on their own. The difference between a $250K practice and $500K or $1M practice is the transition from a sales producer to also being a leader—a leader of teams, a leader of clients, and most importantly, a leader of yourself. You have to get out of your box and out of your own way to move to a higher level of thinking. This will get you to the next level.

OK, so key actions:

1. Select and hire a new team member.
2. Build out your menu of services.
3. Segment your clients into this client-service model.
4. Go see clients with a purpose; have 50 prebooked appointments in the first quarter.
5. Focus on conducting retirement projections for your top 50 clients.
6. Be a leader of a business and a leader of people.

Have a great Thanksgiving, and do something special for (wife's name). I'll ask you about it next time. I'll be mailing a packet to you as well.

Gary

* * * *

In this e-mail I sent to the same advisor a month and a half later, I recap another meeting in which we discussed his practice's growth. This e-mail reiterates how important I felt it was for him to focus on his top clients, present them with a menu of services, ask them for referrals, get his first staff member up to speed on tasks he should no longer be handling, and leverage social media to acquire more clients.

January 14, 2014

Hello, Mike—

Well we are off and running for a new year. Nice work last year, and you are well positioned for an even better year in 2014.

You finished 2012 with $173K production and 2013 with $216K production. That is a 24.8 percent increase. We know the market helped this, but it is not the whole reason. We will target $200K of production and the New Orleans

Circle Trip in 2014. I would suggest a goal of $300K production; that would be a 40 percent increase. I know it's a stretch, but goals are directional and create energy.

We discussed Leann's start and the onboarding process. It is a good design to have her co-house with Jill. Sarah is also a good relationship for you to develop and maintain in the office. I would start identifying those revenue-enhancing activities she can do quickly. We discussed that it will take about six months for you to fully turn the corner on your investment in her. She will require you to be a thoughtful and deliberate leader. It's a real art form to determine how much to give her and how fast. Be clear in your communication and expectations. Be aware of any possible cultural differences in how she interacts with you and others. Be ready to give her recognition and notes of appreciation for behavior you value.

I sent you the menu of services and retirement information. You have made a commitment to visit Alan Westlake in the first quarter. I met with Alan this past Thursday, and he is open and committed to meeting with you. He could be a strong resource for you. Alan also explained how the 2014 compensation program works and how tier compensation changes frequently based on each two-week period. This program rewards practices that sustain growth. Please look into this for our next meeting.

We recapped the six action steps from the notes I took during our November 26, 2013, meeting. It is key for you to have 50 engaged appointments with your top clients by the end of March, then to have 80 by the end of June. These 80 are your top people who are both your best clients and those who need a proven deliverable this year. If you see your top 80 in the first six months, you are going to have a great year. We also discussed providing retirement projections as the theme for the first half of the year. I will be sending to your home address an article I wrote on this topic recently. If you execute only one thing this year that will get you 40 percent growth, this is it.

You mentioned that you did "dentist office" style scheduling for three clients, and it worked! When you see these 80 people in the first six months, get them prescheduled for the second half of the year. It sends a powerful signal to the client that you are prepared and that you are leading them. Teach Leann to do a retirement calculation. I am sure you have simple calculators available to you. I do know Securian has one. Fidelity Mutual Funds also has one, and you may have one with your focus plans.

When you are fully engaged and leading these 80 client families, it will give you an opportunity to make them aware that you are taking referrals. The phrase you and I seemed to like was "I cannot help people if I do not meet them." I would wait for the moment when your client expresses appreciation for what you have done in the meeting and then pivot to saying, "I like helping people have success with their finances, but I can't help them if I don't meet them. Please keep me in mind or suggest people you think I should meet." It's important to at least ask. Don't be concerned about how perfect it is or is not. You will miss 100 percent of the shots you don't take. Also, the sample retirement projection project will open doors for people to want to introduce you to others who may want the same calculation. Let's focus on getting two new in-segment clients in 2014. You need more clients with more money to get you to the $500K level.

Eventually, LinkedIn will help you. Keep me posted on the approval of this tool. Social media is where it's at for marketing. Do you have a WRA website? I recall a fee for this service. Next time we meet, let's discuss LinkedIn and your website.

Please look into the Black Rock calculator for Social Security. This could be a huge value for your clients who are approaching retirement.

We discussed the possibility of you being your own person in your office, and you sent me an e-mail follow-up on this topic. I am concerned that we all become influenced by our environment without even being aware of it. I have a funny story to make the point. I was in a rustic area of South Boston once and walked by a fish market. There was a barrel of live crabs, and they were squirming around on top of each other. What was surprising is that there was no lid on the barrel. So I asked the guy there why the crabs didn't crawl out the top. He said, "It rarely happens. It seems that when one is getting near the top, the others pull that one down. It's why they are called crabs" I wonder in an office if there is a regression to the mean where the lower advisors pull you down so you don't out-achieve them, and the top advisors are too competitive or into themselves to reach down and pull you up. So you will do best by believing in yourself and being your own person. Get the good stuff out of being in an office, but don't let it define you, either.

You asked about leadership books. There are many, and I will admit it: I am a junkie for books on leadership. I benefit most from reading biographies of historical leaders. I read everything I can on Theodore Roosevelt and Lincoln. A couple of books that come to mind are *Mornings on Horseback*, which is about the young Roosevelt, and *Lincoln on Leadership*. You can get these from Amazon. I will send you a book called *Be the First Believer* by one of my fellow leaders at North Star, Ed Deutschlander. You might benefit.

Mike, you continue to make progress that is sustainable and forward-directed. I'm proud of what you accomplished last year and am excited about this next year. I look forward to our next meeting.

Gary

* * * *

A little more than a month later, I followed up with the same advisor via the following e-mail. Here, I address confidence and learning, which we cover in Chapter 6. In Chapter 10, we discuss the concept of "knighting." In this e-mail, I wanted to let Mike know I believe in him. He respects me as a senior person, so I have the ability and obligation to "knight" him.

Thursday, February 20, 2014

Mike,

Great to see you as well. I have read your follow-up e-mail and appreciate those thoughts.

I agree that you have paid your dues and now are seeing a well-deserved uptick of income. This will continue as long as you stay focused on executing on the right things.

Here are some action steps from our meeting and for next time:

1. We need to get a grip on the new compensation plan. Consider visiting with Ted on this to make sure we understand. We should also track your production progress, as we did last year. Let's try to look at YOY as that will take into account those larger IA hits.
2. The right thing to do now is get out to see your top clients. We had set a goal to see 80 by the end of June. Make this happen. It's all about execution.
3. Practice your referral talk all the time ... in the car ... in the shower ... when working out. Watch for the compliment and then pivot into the talk on "I can't help people I don't meet." Review the Life Events Referral talk.
4. Be aware of your office environment. Eagles don't flock. Keep your conversations in the hallway short, close your office door to focus on your blocked times, and consider coming in early several times a week for that great quiet time in the morning. Concentrate on your calendar, scheduling, meeting preparation, and meeting follow-up.

5. I think you and your confidence have grown even in the short time I have known you. You cannot outperform your self-image and you self-image has enlarged. You are a learning animal. I can see how you process and own lessons we have covered. Some people have the same experiences as you but don't learn the lessons they are teaching you. Our experiences and our environment are constantly teaching us something. We have to pay attention!

For the next meeting, let's work on the following:

1. Print out your calendar and bring it with you. I would like to see the next several weeks of activity. Then print out from our next meeting to June 30th. You can do "month at a glance" style. I want to see if your calendar matches your intentions.
2. Print out or list out your top 50 revenue clients. We are then going to go through how you met them, one at a time. I would also like to know their occupations and where they work. We are going to look for patterns and centers of recommendations.
3. Please come with three target markets where you want to concentrate. I know you have the service station owners. Let's look at some others for you may have an interest or affinity.

Let's meet at 7:30 a.m. at the Caribou and include Leann next time. We will work on the three things, and I will be sensitive to keep you in a positive light in front of her. OK?

How about 7:30 on March 11th? I am gone to two different meetings from March 16 to April 1st.

My notes are a bit shorter this time as I don't want to repeat myself, and we covered some of the same topics. I think we have laid out a plan. It's about execution.

Take care,

Gary

I sent the following e-mail to a different advisor to recap seven key action items we discussed in our meeting. The items included first meetings, a model week, marketing strategies, and delegation of some tasks to an intern.

March 5, 2014

Jason,

Great to visit with you today. I wanted to capture seven key points from our discussion:

1. First meetings—You have had 13 first meetings in the past three weeks. Great outcome. These were a product of 450 invitational e-mails that resulted in 22 "yes" responses and then 13 meetings.

2. Result of the first meetings—One is in underwriting now, two are doing fact finders, and eleven were checking their calendars. Zero people said they were not interested (good news). We discussed how to work with those people who said, "I need to check with my spouse." My suggestion is to pencil in an appointment that would work for the three of you, write it on the back of your business card and give it to them, and then have them check with their spouse and get back to you. This creates a covenant to meet. If the meeting doesn't work on their part, it creates an urgency to keep the covenant. They are much more likely to actually get a time that works for all three of you. If we can get the eleven to result in five more sets, your set ratio gets above 50 percent.

3. Adding a corporate professional market—The physician market is great, but it is not infinite. I would suggest that you identify one or two corporate markets you can expand into to increase your prospect base. We used the example of the olive bottle. The first several olives are hard to get out of the bottle, but once you get them out, the others tumble out. Use LinkedIn to get to those first several "olives."

4. Adding dentists to your markets as well—This market is similar to the physician market. Many dentists are also small-business owners, and they can actually be easier to connect with than surgeons and doctors. North Star has a strong track record of success in these markets. Check with some of your peers on how to enter this market.

5. Using a model week—We discussed how you have developed a model week. You prospect and market first thing in the morning when you are fresh, then move on to urgent but less important activity later in the day. We discussed that you want to have four-plus first meetings a week, and these can also be done later in the day. You also discussed that you have

been using Saturdays as administrative clean-up days. The hours you work and the effort you make matters. You will turn the corner in the next 18 months when you duplicate the 40 current top clients to then have 80 of them. Your practice will feel very different.

6. LinkedIn—We discussed three actions for you to take on LinkedIn:
   A. Keep adding contacts on LinkedIn as you are prompted to do so. Be discerning about who you allow into your pool of contacts. Clients and prospects will check you out, so make sure your contacts are successful in their eyes.
   B. Connect with your top 40 clients if they have LinkedIn accounts. When you see who they are connected with, identify three of their contacts you want to meet. Print out their pages and have them ready for the next meeting. Use a script like this: I noticed that we are on LinkedIn together. You have an impressive group of contacts who are obviously also successful, like you. I also noticed that you know Betty Smith at your clinic. Betty appears to be someone who would benefit from the work I do. Do you have any advice on how I could best meet her? I can't help people I don't meet.
   C. Search by organization on LinkedIn. You and I tried Emory University and then saw who our contacts are connected to at Emory. This allows you to connect with them directly or work through the connections you have in common.

7. Leveraging interns—We discussed how an intern could develop lists, send e-mails, and book first appointments from your e-mail campaign and from LinkedIn. Our intern program could give you some great leverage at this pivotal point in your career. Let me know in the next few weeks if you are on board with this.

Jason, good to connect. I will hold you accountable for an average of four first meetings a week, and I will ask you to track your activity so we can analyze where are your strengths in the pipeline and what needs to be tightened. Also remember our discussion about the language to use when you encounter a later-career practicing physician. Youth is on your side because you will be there for them in their retirement.

Gary

Now that you have seen four e-mails I sent to advisors to recap our coaching sessions, here is an e-mail I received from an advisor following a session. This kind of feedback indicates what really resonated with an advisor, and it further seals the advisor's commitment to work on the issues we discussed.

Gary,

Thank you very much for taking the time out of your busy schedule to visit with us! As always, very positive reviews from the other advisors. What I appreciated most was that you took this seriously, asking us questions that got us thinking and requiring us to be prepared. Your experience coaching advisors does not go unnoticed.

One of the things that stuck out most in our conversation was the question, "How would a top client know they are a top client?" I'm getting to a point where there are absolutely people I like to work with—I need to make sure I'm providing an excellent customer experience! Simple things like telling team members who my top clients are (and they need to be helped quickly) and/or making sure I'm proactively reaching out are critical to keeping the clients I've worked hard to get.

The second thing I picked up was to work on systematizing things—"An advisor practice that runs on its own is a thing of beauty and very liberating for the advisor." I believe this has a ton to do with *hiring others*. A successful advisor needs to hire someone who can help him multiply his own time because he is effective at running his portion of the practice.

I'll work on both over the next 30 days.

Have a great week, and we'll talk soon!

Kindest regards,

John

Chapter 11

No supporting documents.

Suggested Reading

Ben G. Baldwin, *The New Life Insurance Investment Advisor*

Paul Batz and Tim Schmidt, *What Really Works: Blending the Seven F's for the Life You Imagine*

Larry Bossidy and Ram Charan, Execution: *The Discipline of Getting Things Done*

Ron Carson, CFP®, CFS®, ChFC®, and Steve Sanduski, MBA, CFP®, *Tested in the Trenches: A Nine-Step Plan for Building and Sustaining a Million-Dollar Financial Services Practice*

Acres of Diamonds: Life-Changing Classics, Russell H. Conwell and John Wanamaker

Chris Crowley and Henry S. Lodge, MD, *Younger Next Year*

Harold Cummings, *Prescription for Tomorrow*

Donna Skeels Cygan, CFP®, MBA, *The Joy of Financial Security: The Art and Science of Becoming Happier, Managing Your Money Wisely, and Creating a Secure Financial Future*

Edward G. Deutschlander and Rich Campe, *Be the First Believer*

Jason Ryan Dorsey, *Y-Size Your Business: How Gen Y Employees Can Save You Money and Grow Your Business*

Financial Planning Competency Handbook, Certified Financial Planner Board of Standards, Inc. (CFP Board)

Tony Gordon, *It Can Only Get Better: Tony Gordon's Route to Sales Success*

Matthew Halloran and Crystal Thies, *The Social Media Handbook for Financial Advisors: How to Use LinkedIn, Facebook, and Twitter to Build and Grow Your Business*

Troy Korsgaden, *Power Position Your Agency: A Guide to Insurance Agency Success*

Troy Korsgaden, *Profit from Change: Retooling Your Agency for Maximum Profits*

Richard J. Leider, *The Power of Purpose: Creating Meaning in Your Life and Work*

Richard J. Leider and David A. Shapiro, *Repacking Your Bags: Lighten Your Load for the Rest of Your Life*

Doug Lennick, CFP®, and Fred Kiel, PhD, *Moral Intelligence: Enhancing Business Performance & Leadership Success,* Wharton School Publishing

Doug Lennick, CFP®, with Kathleen Jordan, PhD, *Financial Intelligence: How to Make Smart, Values-Based Decisions with Your Money and Your Life*

David H. Maister, Charles H. Green, and Robert M. Galford, *The Trusted Advisor*

Morgan W. McCall, Jr., *The Lessons of Experience: How Successful Executives Develop on the Job*

Steve Moore with Gary Brooks, *Ineffective Habits of Financial Advisors (And the Disciplines to Break Them): A Framework for Avoiding the Mistakes Everyone Else Makes*

David J. Mullen, Jr., *The Million-Dollar Financial Services Practice: A Proven System for Becoming a Top Producer*

Nick Murray and John Murray, *Talking It Over, Just the Two of Us: A Guide for the Financial Advisor's Life Partner*

Nick Murray, *Behavioral Investment Counseling*

Nick Murray, *The Game of Numbers: Professional Prospecting for Financial Advisors*

Philip Palaveev, *The Ensemble Practice: A Team-Based Approach to Building a Superior Wealth Management Firm,* Bloomberg

Alan Parisse and David Richman, *Questions Great Financial Advisors Ask... and Investors Need to Know*

Phillip C. Richards, *The Sky Is Not the Limit: Discovering the True North for Your Life's Path*

Phillip C. Richards, *Twenty-Five Secrets to Sustainable Success*

Hersh Shefrin, *Beyond Greed and Fear: Understanding Behavioral Finance and the Psychology of Investing*

Dan Sullivan, *The Good That Financial Advisors Do*

Mark C. Tibergien and Owen Dahl, *How to Value, Buy, or Sell a Financial Advisory Practice: A Manual on Mergers, Acquisitions, and Transition Planning*

Mark C. Tibergien and Rebecca Pomering, *Practice Made More Perfect: Transforming a Financial Advisory Practice into a Business*